Sounds Like Helicopters

THE SUNY SERIES

HORIZONS OF CINEMA

MURRAY POMERANCE | EDITOR

Sounds Like Helicopters

Classical Music in Modernist Cinema

Matthew Lau

Cover: *Apocalypse Now* (1979). Zoetrope Studios / Photofest.

Published by State University of New York Press, Albany

© 2019 State University of New York

All rights reserved

No part of this book may be used or reproduced in any manner whatsoever without written permission. No part of this book may be stored in a retrieval system or transmitted in any form or by any means including electronic, electrostatic, magnetic tape, mechanical, photocopying, recording, or otherwise without the prior permission in writing of the publisher.

For information, contact State University of New York Press, Albany, NY
www.sunypress.edu

Library of Congress Cataloging-in-Publication Data

Names: Lau, Matthew, 1978– author.
Title: Sounds like helicopters : classical music in modernist cinema / Matthew Lau.
Description: Albany : State University of New York Press, [2019] | Series: SUNY series, horizons of cinema | Includes bibliographical references and index.
Identifiers: LCCN 2018052658 | ISBN 9781438476315 (hardcover) ISBN 9781438476308 (pbk.) | ISBN 9781438476322 (ebook)
Subjects: LCSH: Motion picture music—History and criticism.
Classification: LCC ML2075 .L36 2019 | DDC 781.5/42—dc23
LC record available at https://lccn.loc.gov/2018052658

10 9 8 7 6 5 4 3 2 1

For Mom and Dad,
who took us to the movies and violin lessons

"Every new development added to the cinema must, paradoxically, take it nearer and nearer to its origins. In short, cinema has not yet been invented!"

—André Bazin ("The Myth of Total Cinema" 21)

Contents

Illustrations		ix
Acknowledgments		xiii
Introduction: A Fundamental Continuity		1
1	What Happens to an Apocalypse Deferred: Coppola, Herzog, and Schwarzenegger as Readers of Wagner's *Ring*	17
2	The Imperfect Wagnerite: Luis Buñuel and Romantic Surrealism	37
3	"A Film Should Be Like Music": Stanley Kubrick and the Condition of Music	65
4	Too Soon, Too Late, and Still to Come: Jean-Luc Godard and the Ruins of Classical Music	95
5	Before a Winter's Journey: Michael Haneke's Critique of Film Music in *The Piano Teacher*	121
Conclusion: Modernist Cinema's Family Tree		143
Notes		155
Works Cited		157
Index		165

Illustrations

Figure 1.1	Helicopter Valkyries in *Apocalypse Now* (Francis Ford Coppola, United Artists, 1979). Digital frame enlargement.	20
Figure 1.2	Dynamo in *The Running Man* (Paul Michael Glaser, TriStar Pictures, 1988). Digital frame enlargement.	32
Figure 2.1	A surreal Tristan in *L'age d'or* (Luis Buñuel, Vicomte de Noailles/Corinth Films, 1930). Digital frame enlargement.	45
Figure 2.2	Learning to respect private property in Las Hurdes (Luis Buñuel, Ramón Acín/Kino Video, 1933). Digital frame enlargement.	50
Figure 2.3	The bourgeoisie entering paradise in *The Exterminating Angel* (Luis Buñuel, Producciones Gustavo Alatriste/Criterion Collection, 1962). Digital frame enlargement.	55
Figure 2.4	The bourgeoisie at a public bathroom in *The Phantom of Liberty* (Luis Buñuel, Greenwich Film Productions/Criterion Collection, 1974). Digital frame enlargement.	57
Figure 2.5	Window shopping to Wagner in *That Obscure Object of Desire* (Luis Buñuel, Greenwich Films/Criterion Collection, 1977). Digital frame enlargement.	59
Figure 3.1	Private Lawrence and Sergeant Hartman in *Full Metal Jacket* (Stanley Kubrick, Warner Brothers, 1987). Digital frame enlargement.	70

Figure 3.2	Alex reacts to Beethoven in *A Clockwork Orange* (Stanley Kubrick, Warner Brothers, 1971). Digital frame enlargement.	72
Figure 3.3	A razor cuts an eye in *Un chien andalou* (Luis Buñuel, Les Grands Films Classiques/Transflux Films, 1929). Digital frame enlargement.	74
Figure 3.4	Marion's lifeless eye in *Psycho* (Alfred Hitchcock, Paramount Pictures, 1960). Digital frame enlargement.	75
Figure 3.5	The routine problems of space travel in *2001: A Space Odyssey* (Stanley Kubrick, Metro-Goldwyn-Mayer, 1968). Digital frame enlargement.	77
Figure 3.6	Lady Lyndon hears Schubert one last time in *Barry Lyndon* (Stanley Kubrick, Warner Brothers, 1975). Digital frame enlargement.	84
Figure 3.7	Revealing masks in *Eyes Wide Shut* (Stanley Kubrick, Warner Brothers, 1999). Digital frame enlargement.	87
Figure 3.8	Giving up your inquiries in *Eyes Wide Shut* (Stanley Kubrick, Warner Brothers, 1999). Digital frame enlargement.	91
Figure 4.1	Godard listening to his new film in *Prénom Carmen* (Jean-Luc Godard, Sara Films, 1983). Digital frame enlargement.	100
Figure 4.2	Mozart for farmworkers in *Weekend* (Jean-Luc Godard, Comacico/Criterion Collection, 1967). Digital frame enlargement.	114
Figure 4.3	Roxy looks on in *Goodbye to Language* (Jean-Luc Godard, Wild Bunch/Kino Lorber, 2014). Digital frame enlargement.	119
Figure 5.1	Sensing a rival in *The Piano Teacher* (Michael Haneke, Arte France Cinema/Criterion Collection, 2002). Digital frame enlargement.	127
Figure 5.2	The origin of film music in *The Piano Teacher* (Michael Haneke, Arte France Cinema/Criterion Collection, 2002). Digital frame enlargement.	129

Figure 5.3	Waiting her turn in *The Piano Teacher* (Michael Haneke, Arte France Cinema/Criterion Collection, 2002). Digital frame enlargement.	130
Figure 5.4	Departing on her winter's journey in *The Piano Teacher* (Michael Haneke, Arte France Cinema/Criterion Collection, 2002). Digital frame enlargement.	138

Acknowledgments

Joshua Wilner, Wayne Koestenbaum, and Peter Hitchcock supported this project when it was a dissertation and have given valuable advice since. Mark Schiebe and Lily Saint read the earliest drafts. Leah Anderst helped with the revisions when it was almost done.

Eli Spindel and my friends at the String Orchestra of Brooklyn have forced me to keep practicing just to play half as well as they do. Roy Malan has been my most generous mentor of all.

The CUNY Graduate Center awarded me a dissertation fellowship in 2010–11. The CUNY Research Foundation funded this work with a book completion award for 2019–20. The English Department at the CUNY Graduate Center supported my general intellectual development. My colleagues and students at Queensborough Community College have challenged and inspired me to mature as a teacher and writer.

Finally, to my parents, Tom and Diane Lau, and my brother David Lau, my sister-in-law Laura Martin, and my nephew, "the genius," Carlos Martin Lau, you all know how much you mean to me. Like Cordelia, I can only love and be silent.

Introduction

A Fundamental Continuity

"It Scares the Hell Out of the Slopes"

Wagner's "Ride of the Valkyries" in *Apocalypse Now* (1979) is emblematic of the complexity of the role played by classical music in modernist cinema. A complexity that is thus far underappreciated by modern film music scholarship and criticism. As Colonel Kilgore (Robert Duvall) explains it in the film, he plays Wagner from loudspeakers attached to helicopters during an absurd mission to capture the surf break at "Charlie's Point" because it inspires his men and "scares the hell out of the slopes." But rather than intimidating the Vietcong, Wagner lets them know Kilgore and company are coming. Though the music makes victory seem inevitable for Kilgore's cavalry, in the ensuing battle several helicopters are downed, and the enemy is only subdued when air support napalms the jungle perimeter. Kilgore wins the battle, but is less certain of winning the war. "Someday," he muses shirtlessly before a surf, "this war is gonna end."

The decision to use Wagner is often mistakenly credited to director Francis Ford Coppola and assumed to be an ironic allusion to D. W. Griffith's 1915 racist historical epic, *The Birth of a Nation*, and its use of the same music during its climactic Ku Klux Klan cavalry attack on African Americans (Smith 221, M. Cooke 427). In fact, it was *Apocalypse Now*'s screenwriter and former NRA board member John Milius who chose Wagner for the film's infamous helicopter assault sequence. Milius chose Wagner for his screenplay not just to satirize a war adrift or for the irony of the perceived contrast between the music and the machines, but because of the similarity he felt he heard between Wagner's vanguard orchestral timbres and the sounds of helicopters (the emblematic modern vehicle for conventional military forces). An admirer of Wagner's music, Milius observed archly in an interview with Coppola, "Wagner just lends itself to helicopters for some reason."

Milius's idiosyncratic perception underpinning Hollywood's signature image of the Vietnam War is therefore both ironic—drawing attention to itself in a foolish and surreal spectacle—and appropriate—in the way the helicopters sound and act like Wagner's Valkyries as they administer "death from above." Similarly, Coppola's sequence based on Milius's screenplay, as a morally and politically ambivalent masterpiece and the film's true "heart of darkness," both satirizes and celebrates the war as a misguided excess of an empire. The Wagnerian soundtrack could not have been more fitting, for no other composer inspires harsher denunciations or greater reveries. Wagner's legacy remains bitterly contested, with some rejecting his music as fundamentally anti-Semitic and fascist. So, too, if Hollywood's mystification of the conflict is any indication, the United States has yet to come to terms with the bitter legacy of the Vietnam War. *Apocalypse*'s helicopter assault scene brings these disputes together without resolving or diminishing their arguments.

To paraphrase Walter Benjamin, Milius and Coppola used Wagner to capture the history of the Vietnam War not as it really happened—psychological operations ("psy-ops") involved playing rock music from helicopters, not Wagner—but as it flashes up in our cultural memory at a moment of danger ("Theses on the Philosophy of History" 255). The moment of danger was the years just after the war ended when the struggle began to interpret it in Hollywood. Coppola's film contrasts with Hal Ashby's antiwar film *Coming Home* (1978), a love story set away from the battlefield among disillusioned, disabled veterans. Like Ashby, Coppola meant to criticize the war, but to Milius's amusement and Coppola's frustration, the film's signature helicopter assault scene has long since been repurposed as propaganda by the US military and has come to overshadow the film as a whole. As propaganda to inspire soldiers before battle, Wagner's music makes the scene that much more convincing and enjoyable, making victory a foregone conclusion and giving the audience a heroic theme to hum.

When we enjoy *Apocalypse Now*'s signature scene, the pleasure is similar to the ambivalent fascination with Wagner's life and music. "Our love of Wagner," music critic Joachim Kaiser argues, "is as infected as the wound that is suffered by Amfortas," the sinful but ultimately redeemed leader of the knights of the grail in Wagner's *Parsifal* (quoted in Geck xvii). The same could be said for the American public's fascination with

Hollywood films about Vietnam. The love for such films is infected by the tragic consequences of the conflict itself. Like Wagnerians who go on loving his music despite his anti-Semitism and his music's co-optation by the Nazi regime, filmgoers enjoy films about Vietnam despite the troubling facts about the US intervention there. They enjoy them despite the fact that the war was fundamentally about preventing the democratic unification of Vietnam after its war of independence, despite the millions of lives lost in Vietnam and neighboring countries during the war, and despite the ongoing environmental damage from the use of chemical weapons and from aerial bombings campaigns of unprecedented scope (Hirschman et al.).

Apocalypse Now's violent spectacle to procure a surf spot is a microcosm for these depressing underlying truths. But in its irrational use of Wagner's music that all but foils the attack, it also traffics in myths about why the US military was defeated that so many films about the Vietnam War perpetuate: that the US military lost because of its own missteps; and that US forces were really fighting themselves. Wagner's presence in the helicopter assault scene allegorically embodies a variation on these myths: the US military was only playing at war in Vietnam, as when Kilgore relishes his Wagnerian spectacle, and never really fought with everything it had.

Complex examples like Coppola and Milius's Wagnerian helicopter assault show that classical music's part in modernist cinema merits closer inspection. To borrow a metaphor from Kafka, classical music is an ax to break a frozen sea of assumptions about modernist cinema and vice versa: modernist cinema reminds us of underlying truths about classical music. Classical music is often perceived as stuffy and conservative. This is misguided. If there is an elitism to it, it is the democratic kind, an elite status earned by musicians who put in the work to master it. In principle, it is accessible to anyone who starts at a young age and is diligent about practicing. Good examples of classical music's populism are the heralded Sistema program in Venezuela, where any young person can take lessons and join an ensemble through government subsidy; or the now imperiled music programs in US public schools, where I and many others first learned to play.

With the music itself, it is the most original works that endure, not the conservative ones. The canon is composed of the works that test and defy audiences' and musicians' expectations while also remaining recognizably part of the tradition. Modernist cinema's appropriations of canonical classical music remind us of its original vanguard impulse. Such appropriations remind us that, as Arnold Schoenberg noted, canonical classical music remains new music. "In all great works of the great," he writes, "we will find that newness which never perishes, whether it be of Josquin des Pres, of Bach or Haydn, or of any other great master. *Because: Art means New Art*" ("New Music" 114–15).

Film Music Studies Newsreel

Modern film music scholarship and criticism has enhanced the discussion of classical music in film in three interrelated ways. First, it calls for greater appreciation of the diversity and complexity of emotions and meanings resulting from the interaction between cinema and classical music.[1] Second, it describes the long, complicated relationship between opera and cinema.[2] Third, in the most fraught line of inquiry, scholars focus on how the New German Cinema uses ironic appropriations of classical music to critique Germany's Nazi legacy.[3]

These lines of inquiry merit a response that deepens and complicates them. First, of course, the sheer diversity of uses of classical music in films is undoubtedly a point of fact. But in several important, recent studies, the authors and anthology editors state or describe this fact in place of an argument or theory that might suggest how we comprehend the diversity (Joe 24, Stilwell and Powrie xix). While this attention to diversity is admirable and well-intentioned, declining to attempt a more definitive theory can itself become a problem. "All observation," Charles Darwin once noted, "must be for or against some view if it is to be of any service" (quoted in Eldredge and Gould 85). Otherwise one winds up endlessly collecting data ("counting pebbles" in Darwin's image) or, perhaps worse, unwittingly having a theory without knowing or acknowledging it. Along the same lines, Charles Rosen points out that even a bad theory is arguably better than none at all. "A bad theory," he writes, "often provokes an interesting and useful response" (*Sonata Forms*, "Preface").

Second, while the opera and cinema connection is a crucial one, instrumental classical music's representation of the basic paradox of musical expression in its extreme form is key to understanding music's diversity of functions in film. Music's paradox is that it is both inferior and superior to language. It cannot communicate basic information as language can, but it can express, represent, and elicit emotions with degrees of power and refinement that language only begins to approach at its most poetic (Rosen, *Music and Sentiment* 5–6). Music's indefinite message combined with its emotional definitiveness allows it to color situations and contexts in film in such diverse ways, indeed often simultaneously, and is the key to challenging the misconception that modernist cinema's use of classical music is exclusively or primarily ironic.

Third, for comprehending modernist cinema, the category of national cinema is neither general nor specific enough compared with the venerable category of the auteur—the director as the film's author. Nationalism is not general enough because the influences on auteurs are national and international, idiosyncratic and universal. It is not specific enough because directors within nationally defined cinematic movements often make very different films. In the New German Cinema movement, Werner Herzog and Hans-Jurgen Syberberg offer cases in point.

While Herzog's films have been criticized for their dilettantish enthusiasm for Wagner and Romanticism more generally, Syberberg is praised for his ironic flair with both. The truth in both cases is more complicated. The accusation that Herzog's "reevaluation of Romanticism . . . without the component of nationalism" results in a form of self-deceiving liberation overlooks the educational value of many of his documentaries (Hillman, *Unsettling Scores* 137). His documentary about the Bayreuth Festival's 1994 season, *The Transformation of the World into Music*, presents Wagner's work in its historical and living contexts, including a critical account of its anti-Semitic and Nazi associations. (It was Wagner's daughter-in-law Winifred who was a personal friend of Hitler's and cultivated the Nazi regime's ties to Bayreuth.) The film succeeds because of Herzog's clear admiration for Wagner's operas and for the musicians, artists, and tradespeople who keep the music alive. So while he does not neglect Wagner's anti-Semitism and his Nazi co-optation, these extreme right-wing uses of Wagner's legacy do not get the final word because, after all, Wagner's music endures despite, not because of, the Nazi stain.

Meanwhile, when Syberberg flirts with fascism in *Our Hitler: A Film from Germany*, this is considered evidence of his ironic, kitsch sensibility and "stylistic temerity" (Flinn, *The New German Cinema* 7). But as his complaints about the influence of Jews and leftists in reunified Germany and his opinion that Hitler was "a genius, who acted as the medium of the *Weltgeist*" show, Syberberg is being more than ironic about Nazism in *Our Hitler* (quoted in Buruma, "There's No Place Like Heimat"). Ian Buruma's image for Syberberg's relationship to Hitler is as damning as it is incisive: "the fascinating thing is that Syberberg's philosophy . . . is articulated most clearly by a ventriloquist's dummy in the shape of Hitler" (There's No Place Like Heimet"). At the end of Part III of *Our Hitler*, Syberberg ventriloquizes Hitler to rail against democracy and "third class people" while emphasizing that the Nazis helped create Israel ("We got the Jews their state"). Throughout the film, Wagner's music is mined for its rhetorical and expressive power in a way that is similarly more sincere than ironic, more interested in reinforcing Wagner's link to Nazism than in reclaiming him from the association with their atrocities.

A Fundamental Continuity

In varying ways, the examples of Coppola's, Herzog's, and even Syberberg's disturbing film show that it is not enough to say that modernist cinema ironically undermines classical music's expressive power. There is also a fundamental continuity, a *likeness*, between classical music's traditions and the aesthetics of modernist cinema, which can both be regarded to varying degrees as avant-garde in sensibility. Luis Buñuel's lifelong adoration of Wagner is the holotype[4] for the dialectic of irony and continuity between classical music and modernist cinema. For as much as he deconstructs Wagner's music in his early films, Buñuel also saw a deeper parallel in their shared focus on love's subversive power (*My Last Sigh* 219). His early films acknowledge this solidarity by transfiguring the Liebestod from *Tristan and Isolde* (see Sangild, "Buñuel's Liebestod"). He returned to Wagner's music and tropes not frequently but significantly throughout his career, including in the last scene of his last film, *That Obscure Object of Desire*, where the perverse reverie of the hero, Mathieu (Fernando Rey), to an excerpt from *Die Walküre* ends only because an even greater surrealist dream comes true when anarchists bomb a shopping mall.

For a more contemporary example, think of the opening sequence of Lars von Trier's *Melancholia* (2011), where the Prelude from *Tristan* becomes an accompaniment for a slow-motion apocalypse. (Or is the apocalypse a mere accompaniment to *Tristan*?) The *Tristan* Prelude is in a narrow sense the wrong music by Wagner for such a scene (Hello? *Gotterdammerung*?!), but all the same it works. In fact, it is so much the better for the specific story of a depressed heroine who cannot find redemption in romantic love, but finds relief when the other earth, "Melancholia," collides with ours.

Walter Benjamin suggests that extreme cases like Buñuel and von Trier's films are worth greater consideration because they give us more information than typical or average ones. Schoenberg noted something similar about the futility of seeking norms and averages in his comment on the nature of artistic theory. "Theories of art," he writes, "consist mainly of exceptions" (*Theory of Harmony* 11). And Slavoj Žižek similarly begins his analysis of Hitchcock's films with *The Wrong Man* because it is an exception among them. "The only way to reach the underlying law of a universe," Žižek proclaims with his usual aversion to understatement, "is through its exception" ("'In His Bold Gaze'" 211).

Modernism is typified by such exceptionality and extremity. For Fredric Jameson, this challenges a widely held assumption about modernism's origin: that it is a reaction to economic modernization. As Jameson also points out, fundamental modernist works tend to come from the periphery of modernity, not the urban, industrial center. The word itself was coined by Nicaraguan poet Ruben Dario. Joyce's *Ulysses*, the modernist novel, is set in late-colonial Dublin; the South is central to American modernist literature (*A Singular Modernity* 99–105).

The directors and composers examined in this book are similarly peripheral and essential. Richard Wagner rebelled against the conventions of Grand Opera, yet his work is also its summation. To escape Franco's fascist regime, Luis Buñuel went into exile, and the resulting alienation is a key element of his authorial signature (V. Fuentes 160). Thanks to his "offshore" location in the United Kingdom, Kubrick's work is a part of and apart from the Hollywood system. Godard epitomized the French New Wave, but by continuously revolutionizing his filmmaking, he left it behind when its other exponents were finally hitting their stride. Haneke embodies the opposite phenomena. He is a late (and Austrian) arrival in the New German Cinema, providing its extreme version, thanks to doses of Kubrick's coldness and Godard's censorious melancholy, mixed with a directorial sensibility honed in television.

Standing to a degree outside their social contexts allows these directors to identify key modern historical conjunctures. In his critiques of the bourgeoisie and Catholicism, Buñuel notes the left's ongoing struggle against the fascism which was never defeated in his homeland (and that is newly resurgent today). For Kubrick, key conjunctures are the French Revolution, World War I, the Cold War, and the Vietnam War. Godard is fascinated with the New Left, anticolonial struggles, and the 1960s and their aftermath. Haneke's vision is defined by an overriding sense of discontent with the end of history, with life after the triumph of global capitalism in 1989. In each of these contested interpretive fields, classical music becomes not a nostalgic voice from a golden age, but what it always has been—an enigmatic historical commentator on and participant in the ongoing dramas of economic modernization, political modernity, and cultural modernism.

In an interview with Carlos Fuentes in 1973, Buñuel's reflections on the heady days of his youth are characteristic of vanguard artists' sense of their contribution to the drama of history.

> Forty years ago, everything was very clear-cut. We thought we knew the issues. There was a defined line, moral, artistic, political; it all went together, a new art that would

enlarge conscience and sensibility, along with a revolutionary politics . . . We could then attack the bourgeoisie, surprise it, because it was so sure of itself . . . Now that's all changed . . . The media . . . make everything innocuous, fashionable. Just before he died, Breton told me: "Dear friend, it is no longer possible to scandalize anybody." Maybe he was right. (quoted in C. Fuentes, "The Discreet Charm of Luis Buñuel" 70)

The essential element here is the scope of Buñuel's ambition. His art was to be more than just art—it was to be an attack on philistine sensibilities and the political order sustaining them. If it is, as Buñuel speculates, no longer possible to provoke the scandals of old with one's attacks, and increasingly difficult to "enlarge conscience and sensibility" among desensitized consumers, that has not stopped the most ambitious and politically conscious of auteurs from trying. The fact that this ambitious approach to cinema persists signals that modernism itself—despite reports of its demise—has yet to be relegated to the dustbin of history.

To sum up: there is a fundamental continuity between classical music and its associated aesthetic ideals and some of the most significant modernist cinema; and, in both hidden and more obvious ways, modernist cinema renews the subversive energy of classical music masterworks. In this way, this book casts classical music in a more central role in the history of modernist cinema than has been previously proposed.

Its central role for classical music is part of what makes modernist cinema's sense of history distinct. Cinema's most frequent effect on historical subjects is to bring them back to life through realist aesthetics of verisimilitude and reenactment. Modernist cinema's interaction with classical music points to two different historical effects beyond this often misleading historical realism. In both the way it renders the "deep time" of the cinema's art-historical prehistory and the way music triggers memories and associations in qualitatively different ways than images and language, classical music is cinema's historical repressed returning. The effect of music on our lives, in other words, is both an older and a more transient form of experience than that of glimpsing moving images on screens. It is both more ancient and more immediate than encounters with moving images.

Its combination of emotional immediacy and art-historical "deep time" makes classical music modernist cinema's figure for the eternal. Baudelaire defined modernity in art as "the transitory, the fugitive, the contingent" and contrasted it with the "other half of art . . . the eternal and the immutable" ("The Painter of Modern Life" 13). Benjamin went a step further by identifying the two. "The eternal," he proposes, "is in any case far more the ruffle on a dress than some idea" (*Arcades Project* 69). If Benjamin's metaphor works as a figure for eternity, it is because intuitively at first it does not. Like a transient musical performance, nothing could be less eternal than a superfluous ruffle on a dress. But then one remembers the venerable solution to this paradox. The traditional shrug accompanies it. The yawn of boredom follows. The more things change, the more they stay the same.

Again and again modernist cinema manages to shrug off boredom and enliven such clichés in a process film critic André Bazin describes as progress won by cycling back to cinema's origins. "Every new development added to the cinema must, paradoxically, take it nearer and nearer to its origins. In short, cinema has not yet been invented!" (*What Is Cinema?* 21). Modernist cinema is thus original in a double sense: its new developments are original, as are its returns to its origins to find them. And to an underappreciated extent, those origins are in classical music. "Wagner?! God, again?!" one can easily imagine the technician in charge of temp tracks asking. "Yes, Wagner again," the figures in this book reply, "but we will make it new"—just like it felt originally, when the cinema had yet to be invented.

Coming Attractions

Chapter 1—"What Happens to an Apocalypse Deferred"—expands on musicologist Deryck Cooke's insight that while Wagner the philosopher believed in a bygone "golden age," the story of *The Ring* itself posits no such prehistorical period (258). *The Ring*'s afterlife in modernist cinema adds another level of critique to Wagner's own unconscious self-criticism of his philosophy in his art. While *The Ring* hinges on Wotan's decision to forsake power, its key appropriations in modernist cinema feature authorities clinging to power at all costs. At the same time, the visions of directors like Griffith, Coppola, and Herzog bear witness to the enduring modernity of Wagner's art by associating it with new visions of epochal and apocalyptic events. And in a final analysis, Wagner's vision of timely questionings of authority and subsequent rebellions remain in many ways more radical and subversive than his most significant modernist cinematic appropriations, which often lack the political imagination to see beyond the status quo of looming environmental catastrophe.

Fundamental to Chapter 2—"The Imperfect Wagnerite"—is the observation that Buñuel's most daring films, either in their formal experimentation or in confronting political authorities, all feature classical music prominently. The early masterpieces, *Un chien andalou* (1929), *L'age d'or* (1930), and *Las Hurdes* (1933), feature it most extensively. But Buñuel returned to classical music in *Viridiana* (1961) and periodically thereafter in *The Exterminating Angel* (1962), *The Phantom of Liberty* (1974), and *That Obscure Object of Desire* (1977). All of these films are unique variations on Buñuel's consistent aesthetic—to have modernized and politicized the transformation of the individual through erotic love that in *Tristan* Wagner imagined as fundamentally sacred. Buñuel's modernism is both a critique and a radicalization of the emancipatory political and cultural project of Romanticism—just as surrealism was not so much a rejection of Romanticism and realism as their synthesis.

Chapter 3, "'A Film Should Be Like Music,'" begins with the observation that Stanley Kubrick's films are often at their most historical when they are at their most musical. In particular, Kubrick associates classical music with the historical development of the modern psychological subject. Thus music and the condition of music are central to scenes of indoctrination and of recognition and reversal in Kubrick that relate to historical shifts in human psychology. This complex pattern holds true at a number of crucial junctures, including scenes of indoctrination in *Full Metal Jacket* and *A Clockwork Orange*, traumatic encounters in *Barry Lyndon* and *Eyes Wide Shut*, and sudden mental evolution in *2001*. As Roland Barthes wrote, "The historical meaning of the lied must be sought in its music" (274). The same is true of Kubrick's films, and the historical task of music in his films is to represent repressed psychic histories by both fixing and rupturing the meaning of his films.

Chapter 4, "Too Soon, Too Late, and Still to Come" focuses on Godard's tendency to feature fragments of classical music in his films. These fragments are more than emotive refinements of narrative developments. They are—as fragmentary ruins—signs of the current state of history, which from Godard's idiosyncratic but clearly leftist political standpoint is a matter of immense dissatisfaction. In addition to associating classical music with leftist politics, Godard also associates it with reflections on the history of cinema. From the standpoint of his use of fragments of classical music, Godard's *idées fixes* of leftist politics and cinematic art have occurred both too soon and too late on the stage of history. Godard's films bear witness to this historical noncoincidence of its major ideas and their realization in their abiding sense of melancholy. And yet, at the same time, Godard's use of classical music as source music in the films is often more optimistic and lighthearted in tone. Godard's reference in particular to Mozart has this quality of already being in a future world where work and love are united.

Chapter 5, "Before a Winter's Journey," reads Haneke's film as an anachronistic prequel to Schubert's song cycle *Winterreise*. When Erika

(Isabelle Huppert) hits bottom after her affair with her student Walter (Benoit Magimel), the film ends just as she departs on her winter's journey. At this moment, she resembles the singer in Schubert's cycle and the speaker in Wilhelm Müller's monodrama. She has failed at love and abandoned the other defining characteristics of her life. The main historical implication of Haneke's anachronistic prequel is a desire to return to the prehistory of film music and to go in a different direction, to identify the cinema with chamber music and above all with Schubertian lied rather than opera, yet Schubert's art songs eventually contributed to major reforms in Romantic opera, while chamber music and opera are not as opposed as might ordinarily be assumed. In this way, Haneke offers a critique of film music by searching out one of its origins organically, that is, in a film about the life of a singularly distressed classical musician, one for whom the remedy for her suffering is to become one of classical music's key archetypes while leaving the music itself behind.

The conclusion notes the importance of metaphor throughout the book and analyzes Terrence Malick's 2011 film *The Tree of Life* as an extreme example of modernist cinema's search for origins. It revisits the origins of the universe and life on earth as a prelude to flashbacks to the protagonist's childhood. The film incorporates key classical works at crucial moments, including Zbigniew Preisner's *Requiem for a Friend*, written in honor of his collaborator, the Polish auteur Krzysztof Kieślowski. This leads to a discussion of his *Three Colors* trilogy as a similar attempt to Malick's to incorporate the ideals of the Enlightenment into modernist film. It ends by comparing the film's use of Mahler's Symphony No. 1 and his attempts to keep the classical tradition alive by reinventing it with borrowings from folk and popular music with how Malick's film attempts to renew ancient wisdom in light of scientific discoveries. Like Preisner and Kieślowski, for Mahler and Malick, despite setbacks, the struggle for Enlightenment values continues.

Failing Better at Reading Walter Benjamin

In his controversial treatise *The Philosophy of New Music*, Theodor Adorno attempted to apply Walter Benjamin's philosophical-historical method of literary criticism to the study of music. Benjamin outlines what his method entails in *The Origin of German Tragic Drama*. "Philosophical history, the science of the origin," he notes, "is the form which, in the remotest extremes and the apparent excesses of the process of development, reveals the configuration of the idea—the sum total of all possible meaningful juxtapositions of such opposites. The representation of an idea can under no circumstances be considered successful unless the whole range of possible extremes it contains has been virtually explored" (47). Adorno used Benjamin's method to juxtapose what he saw as two opposed extremes of European musical modernism—Schoenberg and Stravinsky. Their juxtaposition was meant to configure the general idea of new music.

But Adorno's application of Benjamin's method has been shown to have two fatal flaws. First, it is motivated by a bias—what Charles Rosen calls Adorno's "parochialism"—in which Schoenberg represents the heroic continuation of central European musical culture and Stravinsky represents an alien intruder from a marginal culture (Rosen, "Should We Adore Adorno?"). The second problem is that Adorno limits himself from the outset to only two extremes from essentially only one category of modern music: the European avant-garde. Adorno makes this mistake in part because he ignores the crucial second sentence of Benjamin's formulation in his invocation of Benjamin. "The representation of an idea can under no circumstances be considered successful unless the whole range of possible extremes it contains has been virtually explored." Ignoring this stipulation, Adorno refused from the outset to explore the full range of possible extremes. As Rosen observes, "Adorno . . . eliminates from his review all forms of popular music, including jazz, and refuses to consider such contemporary figures as Rachmaninov and Sibelius. Hindemith is dismissed as a reactionary and Bartók given the most cursory treatment. In this way, he reduces the picture of the modern age to two isolated images" ("Should We Adore Adorno?").

Like Adorno, my musical focus is limited to what one would typically refer to as European classical music and could not be considered complete by Benjamin's standard because the whole range of opposed types of music in film is not explored. Perhaps this "better failure," to paraphrase Samuel Beckett, is only an improvement in its self-awareness. But a broader justification for the singular focus resides in the fact that the historical and ontological tension that defines music more generally is at its most extreme in classical music. This tension involves the distance between the ideal of a piece of music and its realization in a performance. "Since the eighteenth century, the almost absolute separation between composer and performer has exacerbated the inevitable tension between conception and realization that exists even on the level of improvisation. It has placed the work of music beyond realization but within the range of everyone's imagining" (Rosen, "The Aesthetics of Stage Fright" 10).

Modernist cinema heightens this tension between idea and realization by associating recorded realizations of music with its own ideas and contexts. Paradigmatically, modernist cinema displaces musical works to new contexts and thereby estranges them still further from their abstract idealization. Even with modern or contemporary classical music—whose history coincides with that of the cinema—modernist cinema often associates it with historical settings at variance with its own social context. Kubrick's *2001* is a good example. Ligeti's *Atmosphères* is rendered in the future tense, as a soundtrack for the film's mystified version of the evolution of human consciousness, while the "Kyrie" from his *Requiem* becomes a recurring leitmotif for the eternal monolith's interventions in human history. Similarly, in Kubrick's *Eyes Wide Shut*, the second movement from Ligeti's *Musica Ricercata*, meant as a Cartesian search for musical first principles by Ligeti, stands for a remnant from the Second World War in a film otherwise hailing, in terms of both its production and its historical imagination, from after the end of the Cold War, adapted from a novella from before either war began. In both cases, Ligeti's music's fuller realization, in the sense of reaching an audience of millions, dealt a blow to its absolute idealization. This is apparent in the way these pieces of Ligeti's music occupied a strange place, at least among cinephiles, where it is practically impossible to hear them without thinking of Kubrick's films. In this sense, Kubrick's use of these pieces has altered the very idea of them.

Such examples echo an unusual phenomenon in music history where vanguard pieces exist in advance of the conditions for their performance. Charles Rosen develops this point through an analogy with the history of the watermill (see Bloch, "The Advent and Triumph of the Watermill"). For Rosen, the history of the invention and belated exploitation of watermill technology is a model for how music develops relatively independent of its social context. Despite its immense benefits for productivity, the watermill was not fully integrated into Roman society until approximately five centuries after it was invented in the first century BC, and then it persisted as a means of production long after it was no longer the best option, well into the nineteenth century. These disjunctions were due to the exploitative conditions of labor relations in both eras. "As slavery declined," Rosen notes, "the expense of building watermills paid for itself, above all when the lord who owned the water rights could make his tenants pay for grinding their grain . . . When steam power provided an even more practical way of making flour, the water mills continued to be used because the local lord could force his tenants to continue bringing the grain to his mill" ("From the Troubadours to Frank Sinatra"). From this, Rosen concludes that "the processes of invention and exploitation are out of phase. Inventions arrive before they are needed and continue to be employed when they are no longer useful. The history of society and the history of scientific invention do not fit neatly together" ("From the Troubadours"). The same is true in music history. "Bach's great Mass in B minor was never performed during his lifetime: as a Catholic Mass, it could not be played in a Protestant church, and the use of an orchestra was forbidden in Catholic churches during Bach's lifetime, although he hoped it might eventually be possible" ("From the Troubadours").

As in music history, so too for classical music's role in modernist cinema: the music and the film's contexts are out of phase. Most often in modernist cinema, classical music is an older art persisting in stories set in modern and contemporary times. One such example occurs in Michael Haneke's *The Piano Teacher* and features the "Andante con Moto" from Schubert's Piano Trio in E flat. After the film shows musicians discussing phrasing for the piece in rehearsal, they begin the piece again, but abruptly, as the music continues as a sound bridge, the scene shifts to Erika (Isabelle Huppert), the titular piano teacher, exiting an elevator in a mall in Berlin. The shock of the ensuing sequence is due not simply to the way the music feels out of place, the way it seemingly belongs to a more refined environment than a mall full of bratty teenagers who nearly trample Erika. The greater shock is that the music perfectly suits the story and images at this point. As the scene proceeds and Erika enters a sex shop and then a private viewing booth, the many parallels between changes in the Schubert and the film make the entire situation that much more revealing. It is as if Schubert's trio was written nearly two hundred years ahead of its time, and its melancholy message were only fully expressed as an accompaniment for the exploration of sexuality in the alienated context of late-stage capitalism.

Auteurs Say "Fuck It"

Auteurism's modernist rebellion began with François Truffaut's 1954 polemic "A Certain Tendency of the French Cinema," which challenged the French film establishment's "Cinema of Quality" on the grounds that its purported psychological realism was neither psychological nor realistic. For Truffaut, this was because the "Cinema of Quality" upheld bourgeois values rather than satirizing them, as had the literary canon of psychological realism. For Truffaut, the director, not the screenwriter, was the true author of the film, and auteurism became a tool for exploding an old, and creating a new, canon of French and American directors in the stifling creative environment of the French film establishment after World War II. Liberating experiments in personal style by New Wave and Left Bank auteurs followed, including Truffaut's own early masterpiece *The 400 Blows* (1959). Such films sparked similar rebellions in German cinema and Hollywood and continue to reverberate across world cinema up to the present.

As Hollywood's modernist period, the Hollywood Renaissance of the 1970s was the heyday for auteurism's directorial control of production and a high-water mark in the industry in terms of originality and diversity. Peter Biskind's description of the era is appropriately nostalgic. "The thirteen years between *Bonnie and Clyde* in 1967 and *Heaven's Gate* in 1980 marked the last time it was really exciting to make movies in Hollywood, the last time people could be consistently proud of the pictures they made, the last time the community as a whole encouraged good work, the last time there was an audience that could sustain it" (*Easy Riders, Raging Bulls* 17).

Coppola's description of an artistically inclined director's dilemma on the set of *Apocalypse Now* is of note because it dates from the beginning of the end of the Hollywood Renaissance, and the end of the heyday of the auteurism that Truffaut's writings and films had begun. Facing financial ruin, creative difficulties, and negative press, Coppola summoned his vision of a director at the moment when his career had become emblematic of Hollywood's divorce from the perceived risks of auteurism. "Nothing is so terrible as a pretentious movie," he begins bitterly.

> I mean a movie that aspires for something really terrific and doesn't pull it off is shit. It's scum. And everyone will walk on it as such. And that's why poor filmmakers in a way . . . their greatest horror is to be pretentious. So here you are, on the one hand, trying to aspire to really do something. And on the other hand, you're not allowed to be pretentious. And finally you say fuck it. I don't care if I'm pretentious or I'm not pretentious . . . or if I've done it or I haven't done it. All I know is that I am going to see this movie and that for me it has to have some answers. And by answers I don't mean just a punch-line; I mean answers on about forty-seven different levels. It's very hard to talk about these things without being very corny. You use a word like self-purgation or epiphany and they think you're either a religious weirdo or an asshole college professor, but those are the words for the process, this transmutation, this renaissance, this rebirth, which is the basis of all life. The one rule of all men from the time they were first walking around and looking up and scratching around for an animal to kill . . . the first concept that I feel got into their head was the idea of life and death; that the sun went down

and the sun went up. When they learned how to make a crop and then in the winter all the crops died, the first man must have thought, "Oh my god, this is the end of the world." And then all of a sudden there was spring and everything came alive and it was better. And I mean after all, look at Vietnam. Look at my movie. You'll see what I'm talking about.

This "pretentious" speech has roughly three parts. First, it begins with a summary of the process by which a director overcomes his fear of being pretentious. Second, it includes a satirical and self-deprecating moment that marks the threshold of pretentiousness, with Coppola naming its stereotypical residents ("religious weirdos and asshole college professors"). And third, it takes flight into a pretentious, mythological anecdote that ends with the non sequitur of Coppola insisting that one simply view his film to comprehend the forty-seven different levels of meaning.[5]

Like Coppola, the principal directors discussed in this book have, in various ways, said "fuck it" to being pretentious so that their films might at least mean something to themselves. Of all the ways auteurs risk being pretentious, using excerpts or fragments from classical music is among the most obvious. At such pretentious moments, the classical music expropriated comes close to being reborn. Except that it has never died, but continued to develop interdependently with other modern historical processes.

On account of its stubborn persistent after its initial periods and contexts, classical music in modernist cinema bears a family resemblance to Gloria Swanson's immortal performance as Norma Desmond in Billy Wilder's *Sunset Blvd.* (1950). Desmond is a star from the silent era whose time has passed. When it becomes clear that her planned comeback has failed, she reacts by shooting the messenger, her lover Joe Gillis (William Holden), and retreating into psychosis. In one of Hollywood's great endings, murdering Gillis inadvertently fulfills Desmond's greatest wish. She finally reappears on the biggest stage of all when she descends the staircase in her mansion under the delusion that the news cameras are filming her latest movie, not her downfall. Like Desmond at this moment on the staircase, there is something sublimely defiant about supposedly outdated, "irrelevant" classical music's persistence in modernist cinema. And like Desmond, classical music in modernist cinema is ready for its close-up.

1

What Happens to an Apocalypse Deferred

Coppola, Herzog, and Schwarzenegger as Readers of Wagner's *Ring*

The Usual Way with Wagner

THE INTERDISCIPLINARY, CULTURAL studies approach to Wagner is no longer the rebellious road less taken it was a generation ago. In fact, today its prominence invites caricature. "The usual way to write about Wagner," music critic Alex Ross notes sardonically, "is to proceed from the world-historical level, musing on some combination of Aeschylus, the Icelandic sagas, Shakespeare, 'Faust,' Beethoven's Ninth, Schopenhauer, Nietzsche, George Bernard Shaw, Theodor Herzl, Adolf Hitler, 'Apocalypse Now,' and Bugs Bunny" ("Secret Passage"). While this world-historical approach is "an absorbing game" for Ross, the trouble is that "at the end of the day it leaves little space for the music, which is the ultimate source of the spell that Wagner continues to cast upon the world" ("Secret Passage").

But while Ross is right to lament the lack of attention to the details of Wagner's music in the cultural-studies approach, his subsequent interpretation of a unique orchestral "microlude" near the beginning of Act II of Wagner's *Die Walküre* moves from the musical details to the "world-historical level." Thus, by the end of his article he is citing not Nietzsche and Bernard Shaw, but two of their present-day equivalents:

philosophers Alain Badiou and Slavoj Žižek. Following Badiou, Ross dissociates Wagner from his Nazi appropriation by emphasizing that Wotan, the leader of the gods, willingly resigns from power in Act II of *Die Walküre*. Coming on the heels of the key "microlude" in Act II, Wotan's "soliloquy undercuts everything that is popularly associated with the term 'Wagnerian.'" "It is a deconstruction of power, a dismantling of grandeur." Then, in an outstanding example of "the usual way," Ross reports the comments of the German maestro Christoph von Dohnányi, whose father and uncle both died in concentrations camps for participating in the German resistance. "I don't blame any Jewish person," Dohnányi tells Ross, "not *any*, who would say, 'Wagner's music might be great, but I don't want it' . . . But when I really think about Wagner I don't discover anything that had to lead to Hitler. And what happens here [in the resignation soliloquy] . . . is not something that a Fascist could have written. Because . . . it is a 'giving up' thing" ("Secret Passage").

There are several reasons why Ross's interpretation of *Die Walküre*'s key "microlude" in Act II still ends up musing on a "world-historical level." At the most general level, history is the ultimate destination for even purely formal analyses of music. "Even the most technical description of music will bring us eventually to history," Charles Rosen observes. "No doubt the relationship between analysis and historical interpretation is reciprocal, a movement back and forth generally called hermeneutic" (*Frontiers of Meaning* 125). But while the interpretation of a musical text and its context is reciprocal, Rosen, like Ross, insists one begin with the music because "the essential condition of music is its proximity to nonsense, its refusal from the outset of a fixed meaning." Music's proximity to nonsense "is why," for Rosen, "starting with historical interpretation in order to explain the formal aspects of music is certain disaster: it is too easy to convince ourselves that anything we say is true, and too hard to convince anyone else" (125). In this light, the strength of Ross's "world-historical" interpretation of Wagner resides in how it starts with the music of *The Ring* and addresses historical and political questions not in advance, but as they arise from an immanent analysis of the opera's music. But in the case of Wagner, philosopher Lydia Goehr argues that politics and history are even more inevitable when interpreting his music because "with an impact unparalleled [Wagner] demonstrated in theory and in practice the wide-ranging significance of thinking about philosophy and politics in terms of music, and music in terms of philosophy and politics" (1–2).

Thus the "world-historical level" is inescapable in the course of musical interpretation; the question is whether one starts with the details of the music or with politics and history. Rosen and Ross make a compelling cases for why one ought to begin with the music. But in the case of Wagner, this method is not without its limits. Ross's music-focused reading proves a negative—that Wagner's *Ring* is not a proto-fascist work—but he does not advance very far in saying what then Wagner stands for more generally in *The Ring*. "The music offers hope," he argues, "nothing more." In fact, *The Ring*'s story itself offers more: an allegory for modern industrial class warfare and the revolutionary heroism needed to resolve the conflict and bring about a new nonhierarchical society, identified long ago by George Bernard Shaw.

Modernist cinema's interpretation of Wagner's music starts simultaneously with both the music and the world-historical level. They both come first. The music comes first because Wagner's music is the particular feature of his artistry that modernist film excerpts and repurposes. Auteurs want us to hear his music in new contexts of their choosing. But the film's new context simultaneously predominates. The new context for Wagner's music transforms its significance. These filmmakers have in effect already convinced themselves, as Rosen warns against, that the new historical context of their film is what the music now means, and these new contexts alter the significance of the music away from Wagner's intent.

Because of its attention to both the music and its new context, modernist cinema offers a perspicacious critique of the political philosophy entailed in Wagner's *Ring*. The modernist appropriations of Wagner's *Ring* admonish its naive belief that those in power would through reason alone reach a moment of voluntary resignation like Wotan's. But in this way modernist cinema's critique continues a process Wagner himself began in *The Ring* when the tetralogy abandons a central theme of Wagner's own avowed political philosophy: that there was a golden age in human prehistory. "In the tetralogy," musicologist Deryck Cooke notes, "the question of how [the fall from the golden age] actually happened in prehistory, and of what primitive humanity and its first societies were like, are ignored as the irrelevancies they are" (257). By contrast, Cooke notes, "Wagner simply confronts us with Wotan and his rune-laden (law-laden) spear, as a pure symbol of the existing immemorial authoritarian state-ruler" (258).

In his music's afterlife in modernist cinema, Wagner's wisdom in abandoning the golden-age premise devolves into cynicism. For Coppola (and Milius) and Herzog, Wotan-like authoritarians do not resign from power. But because of the disobedience and unruliness of the tetralogy's protagonists, Brünnhilde and Siegfried, Wagner's *Ring* remains a subversive and progressive political allegory surpassing Coppola and Herzog's implicit cynicism. The principle animating this disobedience is noticeably absent from the modernist films discussed in this chapter but oddly present, albeit in a distorted form, in the Arnold Schwarzenegger cult film *The Running Man* (1987). According to tradition, this subversive force is called love.

Figure 1.1. Helicopter Valkyries in *Apocalypse Now* (Francis Ford Coppola, United Artists, 1979). Digital frame enlargement.

A Helicopter Assault on Cinema's Origins

Today, the helicopter assault scene in *Apocalypse Now* and the memorable role of "Ride of the Valkyries" in it overshadow the film as a whole in the cultural imagination. As a result, the larger satirical framing of the scene and the ostensible antiwar intentions of the film have been obscured. In this depressing circumstance, two of today's most perceptive film music scholars, Mervyn Cooke and Matthew Wilson Smith, both make the well-intentioned but ultimately inaccurate inference that *Apocalypse Now* uses "Ride of the Valkyries" to allude to and criticize D. W. Griffith's *The Birth of a Nation* and its racist "Ride of the Klan" sequence, where members of the Ku Klux Klan rescue white women from marauding African American men to the tune of Wagner's "Ride" (M. Cooke 427, Smith 221). But neither director Francis Ford Coppola nor screenwriter John Milius refers to *The Birth of a Nation* as an inspiration, satirical or otherwise, for the idea of including Wagner in this scene. And while, though unintentional, the helicopter assault scene's resemblance to the climax of *The Birth of a Nation* is significant (more on this in a moment), the scene's true satirical allusion is immanent and obvious: it criticizes what film critic Michael Wood calls "the casual everyday lunacy of the war in Vietnam" ("Bangs and Whimpers").

During a conversation, Milius comments to Coppola that the scene is not an ironic rebuke of *Birth*'s glorification of the Ku Klux Klan, but an inspiration born from a genuine enthusiasm for Wagner's music:

MILIUS: Well, when you listen to his music and I loved Wagner, it just lends itself to helicopters for some reason [laughing].

COPPOLA: How did you come up with that? Because that was an early idea wasn't it?

MILIUS: Yeah, when I wrote the script the two things that I thought about all the time were Wagner and The Doors because I wrote the script entirely to Wagner and The Doors.

Milius wrote the screenplay listening to the Doors and Wagner, and naturally enough they both ended up as music for the film. Any allusion to *The Birth of a Nation* is, in this light, at most an unconscious one on Milius's part. Furthermore, Milius is definitely not as self-evidently antiwar in his politics as Coppola. Though difficult to categorize, Milius is normally seen as a major libertarian or conservative figure in modern Hollywood, having written and directed, among others, the kitsch anticommunist cult film *Red Dawn* (1984). The title *Apocalypse Now* itself speaks to Milius's irreverence toward the pieties of the 1960s countercultural left. It originated as his retort to the hippie slogan "Nirvana Now."

As he continues to discuss the idea of using Wagner during the helicopter assault scene, Milius's uncritical enthusiasm for the US military is hard to miss:

MILIUS: Oh yeah, that whole scene . . . I thought the Wagner worked. I knew that would probably work. And I knew that they did have psy-ops where they did, you know, put out speakers and play things . . .

COPPOLA: But they didn't play Wagner.

MILIUS: They didn't play Wagner; they played rock n' roll and stuff like that. But I really thought the Wagner would work. I thought that it would be, you know, something that fit with helicopters and a helicopter assault. And it worked so well that you can't do a helicopter assault anywhere in the world today without using Wagner.

COPPOLA: [laughing] That's true.

MILIUS: During Desert Storm, when the 101st landed behind the Iraqi lines, they had the helicopters flying over with the

Wagner before the other helicopters came, so that everyone could hear the Wagner and run away from "Ride of the Valkyries." And the same thing in 2003 when they invaded, every time the Apaches would go ahead they would put on the Wagner.

Milius takes so much pride in his scene's role in actual combat operations that he exaggerates its role. In fact, reports from the early days of the Iraq War described soldiers listening to "Ride" not while going on raids, but before.

> Psyched up by the blaring Wagnerian "Ride of the Valkyries" of *Apocalypse Now* fame, hundreds of American soldiers raided the homes of suspected Iraqi guerrillas yesterday in the western city of Ramadi. Troops with the 124th Infantry Regiment crashed their vehicles through metal gates in the city 60 miles west of Baghdad and rounded up Iraqi men at gunpoint, scribbling codes on their skin with marker pens as women howled in anguish. (Shin)

Fittingly, but also drearily, these soldiers have a more accurate understanding of the spirit in which Milius wrote the scene than film scholars in search of satiric allusions to cinema history.

But at a level beyond Coppola and Milius's intentions, *The Birth of a Nation* and *Apocalypse Now*'s varying degrees of indebtedness to Wagner make for an instructive comparison for considering the tendencies of modernist cinema. *Birth*'s composer and music director, Joseph Carl Breil, used "Ride" as part of an innovative musical score consisting of compiled folk and popular music, classical music excerpts, and original musical cues. Breil's score won acclaim for its pioneering use in film music of Wagnerian leitmotifs: short, recurring musical ideas associated with characters and themes (love, revenge, etc.) that lend both emotional resonance and, when repeated, dramatic coherence to a story. Thanks in no small part to the influence of *Birth*, leitmotifs eventually became part of the standard approach to film scoring.

Film historian Tom Gunning calls the type of filmmaking inaugurated by films like *Birth* "the cinema of narrative integration." Such films, as Gunning's name suggests, subordinate cinematic spectacle to traditional elements of storytelling, including character development and unity of action; such films were also longer than earlier films, with higher production values (including in the music department), and were ultimately more profitable on account of the higher ticket prices they commanded (Gunning, "Early American Film" 256–58; Lenning 121–22). As recurring, short musical ideas to link events distant in time, leitmotifs were especially important to the cinema of narrative integration, and have remained so for Hollywood film scores up to the present.

The irony of Wagner's "Ride of the Valkyries" in *Apocalypse Now* is that the film uses this music in a way opposite to Wagner's main line of influence on narrative cinema. Because the music occurs only once, it is not a leitmotif and does not aid narrative coherence as leitmotifs typically do; in fact the use of Wagner undermines narrative coherence. The helicopter assault scene and Robert Duvall's masterful performance are superfluous to the film's main story of Willard's mission to assassinate Colonel Kurtz. But as a surreal musical spectacle, it has become the most memorable part of the film. In this way, *Apocalypse Now*'s helicopter Wagner sequence returns to an original cinema aesthetic, where the spectacle was primary and the narrative secondary, a moment in the development of cinema to which modernism's avant-garde has remained faithful throughout the history of the medium (Gunning, "Cinema of Attractions" 57).

At the same time, the scene represents a sad sort of political progress: it updates *Birth*'s malevolent, racist nationalism. Indeed, it is the shared racist, nationalist element that is probably the source of the erroneous inference that the helicopter scene satirically alludes to *Birth*. In both films, a nation is implicitly a community unified by its opposition to a falsely characterized enemy.[6] And each film is a sign of the times in its version of this nationalism: at a moment when the Ku Klux Klan was reemerging, *Birth* depicts white America fighting the black enemy within; *Apocalypse* depicts a multicultural American army fighting a racialized enemy abroad. The evolution of this nationalism in the Cold War–era setting of *Apocalypse Now* involves a broadening of who counts as American and also a broadening of the threat to the American way of life.

In both cases, this extreme nationalism reaches its pinnacle in the mythical connotations of "Ride of the Valkyries." The use of "Ride" equates the Klansmen in *Birth* and the Air Cavalry in *Apocalypse* with the gods rather than their human counterparts on the battlefield. Traditionally, Valkyries do not participate in battle but, like Kilgore's cavalry, administer "death from above." In *The Ring*, they are responsible for bringing the bravest of the fallen warriors to Valhalla to await the battle at the end of the world, at which time Wotan will need their help defeating Alberich. Griffith's film equates the Klansmen with this race of gods who do not so much engage in a battle with equals as they sweep in to disperse their enemies without the possibility of being harmed themselves. The same can be said of the Valkyries of *Apocalypse Now*, except their invincibility is located in one character in particular, Colonel Kilgore, of whom Captain Willard notes, "He had a weird light around him. You knew he would come out of this without a scratch."

From Subversive Love to Class Struggle

In his skeptical attitude toward Kilgore, Willard's predicament bears a family resemblance to Brünnhilde's quandary when "The Ride of the Valkyries" first takes place at the opening of Act III of *Die Walküre*. In Act II of the opera, Brünnhilde has defied her father, Wotan, by coming to the aid of Wotan's half-human son, Siegmund, in a fatal duel with Hunding, the villainous husband of Sieglinde, Siegmund's twin sister and lover. Wotan first orders Brünnhilde to protect Siegmund and guarantee his victory over Hunding. But after Wotan's wife, Fricka, insists that Hunding win the fight, Wotan orders Brünnhilde to ensure Siegmund perishes. But when she encounters Siegmund and Sieglinde and is moved by their love for one another, Brünnhilde changes her mind and aides Siegmund. Only Wotan's personal intervention finally destroys him, and Act II ends with Sieglinde and Brünnhilde fleeing an angry Wotan.

As Act III opens and "The Ride of the Valkyries" occurs, it is for both the first time in the opera and the last time in the lives of the Valkyries. Brünnhilde's panicked arrival undermines her sisters' joyous performance of their song, and they are afraid for her when they learn she has defied their father. Brünnhilde's punishment is a harsh one: Wotan makes her mortal, imprisons her in a fire cell, and casts a sleeping spell over her. The rest of the Valkyries disperse, never to assemble again. But Brünnhilde succeeds in saving Sieglinde, who escapes with her unborn child, Siegfried, the hero in the final two operas in the tetralogy.

Apocalypse's "Ride" is a version of *The Ring*'s but without the idea of love as a force challenging the status quo. Coppola himself acknowledged the lack of love in *Apocalypse Now* and its relation to the film's openness to its eventual pro-war cooptation. "It is clear that if you want to make a real antiwar film you have to be far from the battlefield," he notes, "because if you show battle you are in a sense exciting people even though it's horrible . . . If you want to make a film that's antiwar, it has to be about love and it can't be near a battlefield."

In place of such a love story, Willard, who because of combat trauma is no longer capable of love, can only stare in bewilderment at the modern Valkyries of Colonel Kilgore and his men and then continue to carry out his mission to find and assassinate the renegade Colonel Kurtz. This shows how Willard is not as subversive as Brünnhilde. Through her love for her father and her regard for Siegmund and Sieglinde's love for each other, she realizes that being disobedient to Wotan's explicit orders and sacrificing her immortality is the only way to fulfill her higher ethical duty to her inner moral law and to her father's true wish to resign from power.

Despite the veneer of rebellion in his drug and alcohol binge at the beginning of the film, Willard obediently follows orders and completes his mission to kill Kurtz. By contrast, Brünnhilde disobeys Wotan and carries out what she believes to be her true duty, which she has discovered thanks to witnessing redemptive love. In a more Wagnerian version of *Apocalypse Now*, Willard—inspired by the patriotism and selfless love of a Vietcong Siegmund and Sieglinde he encounters by chance—would disobey his orders and joins forces with the Vietcong to bring the war to a swifter conclusion. The extent to which such a counterfactual version of the film is impossible, given the commercial and political realities of Hollywood, marks the difference between Wagner's artistic milieu and modern Hollywood.[7] Wagner found a singular patron in the young Ludwig II and was given a free hand to realize his vision. Coppola received none of the usual support from the US military that Hollywood war films rely on because of the perception that his film would be antiwar. He nearly went bankrupt funding the movie himself, only to have it become a signature piece of propaganda.

The irony is even greater in the case of Wagner's legacy. When the Nazis appropriated *The Ring* for their far-right cultural struggle, they distorted an art work whose politics recasts the Marxian class struggle in mythological terms. The Gods are figures for traditional aristocratic and theocratic authority struggling for power with the emergent class of industrial capitalists, represented by Alberich above all, but also by Mime and Hagen. The hero Siegfried, as a by-product of their struggle, is the revolutionary element. Wagner based Siegfried on his friend, the revolutionary Mikhail Bakunin, and in Shaw's reading Siegfried is an anarchist who despite being destined to save the world manages only to precipitate its collapse. The apocalyptic ending of *The Ring* is thus unintelligible from Shaw's progressive socialist perspective. This section of his treatise is subtitled "The Collapse of the Allegory" because the gods and their rivals perish while a socialist order is not brought into being.

But in fact it was in *Gotterdammerung* that contemporary audiences would have been most likely to recognize a class-struggle allegory. When Shaw calls *Gotterdammerung* a mere Grand Opera compared with the other true Wagnerian "Music Dramas" in the tetralogy, he unwittingly makes this point. For the tradition of Grand Opera was widely perceived to entail "naïve and pleasing depictions of the class struggle" (Rosen, *Romantic Generation* 601). "The hero and heroine—rarely seen as tied to their class but characterized only as individuals or else as rising above narrow class interests—are caught between the immoral corruption of the aristocracy and the doctrinaire rigidity or the secret greed of the leaders of the proletariat" (601). *Gotterdammerung* easily scans as another permutation on this naive and pleasing depiction of class struggle, with Wotan and Alberich as leaders of the contending classes, Brünnhilde and Siegfried as the lovers caught in the middle, and the typically catastrophic ending inflated into an apocalypse.

Like Shaw's quasi-Marxian interpretation of *The Ring*, *Apocalypse Now*'s appropriation of *The Ring* follows a pattern of insight and blindness. Its incipient critique of imperialism points in the direction of Wagner's themes of disobedience to authority and fidelity to redemptive love, but falls short of a full articulation of them. While Willard's cynical nihilism has the semblance of rebellion, Brünnhilde's disobedient sacrifice for the higher ethical ideal of love has its substance.

Herzog's Deferred Apocalypse

Werner Herzog's affinities for Wagner's music and the culture of opera more generally are well-known among his devotees. He has directed several productions of Wagner's operas; *Fitzcarraldo* (1982) features the title character (Klaus Kinski) entering the rubber business in a previously inaccessible area of Peru to finance his quixotic dream of building an opera house in Iquitos; and in his documentaries Herzog has turned to Wagner frequently and often insightfully. In addition to one about the annual summer festival founded by Wagner in Bayreuth, *The Transformation of the World into Music*, several major and minor Herzog documentaries include Wagner's music at crucial moments, especially the Vorspiel from *Das Rheingold* and Siegfried's Funeral March from *Gotterdammerung* (Hillman, "Wagner as Leitmotif" 260–64).

For Herzog, documentary realism needs Wagnerian artifice to reach what he calls "ecstatic truth": "There are deeper strata of truth in cinema," he claims. "It is mysterious and elusive, and can be reached only through fabrication and imagination and stylization" ("Minnesota Declaration"). But here, like Wagner, Herzog's philosophy and his art diverge. The deeper strata of truth that Herzog's cinema reaches through fabrication is not mystical but historical—most obviously in his fascination with catastrophes and disasters of historic proportions, but not exclusively in this sense. The true strength of Herzog documentaries is that they often present history from below, from the point of view of unsung people engaged in the necessary business of their daily lives. In this way, Herzog's ecstatic truths remain earthly and human.

An early example of Herzog's Wagnerian artifice serving historical ends occurs in the short documentary *La Soufière* (1977). The film finds Herzog chasing nature to the Caribbean island of Guadeloupe, where a volcanic eruption expected to devastate the island fails to materialize. Significantly, when in the last minutes of the film Herzog reveals that the volcano never in fact exploded, the film becomes otherwise aesthetically maximal to compensate for the lack of the explosion. The images at this moment are from a helicopter shot of the still smoldering volcano, and they are scored to Siegfried's Funeral March from *Gotterdammerung*. In one of his inimitable voice-overs, Herzog notes the inexplicability of the fact that the volcano never exploded before moving on to the true catastrophe he witnessed: the impoverished people who were unable to flee the expected eruption. "The volcano will probably soon be forgotten. In my memory it is not the volcano that remains but the neglect and oblivion in which those black people live. There was something pathetic for us in the shooting of this picture and therefore it ended a little embarrassingly. Now it has become a report on an inevitable catastrophe that did not take place."

In his honesty about his film's failure, Herzog matches the catastrophe for his film with the music for the major catastrophe in *Gotterdammerung*: Siegfried's betrayal and murder by a jilted Brünnhilde. This transforms Wagner's music denoting a catastrophic event into a soundtrack for an expected catastrophe that is inexplicably and indefinitely postponed. Herzog's voice-over emphasizes that the contingencies of nature are less predictable and more chaotic than even scientists sometimes allow for. Contingency is also a theme in the film's social analysis of life on the island, where, as most residents evacuated, the island's indigents remained. Crucially, they are not aboriginal but modern people, structurally unemployed and barely subsisting in the informal sector. The music becomes an appropriate elegy, or song of mourning, both for the film's failure to document the catastrophe that did not arrive and for its success in depicting the ongoing catastrophe of the lives of Guadeloupe's poorest citizens.

The counterpart to the failed catastrophe in *La Soufière* is Herzog's most controversial documentary, *Lessons of Darkness* (1992), where a significant, this time man-made, environmental catastrophe does in fact occur. *Lessons'* catastrophe is the oil well fires set by Iraqi troops as they fled Kuwait in retreat during the First Iraq War, which critics accused Herzog of transforming into a decontextualized spectacle that fails to educate audiences about its subject matter. Instead of explaining why this crime against nature was carried out, its long-term consequences, or how countries other than Iraq might share some of the blame, Herzog reads from The Book of Revelations to accompaniments from *The Ring* and *Parsifal* as footage from helicopters (much of it originally filmed by CNN) documents oil fires as though they were the end of the world.

The film's ironic tone begins almost immediately when Herzog's voice-over assumes the perspective of an extraterrestrial observer. "A planet in our solar system. White mountain ranges, clouds, a land shrouded in mist. The first creature we encountered tried to communicate something to us." The images that accompany these intentionally misleading lines begin with a seemingly primordial landscape with smoke rising from smoldering oil. The next shot is more surreal: a worker in the distance motions to the camera while an oil derrick spews flames many hundreds of feet in the air behind him. The soundtrack's Vorspiel from *Das Rheingold* renders the scene both more sublime and ridiculous.

The opening measures of *Das Rheingold*'s Vorspiel are famous for their use of a pedal point, a single, low droning E flat, developed with orchestral effects but without leaving the overtone series of this fundamental pitch for more than a hundred bars. Coming as it does at the beginning of the tetralogy, this pedal point was meant by Wagner to invoke a primordial world of mythic grandeur. In *Lessons of Darkness*, the music has a similar effect: it is meant to put the events at a distance where they are perceived as cosmological and world-building, as though this whole catastrophe had happened long ago and far away. Such a perspective, while not factual in a strict sense, has a grain of truth to it when one considers the role of catastrophic disasters in the natural history of the planet, such as the death of ancient forests, of which the fossil fuels burning out of control in the film are a prominent remainder.

This sequence is also historical in a Wagnerian sense. It transposes history into mythology, but with persistent, evocative political remainders. *Lessons* uses the music from the beginning of *The Ring* for a film that functions like a new epilogue to *Gotterdämmerung*. The gods have receded, and the humans who remain are tasked with cleaning up the mess. It is significant in this sense that the people featured in the film are not military or political leaders, but cleanup workers and traumatized survivors of the war.

The political and didactic shortcomings in *Lessons* can be traced to its exclusive use of poetic voice-overs. We are never told where the fires are, except in ironic title cards like "Satan's National Park." And when one does learn what happened to certain victims, the film omits basic contextual information about them, such as whether they are Kuwaiti or Iraqi, why they were tortured, and so forth. The obvious conclusion to be drawn from this is that changes in the substance of the voice-overs and the prominence of the film scoring in Herzog are reactions to the surreal quality of the imagery in the film. And yet at the same time, the scenes of the cleanup crew in *Lessons* are hardly less surreal; indeed they are arguably more so. But in these scenes there is no voice-over at all, as if the dignity of such necessary work could speak for itself.

Of all his documentaries, Herzog's documentary on the Bayreuth Festival, *The Transformation of the World into Music*, strikes the right balance between sublime imagery, informative interviews, insightful voice-overs, and musical scoring. Herzog was at Bayreuth in the summer of 1994 to direct a production of *Lohengrin*, and the *Transformation of the World into Music* is based around the interviews with principle figures at the festival that summer: Wolfgang Wagner, Wagner's grandson and the Festival's director; conductor Daniel Barenboim; tenor Plácido Domingo; and other festival staff, including an aged, volunteer fireman, who, in the film's most charming moment, sings along to *Lohengrin* backstage while Herzog illuminates his face with a flashlight. Herzog finds a happy medium in the film between enthusiasm and criticism: documenting the passion of the musicians, artists, and craftsmen involved in mounting performances at Bayreuth while also alluding to the ghosts of Nazi Germany that still haunt the festival.

In this balanced exposition, ultimately the enthusiasm for Wagner's music wins outs. Such is the case in the most trenchant interviews in the film—the first with Wolfgang Wagner, and the second with Barenboim, who is among the most celebrated Israeli musicians of his generation. Both Wagner and Barenboim advocate for the integrity of Wagner's art despite the festival's disturbing past association with the Nazi party. For Wolfgang Wagner, it is the performances in the here and now that matter and not what Herzog calls the "mythos" or "mystical" aura of Bayreuth. If one does not focus on the music in the here and now but opts for the mythos, one falls into the trap of past Wagnerians who saw in his music what Wolfgang ominously calls "the solution to all the world's problems." He speaks from experience; his mother, Wagner's daughter-in-law, Winifred Wagner, had been a close friend and supporter of Hitler and was chiefly responsible for fostering Bayreuth's ties to the Nazi Party. For her son, the business of mounting new performances may not undo the past, but the integrity of such performances can nonetheless speak for themselves.

When Herzog asks Barenboim about the well-known taboo on performances of Wagner's music in Israel, Barenboim gives the consummate answer of a musician. "As silly as it sounds," Barenboim says to Herzog, when the ban is finally lifted, "the important thing is that the music is rehearsed and performed properly." Barenboim continues with comments to the effect that while one must acknowledge Wagner's loathsome anti-Semitism and guilt by association with Nazi crimes, one also cannot reduce Wagner's music to that alone. The Third Reich co-opted the music of Liszt and Beethoven, too. In his most salient point, Barenboim reminds Herzog that when the conductor Arturo Toscanini rejected his 1938 appointment at Bayreuth to protest the Nazis and performed concerts in Tel Aviv instead, the music he chose was Wagner, proof for Barenboim that the association between Wagner and anti-Semitism did not yet exist and is not inherit to the music. To focus too much on the Nazi past, and thereby to prohibit performances in Israel, is to let the Nazis win by giving them exclusive right to music that belongs to the whole world.

By emphasizing the enthusiasm of the people involved in the production of Wagner's operas, Herzog's film suggests that a fuller understanding of Wagner's legacy can only be reached through the labor of learning and performing his music dramas. As in many of Herzog's documentaries, Herzog himself models the beginning of this process of learning about Wagner with his signature mixture of naive curiosity, enthusiasm, and reverence for his subject. His film is his contribution to the work of knowing the music by keeping its performance tradition alive. Here and elsewhere Herzog does not attempt to undermine Wagner's music but to find new audiences for it.

Terminating Wagner

Arnold Schwarzenegger's star persona is not unlike a postmodern version of Wagner's Siegfried, the hero in the latter two operas of *The Ring* whose actions, often unwittingly, hasten the demise of the gods. Schwarzenegger and Wagner's Siegfried are both central European in origin, fearless and invincible when not vulnerable to love, and their hero personas are agreeable to a wide range of political orientations, from the anarchist left to the libertarian right, though Schwarzenegger leans right both in life and in the preponderance of his films. The half-forgotten dystopian sci-fi film *The Running Man* is one of Schwarzenegger's most Siegfried-like roles. Schwarzenegger's Ben Richards has been cast out of the police force for an act of civil disobedience and joins the resistance's fight for control of the communications system in the film's authoritarian future. Like the more acclaimed *Total Recall* (1990), *The Running Man* is thus an important exception to Schwarzenegger's films' usual cynical tone (Freedman 544–46). Instead, Schwarzenegger's fearless character, like Siegfried, is continually caught in the plots and designs of those who mean to exploit his charisma and talent for violence.

"The Running Man" is a hit show in which "Stalkers" hunt and kill "America's Most Wanted." The film repeatedly satirizes the bloodlust of the show's audience when they cheer for brutal murders as though they were wholesome fun. It also criticizes the sanctimony of the game show host, Damon Killian (Richard Dawson). Publicly interested in justice and morality, behind the scenes he mocks his viewers' intelligence while pursuing higher ratings even if it means breaking the law. These attempts at satire are strange and ambiguous, and wholly different in tone from the Stephen King novel on which the film is based. They corroborate the film's antiestablishment theme of the oppressed overthrowing an authoritarian regime. But under the weight of so many failed attempts at humor (beyond Schwarzenegger's customary one-liners), the film devolves into absurdity, as though the price for delivering an ostensibly left-wing political message is paid by the film becoming incoherent and ridiculous. Nevertheless, in the film's antiauthoritarian politics and satirical tone, it distantly echoes Wagner's *Ring* and *Apocalypse Now*, but the faint traces of both are deformed, repeating as farce.

Set in a dystopian United States in 2017, the film begins with a counterfactual version of Willard's trip aboard Kilgore's helicopter in *Apocalypse Now*, but displaced from the periphery to the core of the US Empire. Unlike Willard, who only looks on in disbelief, Ben Richards disobeys orders by refusing to fire on a food riot in Bakersfield, California. Richards's punishment is swift and merciless. He is convicted for carrying out the massacre he alone tried to prevent. After he leads a successful prison break, and he and his fellow escapees find their way to the resistance network's lair, Richards is greeted coolly on account of his former profession in law enforcement and his notoriety as "The Butcher of Bakersfield." Richards assures the resistance that the feeling is mutual. "If you're not ready to act," he tells them, "give me a break and shut up."

Richards finally joins the resistance after he and his fellow escapees are recaptured and forced to participate in "The Running Man." As they escape death traps and dispatch the Stalkers pursuing them, his fellow contestant Weiss (Marvin McIntyre) realizes that the security system for the country's entire communications network can be hacked from an "uplink" stationed within the game show's designated battlefield, its "game zone." At first Richards is uninterested in the possibility for the resistance presented by this, but when angered by the death of his friends, including Weiss, the opportunity to "jam the network" becomes a way of avenging his losses.

At this crucial moment, when Richards's survival in the game zone takes on greater political significance, Wagner enters the film by way of

Dynamo, a Valkyrie-cum-professional-wrestler whose schtick is to sing opera while he dispatches his victims with weaponized electric shocks. The character embodies kitsch in actor Erland van Lidth, who was trained as an opera singer and served as an alternate on the 1976 US Olympic wrestling team, in this way developing a celebrity persona not unrelated to Schwarzenegger's, both being European émigrés who entered Hollywood through the side door of relatively obscure sports. Van Lidth was a good but not great wrestler who won a few small but memorable roles in mainstream films before his untimely death at thirty-four.

Dynamo enters the game show singing a 1980s version of "Ride of the Valkyries" arranged by Harold Faltermeyer, the man synonymous with the "synthpop" style then fashionable in Hollywood and the composer of themes for *Beverly Hills Cop* (1984) and *Top Gun* (1986). For devotees of kitsch, Faltermeyer's "Ride of the Valkyries" is a charming failure. If Wagner's original was ahead of its time, this version is already dated. Correspondingly, when Dynamo enters into combat with Richards, his distracting singing and bulky technological prostheses seal his fate. Preoccupied with his own singing, Dynamo follows Richards up a trash heap, where his car overturns, trapping him inside. Studio and home audiences call for his execution, but Richards spares his life, invoking humanitarian morality, not politics, in his decision: "I won't kill a helpless human being, not even sadistic scum like you."

Figure 1.2. Dynamo in *The Running Man* (Paul Michael Glaser, TriStar Pictures, 1988). Digital frame enlargement.

Allegorically, Richard's struggle against Dynamo is a contemporary ideological struggle (one that distantly echoes Wagner's *Ring*'s) in which the two sides of the ruling ideology meet in a cultural transposition and both sides lose. Richards is a libertarian moralist outwitting his superiorly equipped opponent but failing to recognize the larger context of the revolution (until Weiss's death in the next scene). Dynamo embodies the modern state's "law and order" fantasy gone awry: he is a clownish fascist, made more vulnerable by the technologies that should have advantaged him. Richards is right not to kill Dynamo during their encounter, not at a moral level, but because he represents the cartoonish fascism and law and order aspects of Schwarzenegger's own celebrity persona.

Musically, Dynamo's failure to defeat Richards marks the synth-pop style as an outer historical limit of Wagner's musical influence in modern cinema—the point where "Ride" spells defeat instead of victory. Perhaps the time has come then, as Alex Ross suggests, to return to Wagner's music without the baggage of its modernist and postmodern cinematic and cultural afterlife that burdens our understanding like Dynamo trapped in his Valkyrie car after Richards discards him. Except that such a move would be antihistorical and therefore anathema to the philosophies of both Wagner's music dramas and their afterlife in modernist cinema. *The Running Man* recoups the redemptive, emancipatory politics of the *Ring*, but the mark of historical difference is that it appears as a farce. Yet Wagner's *Ring* and its subversive political allegory remain an intimidating presence for any modern artist or critic, if only they can be remembered appropriately, as modernist cinema, sometimes in its very failures, sporadically but brilliantly suggests.

Coda: Witchcraft of This Sort

It is instructive to compare the co-optation of Wagnerian leitmotifs by modernist directors with the reception of Wagner in France in the nineteenth century and with Brecht's epic theatre in the twentieth. In each case, only a few drops of Wagner's artistic legacy, like an essence for cooking, seem necessary to advance the causes of modernist art and thought. While for Coppola and Herzog excerpts from Wagner's music are primary, "ideas rather than music were of crucial importance in attracting a number of important French literary figures to Wagner between the early 1860s and the late 1880s" (Bujić 223). Mallarmé's sonnet "Homage to Wagner" represents an extreme case in this tradition; his laconic tribute is colored with resentment. In contrast to Mallarmé's other homages, which begin at the respective tombs of Poe, Baudelaire, and Valéry, the homage to Wagner begins at the funeral of Mallarmé's own poetry. The burial is unceremonious, with his poetry entombed "in a cupboard-nook." This is because Mallarmé's defeat is "the god" Wagner's victory. Mallarmé has Wagner gloat about it: "smiling loathe original uproar." He saw in Wagner's idea of massive spectacles something that a sonnet or any poem for the page could not compete with, at least not on Wagner's terms.

Brecht's epic theater poses the greatest challenge to Wagner on his home turf of dramaturgy. For Brecht recognized that criticizing the pervasive influence of Wagner's Gesamtkunstwerk ("total work of art") was essential to promoting his original conception of theater.

> So long as the expression "Gesamtkunstwerk" . . . means that the integration is a muddle, so long as the arts are supposed to be "fused" together, the various elements will all be equally degraded, and each act as a mere "feed" to the rest. The process of fusion extends to the spectator, who gets thrown into the melting pot too and becomes a passive (suffering) part of the total work of art. Witchcraft of this sort must of course be fought against. Whatever is intended to produce hypnosis, is likely to induce sordid intoxication, or creates a fog, and has got to be given up. (quoted in Koss 254–55)

Brecht is usually read here as casting the Gesamtkunstwerk as the foil to his epic theater, which seeks to make relatively precise political points, not to intoxicate its audience. In *The Threepenny Opera*, robbing a bank is nothing compared to managing one, while gangsters parade around like statesmen and vice versa. To drive such points home, Brecht and Weill avoided the endless melodic style of Wagner, calling their *Threepenny Opera* "a play with music" and keeping its strong musical numbers relatively distinct from the development of the story.

But Brecht also conditionally accepts the idea of a Gesamtkunstwerk. "So long as . . ." is a key beginning. Brecht is not against the Gesamtkunstwerk a priori. Wagner's muddled version is contingent, not essential. "Witchcraft *of this sort* of course must be fought," but another sort of might retain the artistic integrity Brecht requires and attain the change in political consciousness he seeks. And this change is not all that different from that of Wagner's *Ring*, where traditional authorities wither away.

So if Brecht in a way remains Wagnerian, how to be Brechtian, how to pointedly awaken the spectator's political consciousness? Film critic Raymond Durgnat argues that "in his detachment from his own lyricism, Buñuel is more Brechtian than Brecht" (16). For Durgnat, Brecht's famed alienation effects "in practice delight us aesthetically" and therefore undermine their alienating purpose by continuing to charm and bewitch. Buñuel achieves the political and moral point making Brecht prized not with alienation effects but "because the complexity of his characters and of their predicaments, and the sardonic restraint of his style, force the spectator to careful moral judgements at every turn" (16). Indeed, Buñuel used Wagner in a Brechtian way, repurposing his music for political ends that, at the end of the day, are not all that different from Wagner's own.

Buñuel's critique of Wagner's *Tristan* seeks to politicize music from a story that Wagner saw as fundamentally sacred. But, like *The Ring*, *Tristan*'s other main theme is subversive love that defies authority. Buñuel's early films, *Un chien andalou* and *L'age d'or*, both resemble *Tristan* in their attacks on Victorian erotic and therefore political norms. Similarly to Coppola and Herzog, who modernize Wagner's music's context, but whose implicit criticisms of it only attest to the power of the original, Buñuel's radicalization of Wagner's *Tristan* is also an act of restoration. Though in the wrong hands the star-crossed lovers' trope becomes a stultifying cliché, with Buñuel and Wagner it retains its power both to liberate and to shock.

2

The Imperfect Wagnerite

Luis Buñuel and Romantic Surrealism

"An Essential Margin of Nonconformity"

As TOUCHED ON IN PREVIOUS CHAPTERS, classical music is fundamental to Luis Buñuel's most radical films, especially Wagner's music and particularly *Tristan and Isolde*. From *Un chien andalou* and *L'age d'or*, which rewrite Wagner's *Tristan* as hallucinatory dreams, to the last scene from his last film, *That Obscure Object of Desire* (1977), where Siegmund and Sieglinde's love duet from *Die Walküre* collides with an anarchist bombing of a mall, Buñuel imagined provocative new contexts for Wagner's notion that "love is not merely an urgent dramatic force in life, but the compelling higher reality of our spiritual universe" (Kerman, *Opera as Drama* 160). Like Wagner, Buñuel recognizes the socially destabilizing and liberating elements of love. But he also attacks romantic love as a harmful bourgeois palliative.

Just as surrealism is a radical synthesis of romanticism and realism, so too Buñuel's critique of Wagner's ideal of romantic love radicalizes Wagner's own emancipatory political and cultural project. Buñuel uses Wagner's music (along with that of Brahms, Handel, and others) to remind us of romanticism's central thesis: this is not the best of all possible worlds. "In any society, the artist has a responsibility," Buñuel argues, ". . . they can keep an essential margin of nonconformity alive . . . An artist describes real social relationships with the purpose of destroying the conventional ideas about those relationships, undermining bourgeois optimism and forcing the public to doubt the tenets of the established order" (quoted in C. Fuentes 71).

As these comments indicate, the high modernist period of the early twentieth century was a simpler time in some respects. Psychoanalytic insights were not yet clichés (though they never are in Buñuel's hands), and leftists were an organized political and cultural force on a global political stage where fascism was a real and eminent danger. The foregoing is written not with nostalgia for this time, but with a sense of renewed purpose in light of the reemerging threat of fascism after the failure of neoliberalism to secure basic economic dignity for the vast majority of humanity.

The scholarly literature dutifully mentions the key instances of classical music in Buñuel's films and describes them as ironic (e.g., Hammond, *L'age d'or*; Williams, *Figures of Desire*). They deserve greater consideration, both because of how crucial the music is to the films in which it appears and because his intent in excerpting classical music is not just ironic but also fundamental for modernism's politicization. Buñuel appropriates classical music—one of the best symbols of bourgeois refinement—as a tool to shock and skewer bourgeois culture. As his fascist opponents realized, this was more than a rhetorical game or prank. Buñuel's satires were attacks on the cultural front in the conflicts that forced him into exile after Franco's victory in the Spanish Civil War, embroiled Europe until the end of World War II, and endured in Buñuel's homeland for the rest of his life.

It is a commonplace of modern cultural history to note how some of the most vile, murderous regimes were capable of great musical refinement, the Nazis being chief among them. Buñuel's use of classical music is an antidote to the hypocrisy of playing string quartets after a hard day's work at the concentration camp. Buñuel's classical music shines a critical light on both the neuroses resulting from sexual repression and the false cure of libidinal desublimation proposed by consumerism (which Adorno called psychoanalysis in reverse). But, on the other hand, Buñuel avoided the other extreme represented by Leninism's supposed rejection of classical music altogether. Like Wagner, Buñuel left his greatest contributions to the cause of nonconformist, free expression in his art. But, unlike Wagner, he never wavered in the left-wing political orientation of his rejection of the status quo.

Dreaming Tristan and Isolde

In his memoir, Buñuel's describes the premiere of *Un chien andalou* as an unexpected triumph. "I was a nervous wreck," he writes. "In fact, I hid behind the screen with the record player, alternating Argentinian [sic] tangos with *Tristan and Isolde*. Before the show, I'd put some stones in my pocket to throw at the audience in case of disaster . . . I expected the worst; but, happily, the stones weren't necessary. After the film ended, I listened to the prolonged applause and dropped my projectiles discreetly, one by one, on the floor behind the screen" (*My Last Sigh* 106). The immediate and enduring success of *Un chien andalou* with the public is worth further reflection. A truly shocking film will likely retain this quality, but what has made it connect with audiences from the beginning? The answer resides in the way it draws on both great styles of the silent cinema. The film is both a spectacle and an integrated narrative.

Tom Gunning suggests that with the ascendancy of the narrative integration style, "the cinema of attractions does not disappear with the dominance of narrative, but rather goes underground" ("Cinema of Attractions" 64). *Un chien andalou* should be thought of as one of the great returns of this cinematic repressed, but combined in novel ways with the narrative integration style. The film's surrealism is not just groundbreaking but also familiar in its emphasis on spectacle over storytelling. But it also notes the ascendancy of narrative integration in its reliance on Wagner's Liebestod in its two most coherent instances of narrative arc building to a climax and resolution. Furthermore, rather than a contingent weakness, as was often lamented of incongruous musical numbers improvised by wayward silent film accompanists, Wagner's Liebestod and the film's tango numbers are an intended, absurdist juxtaposition of popular and classical musical extremes. But as opposites, they share an identity. "Both *Tristan und Isolde* and Argentine tangos were easily recognizable at the time as the high- and low-culture pinnacles of musical sensuality" (Barlow 43–44).

In the finale of *Tristan*, Isolde sings the Liebestod over Tristan's dead body, and then, overcome by grief and the physical toll of her performance, she dies of love. This is typically read as an act of spiritual (rather than carnal) consummation in which the lovers vanish into a purely musical realm. In a quasi-Marxian, materialist variation of this benchmark interpretation, Slavoj Žižek argues that the musical climax obscures the "cold hard facts" of the story. "In *Tristan*, the ultimate truth does not reside in the musical message of passionate self-obliterating love . . . but in the dramatic action itself . . . In music, it is as if the two lovers die together, whereas in reality, they die one after the other, each immersed in his or her own solipsistic dream" (*Opera's Second Death* 123).

But to understand Buñuel's use of Wagner's music, it is useful to recall an even colder, harder fact. The music from the end of Wagner's opera, widely known as the Liebestod, was not called that by Wagner himself.

Contrary to popular belief, *Tristan und Isolde* does not end with a Liebestod, or "love-death." In the final minutes of the opera, Isolde indeed collapses, lifeless, after singing an aria of serene ecstasy over Tristan's body. But Wagner called that monologue Isolde's "Transfiguration." He applied the word "Liebestod" to the music of groping longing that appears in the Prelude and recurs in Act I, as the lovers partake of the potion that they mistakenly believe to be poison. It was Franz Liszt who, in an 1867 piano paraphrase, dubbed the ending "Isolden's Liebes-Tod." In its original context, Liebestod indicates a death that turns into love. The later usage implies the opposite, a love that turns into death. The misnomer is particularly ironic because the dying Isolde never mentions death: instead, she hears Tristan's voice immortally resounding. Her transfiguration unveils a metaphysical realm indistinguishable from music itself. (Ross, "Wagner Weekend")

In light of these corrective comments, the genius of Buñuel's use of Isolde's "Transfiguration" in *Un chien andalou* comes into focus. When the film's male lead (Pierre Batcheff) survives his own death several times and continues pursuing his ambivalent lover (Simone Mareuil), the film enacts a surreal version of Wagner's notions of a transfiguration and of a "death that turns into love." The leitmotif-like repetition of the music (an abbreviated version of the Liebestod occurs twice in the twenty-minute film) and the death and rebirth of the character are a prototype for the theme of Buñuel's mature films.

In the film's first instance of the Liebestod (in Liszt's sense), Batcheff's character dies near the beginning of the music, and Mareuil's character rushes out of the apartment to cradle him on the street where he expires. In grief, she retreats into the apartment and begins, not unlike Isolde at the end of the opera, to try to imagine him and will him back into being. She arranges the nun's habit he had worn in drag on the bed, but he reemerges to her left dressed normally. Ants famously crawl out of a hole in his hand, and the close-up on his hand moves through a series of associative match cuts—first to an armpit, then to a cactus, and finally back to the street where he died—as a crowd encircles a detached hand being poked at by a woman in drag who vaguely resembles Batcheff. The rapid montage of shots corresponds to the increased pace of the music as it reaches its climax.

At the climax of the music, Batcheff and Mareuil appear in the window of the apartment above the scene. They observe the young woman as she pokes at the severed hand (a Freudian symbol of castration). As the music gradually begins to resolve and the crowd around her disperses, a police officer places the hand in a box (another sexual symbol for Freud) and gives it to the young woman. Entranced, she lingers in the street clutching her box, oblivious to the danger of passing cars. When she is hit and killed by one, this arouses Batcheff, who begins to aggressively pursue Mareuil while the music switches abruptly to tangos. The film is ambiguous about the extent to which his desire is fulfilled. As he fondles her breasts and they transform comically into buttocks, his expression is ecstatic, but when she pushes him away and prepares to defend herself against his advances, he is suddenly and inexplicably prevented from further assaulting her by being compelled to pull two grand pianos with dead horses inside them toward her.

As if this were the wrong version of him, while she hides from him in the next room, another version of him appears in the suit of clothes she had previously laid out. An intertitle indicates that it is it now "around three o'clock in the morning," and when someone rings the door and she lets him in, the person begins berating the new, docile Batcheff. This father figure gets him out of bed, throws away the nun's habit he had been wearing, and makes him stand with his head against the wall in punishment.

The next title card—"Sixteen years earlier"—makes the following images a flashback (to the extent that time is operating linearly at all). In slow motion and to the sound of the Liebestod again, the father figure character is revealed to be another, competing version of Batcheff. He approaches a school desk and picks up several notebooks and hands them to his other self. They immediately transform into guns, and as he tries to leave the room, the now armed version of himself commands him to turn around and put his hands up. At the second climax of the Liebestod, he shoots his fatherly self repeatedly. The scene cuts to a wooded area as the father version collapses; with his dying gesture, he claws at a woman's naked back.

In the next scene, Mareuil reappears in the apartment, as does the tango music. The camera focuses on a death's-head hawkmoth, and Batcheff, having survived death again, reappears in front of her. He covers his mouth, and when he uncovers it the hair from her armpit appears on his face. In disgust she exits the room and walks, dreamlike, onto a beach where she finds a new, more agreeable beau. They wander along the shore until they find what appears to be the remnants of the box that contained the severed hand from the first Liebestod sequence. The damaged box is like the ghost of Batcheff that she cannot escape. After another poetic intertitle, "In Spring," the film ends abruptly with an image of Mareuil and Batcheff dead and half-buried in the sand.

That Buñuel uses Wagner's music not once but twice to show death and transfiguration shows both his dependence on Wagner's music and his independence from its underlying metaphysics. It shows him emerging from the shadow of the master and finding what would become his films' principle theme: the inexplicable frustration of a desire. In *The Exterminating Angel* (1962), the dinner guests are unable to leave a party at the end of the night and persist in the salon for days. Conversely, in *The Discreet Charm of the Bourgeoisie* (1972), the couples are continually prevented from sitting down to dinner in the first place. And in *That Obscure of Object of Desire* (1977), Mathieu (Fernando Rey) is never able to consummate his relationship with Conchita (Carole Bosquet and Angela Molina), who is played, in an inspired detail, by two different actors. In these mature films, a metaphysical element beyond normal reality intrudes in the transfiguration of everyday experiences into impossible scenarios.

In *Un chien andalou*, by contrast, the frustration of the desire is not yet raised to an absolute, nor is the absurd premise delivered deadpan. Instead, these principles are only taking shape, and correspondingly, the scaffolding of Wagner's transfiguring music is still visible on the exterior of Buñuel's cinematic edifice. The film has its cake and eats it too: fulfilling the desire for death and rebirth at the climax of both renditions of the Liebestod and then having Batcheff survive and repeat the process. In Buñuel's mature films, the longed-for goal is not so easily, let alone repeatedly, had. Correspondingly, Buñuel does not repeat Wagner's music as a quasi-leitmotif again (with the exception of his *Wuthering Heights* [1954], in which case Buñuel did not control the final cut and was distressed by the producers' decision to use Wagner's music as a series of ubiquitous leitmotifs).

So while Buñuel reminds us that Wagner's initial notion was not one of love that turns into death, but a transfigured death that becomes love and desire reborn, still the repetition of the music and the tableau to end the film alter Wagner's aesthetic. The music loses its effect, and the ending of the original opera in a purely musical realm cannot be. One notes in this undermining of the music and the opera's original dramatic logic what Wallace Stevens once called the degeneration of nobility in modernist art because of "the pressure of reality" (13). In *Un chien andalou*, this pressure comes from the reality of the libidinal unconscious, where once is never enough.

The Golden Age as Its Opposite

L'age d'or, Buñuel's next film, also relies heavily on Wagner's *Tristan* and continues to radicalize the opera's idea of transfiguration. But in *L'age d'or*, Buñuel's notion of transfiguration is more clearly dialectical: he combines Wagner's musical sublimation of love with regression to infantile sadomasochism. The film's title is also a radicalization of Wagner's cosmology in *The Ring*. In both cases, no "Golden Age" exists (despite Wagner's own postulation of such an era in his writings). But while in *The Ring*, before Wotan cuts his spear from the Tree of Life, "there were no events, but only the unconscious world of nature" (D. Cooke 248), for Buñuel, this preconscious natural environment is a Darwinian one of competition in the struggle for existence. This is clearly visible in the documentary segment at the beginning of the film, where a scorpion kills a rat and "nature, red in tooth and claw" is invoked in contrast to Wagner's slumbering world of preconscious nature.

Like its expanded, quasi-Darwinian cosmology, the soundtrack of *L'age d'or* expands beyond Wagner. Buñuel "raided the classics," beginning with Mendelssohn's Fingel's Cave as the accompaniment for the nature documentary segment, followed by excerpts from Mozart's Ave Verum Corpus, the third movement of Beethoven's Fifth Symphony, and the first movement of Schubert's "Unfinished" Symphony, among others. Among these works, the Mendelssohn stands out because it is the first piece heard in the film and because it accompanies the film's implicit Darwinian critique of Wagner's cosmology in *The Ring*. It also stands out in this context because Mendelssohn was the principle target of Wagner's infamous essay "Judaism in Music." The essence of Wagner's polemic against Mendelssohn is that while he is clever and talented, on account of his Jewishness his music fails to depict deeper, universal human feelings (Wagner 94). Buñuel's use of Mendelssohn turns Wagner's prejudiced view on its head. Mendelssohn's heartlessness (in Wagner's account) makes him a more suitable composer for depicting the unsettling truth of the Darwinian universe: that the natural world is fundamentally amoral and not a guide for moral or ethical behavior. Similarly, *Tristan*'s role in the film is a rewriting of its significance so that its sense of love is also amoral, by turns infantile and sadistic.

The film is divided into three narrative segments: first, what the written summary of the film its producers used to bypass censors calls "several scenes of the great outdoors,"[8] followed by the main part of the film at a fashionable soiree, and a final brief coda that alludes to Sade's *120 Days of Sodom* in what remains an unsurpassed moment of surrealist shock effect. The thwarted sexual encounters between the principle couple (Gaston Modot and Lya Lys) are the one constant between the initial great outdoors scene and the soiree. When the great outdoors sequence ends with Modot's and Lys's characters shocking the dignified guests by groping each other in the mud, the soundtrack for this surreal spectacle is the film's first excerpt from *Tristan*. Their attempt at lovemaking is thwarted by both the pious crowd and nature itself when a belching noise interrupts *Tristan* and a non sequitur shot cuts to bubbling mud. Modot's and Lys's characters' frustrated sexual encounter continues at the soiree until Modot's character is finally able to retreat with Lys to a secluded spot on the grounds of the chateau for their infantile interpretation of *Tristan*.

The film ironically undermines the music from *Tristan* and Wagnerism more generally in three ways. First, formally, Buñuel includes the orchestra in the film itself, which is the opposite of Wagner's emphasis on the invisibility of the orchestra in the pit below the stage. Second, what transpires between Modot's and Lys's characters during the Liebestod is a repressive desublimation of the longing described by the music of *Tristan*. Their characters give way to strange impulses that essentially mock bourgeois society's most venerable transgression: the rendezvous of an illicit affair. Finally, the music itself is interrupted when the conductor, as a figure for an impotent and obscene paternal authority, approaches the couple and replaces Modot as Lys's lover.

But all this negation of Wagnerism and his music also confirms what it endeavors to deny: namely, the extent of Wagner's influence on Buñuel. Freud argued that such "obstinate denial" (Verneinung) allows for a repressed wish to surface on the condition that it is negated. Buñuel's wish concerning Wagner is clearly an Oedipal one. Correspondingly, the film ends with an apparently blasphemous vision of Christ as a menacing Oedipal father. After Lys rejects Modot in favor of the conductor, the film enters a coda section where it switches scenes and transports us to the conclusion of Sade's *120 Days of Sodom*. The novel's four libertines, who have kidnapped and repeatedly tortured and raped their victims for months, are seen leaving the chateau that is the scene of their crimes, except that Buñuel has made Christ one of the sadistic perverts. As shocking as this appears, Buñuel's depiction of Christ as a sadistic pervert is more heretical than blasphemous. Like Buñuel's famous quip, "I'm still an atheist, thank god," the shock value of the ending is predicated on a belief in Christ, however attenuated or disavowed.

Because Buñuel places the orchestra in the film as part of the drama, Wagner's music is central to how the film arrives at its heretical vision of Christ as a sadist. While Modot and Lys finally retreat to a secluded section of the estate's grounds, the orchestra tunes up and the other guests begin to congregate for its performance. Modot passionately and awkwardly embraces Lys, but just as the orchestra has yet to begin its performance, she will not let herself be kissed. Instead, in a first nod to infantile sexuality, they stick their hands in each other's mouths. The moment is both horrifying and funny, especially when she apparently bites off his fingers and he rubs her face with what's left.

After this "overture," the conductor steps to the podium for the downbeat of the Liebestod. But throughout the performance, to the evident frustration of the musicians, the couple misread the music as a call not to transcend but to continue their infantile sadomasochism. In the midst of their first kiss, Modot pauses in distraction, and Lys realizes to her evident dismay that she is second place to the foot of a statue adjacent to her head. After several further delays, they finally begin to fondle each other in a manner more suitable for the music and adult sexuality. But it is as though they have missed their entrance and are desperate to catch up to the orchestra. As a result, they rush and ruin the climax. As the music builds to its apex, Lys proclaims, "I have waited a long time for this." But "this" is not what one expects. "What joy to have our children murdered," she clarifies. Turning around, she sees her fantasy realized in a distorted form: Modot's eye is gouged and bleeding. "My Love! My Love!" he cries, as his symbolic castration coincides with the music's climax.

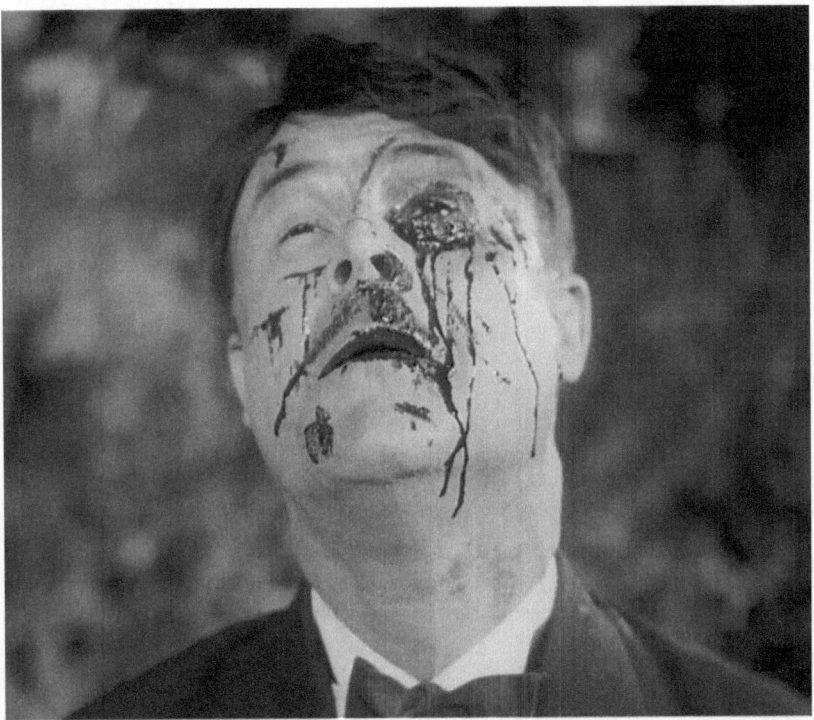

Figure 2.1. A surreal Tristan in *L'age d'or* (Luis Buñuel, Vicomte de Noailles/Corinth Films, 1930). Digital frame enlargement.

This grotesque spectacle proves too much for the musicians. The conductor throws his baton in frustration and, to the dismay of the audience, walks off toward the couple. Seeing his distress, Lys rushes toward the maestro, and they begin kissing while the film's score shifts abruptly to a primitive, ritualized drumming that, in another instance of regression, recalls the drums of Buñuel's childhood home in Calanda and their symbolism of Christ's death (*My Last Sigh* 19). Modot, dismayed, his infantilization deepening, storms inside while the soundtrack returns one last time to Wagner. But then the martial drumming begins again with renewed vigor as an enraged Modot defenestrates Christian and other religious fetishes.

From here it is on to Christ and Sade as the underlying essence of Wagner's *Tristan*. Buñuel's film believes that when one desublimates Wagner's transcendent music, one arrives at this radical image for bourgeois ethical life: Christ as the Urvater, a God whose ultimate ethic is to pursue enjoyment without limits, just as in the religion of capitalism one pursues profit without limits. In the final scene of the film, Christ murders a young girl offscreen and returns with a look of unspeakable joy on his newly clean-shaven face.

In the film's shift from Wagner to Sade, there is both regression and progression. There is a putative moral regression, and the change to primitive drumming on the soundtrack corroborates this aesthetically. But there is also progress from infantile sexuality as acted out by Modot's and Lys's characters to something more like adult sexuality, albeit in an extreme form of sadism. It is as though the film punishes them for their misreading of Wagner as a soundtrack for infantile eroticism by teaching them an advanced lesson from the textbook on adult sexuality. But more disturbingly, there is arguably moral progression in the reference to Sade, an early martyr in the fight against bourgeois hypocrisy in sexual matters. Furthermore, in Buñuel's use of both Wagner and Sade, he suggests that when an extreme degree of artifice is needed to stimulate sexual desire, it implies an underlying impotence. Sade himself emphasized this fact about his torturers in *120 Days*: their extreme cruelties were desperate acts to overcome their own impotence. Similarly, here and throughout his films, Buñuel's reference to Catholicism repeatedly emphasizes the impotence of faith when confronted by a harsh reality, above all in *Nazarín* (1959).

At the same time, Buñuel's sadistic version of Christ recalls his famously strident statement: "Do not think that I came to bring peace on Earth; I did not come to bring peace, but a sword . . . a man's enemies will be the members of his household. He who loves father or mother more than Me is not worthy of Me; and he who loves son or daughter more than Me is not worthy of Me" (Matthew 10:34–39). Buñuel invoked these lines at the end of *The Milky Way* (1969), his film that revisits the history of heresy as two pilgrims make their way toward the Shrine of Saint James in northern Spain. In the last minutes of the film, Christ recites these lines and then performs a miracle—making the blind see—only to have the miracle wear off almost immediately. The impotence here is not only Christ's but also the blind men's. He had stipulated that the miracle will only work to the extent that they believe. God and believers alike are thus united in culpability for the miracle's failure.

In *L'age d'or*, Buñuel's picture of Christ as an impotent sadist suggests a historical and political ambivalence. For the surrealists, Sade was a hero, a main figure in their canon. So making Christ part of a sadistic scenario means claiming him as part of their subversive tradition as well. For Buñuel in particular, putting Christ in the surrealist canon should be understood as an accusation against a Catholic Church that would five short years later ally with General Franco's fascist forces seeking to overthrow the elected government of the Spanish Republic. His next film, *Las Hurdes: Tierra Sin Pan* (1933), would be even more politically provocative and accusatory toward the Spanish state. Corresponding to the film's political intensification, Buñuel's shift from Wagner to Brahms as the primary musical background in *Las Hurdes* should be understood as an aesthetic intensification.

Land without Brahms

As Buñuel's only documentary, *Las Hurdes* emphasizes the realism in surrealism as his two previous films had not. Drawing on Maurice Legendre's popular ethnographic study of the remote Las Hurdes region in central Spain, Buñuel argued that his aim in the film "was to objectively transcribe the facts offered by reality without any interpretation, less still any invention" (*Unspeakable Betrayal* 217). But the film's inventive interpretation is hard to miss, and while staging and artifice in general are, ironically, among the oldest traditions of documentary filmmaking, *Las Hurdes* nevertheless represents an extreme case. Most famously, the film stages the death of a goat by dropping it over the side of a cliff and exaggerates the extent of the villagers' various maladies. In a corresponding instance of artifice, the film excerpts the majority of Brahms's Symphony No. 4, Opus 98 (1884) for its musical score. Thus *Las Hurdes* presents its subject through the distortions of a nightmare accompanied by Brahms.

Brahms was the most erudite of all composers in the late nineteenth century (Rosen, "Brahms: Classicism and the Inspiration of Awkwardness" 162). His Symphony No. 4 exemplifies two essential qualities of his style, economy and symmetry, which firmly position Brahms as a traditionalist (Firsch 119–22). Wagner, by contrast, was the iconoclast who created "artworks of the future," which were not, like the majority of Brahms's great works, purely instrumental works. But one should reverse the usual assumption that Brahms is the traditionalist and Wagner the revolutionary to understand the appropriateness of Brahms's music for *Las Hurdes*. It was already Arnold Schoenberg, in his essay "Brahms the Progressive," who praised Brahms's music for its innovations in orchestral timbres and rhythmic complexity. On the other hand, like many revolutionaries, Wagner described his innovations as a return to origins, in this case to ancient Athens, when, according to Hellenist doctrine, art was at the center of civic life.

The dominant interpretation of Brahms's Fourth's role in *Las Hurdes* is that it is "completely incongruous" (Russell 103). But, as with his use of Wagner, there is also a fundamental continuity between the music and Buñuel's disturbing new context for it. Like Buñuel's description of the region in *Las Hurdes*, Brahms music has an ugly beauty that distinguishes it: an awkwardness that results from its primitive, angular motifs and its irregular rhythmic emphases, and a sense of frustrated expectations that resembles Buñuel's sense of the lives of the rural villagers of the region.

Brahms's awkwardness shows both his debt to the past and how he transformed his sources. Beethoven and Haydn both used simple motifs to complex effect, but "Brahms chose material that even Beethoven might have considered unpromising: simple relationships that were ugly, awkward, resistant to development. He knew that the awkward could be made radically expressive, and how it could be exploited" (Rosen, "Brahms: Classicism and the Inspiration of Awkwardness" 177). From Schumann, Brahms took and developed the notion of dislocating the rhythmic relationship between melody and bass. But while, for Schumann, this dislocation was often total and consistent, Brahms's practice is rarely as schematic or regular. Charles Rosen's metaphor for the frustrated expectations of Brahms's music is one of infestation. "I mean this as no criticism, but in Brahms the relationship of consonance and dissonance is constantly eaten from within as if by termites. His music is full of holes, of frustrated expectations; this gives it its very unusual quality, and explains why nobody mistakes a piece by Brahms for one by the composer that he seems to be ostentatiously imitating" ("Brahms the Subversive" 159). This infestation is the sine qua non of Brahms's music, and the frustration in which it is rooted makes it an apt accompaniment for a film about a difficult place to live.

The struggles of the people of Las Hurdes also find an apt parallel in the way Brahms's music manages to be monstrously difficult without sounding like it. "It is something of a feat," Rosen comments, "to compose music so difficult that makes so little impression of virtuosity . . . Brahms had a decided preference for an awkward difficulty over a flashy one. The Lisztian pianist triumphs with ease over difficulties . . . the Brahmsian pianist remains engaged in his struggle, and will always seem buried in the musical material, and at moments overcome by it" ("Brahms: Classicism and the Inspiration of Awkwardness" 169). With his music's key features in mind—its awkwardness, its frustration of expectations, and its sense of unrelenting struggle—one can see why it makes a fitting soundtrack for a film that enhances its already difficult material with gestures toward surrealism. No wonder Buñuel himself felt that the symphony fit perfectly with the film and claimed to have been whistling it during editing (Gubern & Hammond 178).

The two major cuts Buñuel introduces in his arrangement of the symphony for the permanent version of the soundtrack (added in 1960) enhance its sense of struggle. First, the film completely cuts the third movement, the symphony's ray of sunshine in an otherwise "downright grim" affair (Frisch 127). Such a joyous movement is simply inappropriate for Buñuel's bleak picture of the economic and social conditions in Las Hurdes. Excluding this movement makes the piece more consistent (if less varied and complex), while also heightening its noted archaism. (The fourth movement, for instance, uses the baroque-era dance form of a passacaglia, which features variations over a short, repeating harmonic progression.) With reduced versions of the first and fourth movements as a prologue and conclusion, and the long second movement at the center of the film, Buñuel gives the entire symphony a pre-classical A-B-A' structural scheme. The abridged first movement is the A, the second movement the contrasting B section in the parallel major key, and the abridged finale, with its return to the first movement's E minor key signature, becomes A' with a coda.

The second significant cut occurs about nine minutes into the film and is also the score's only significant moment of silence. The music at this moment is from the second movement, and the film's arrangement alters it significantly. The film's version of the second movement begins at bar 87, proceeds to bar 106, and then after a pause begins at the beginning of the movement. When it pauses mid-phrase, around bar 106, the ensuing fifteen seconds or so feel suspenseful both because of the music's omnipresence until this point and because it is one of the film's only moments of real dramatic uncertainty and suspense.

The scene is a dismal schoolroom full of eager but malnourished students. The narrator claims to have opened "at random" a book of maxims and asked a top student to write one on the chalkboard. The shot of the student beginning to write on the blackboard coincides with the silence before the initial statement of the regal first theme in the brass. While he writes, the film intercuts with the faces of malnourished children diligently copying the words, and the viewer must wait in suspense to see what the maxim says. The students' enthusiasm is painful to see, and when the maxim—"respect the property of others"—is finally revealed on the chalkboard, it is no less authoritative than the Brahms fanfare that opens the second movement. The narrator's commentary gives the maxim a global significance. "It's the same all over the world. Respect other people's property." This commentary is both an objective description and a bitter indictment of the legal and moral underpinning of the social order. Respecting other people's property needs to be taught above all to those without any, to children like these. Fittingly, the image of the young boys transcribing the maxim was used in leftist propaganda both before and during the Spanish Civil War (Mendelson 85–88).

If one were to use a metaphor to describe the close relation of the Brahms to *Las Hurdes* at this key moment, one could say that they are like residents of the same town who lead totally different but inextricably bound lives. Like Don Pepe in Buñuel's *El Bruto* (1953), the Brahms is

Figure 2.2. Learning to respect private property in Las Hurdes (Luis Buñuel, Ramón Acín/Kino Video, 1933). Digital frame enlargement.

the boss of the town—calling for the respect of others' property. The inhabitants of the region are, like the Don's bastard son Pedro the brute, Brahms's exploited offspring whose lives are not nearly so enriched as to include classical music directly, or indeed music of any kind. "Strange, but we never heard anyone singing in Las Hurdes," Buñuel's narrator says pointedly over the film's first images of daily life in the region. But given the aesthetic analogies between Brahms's Fourth and the film, one can understand Buñuel's narrator's sad comment in a new light. Of course, they were not singing in Las Hurdes, but it was not just because they were poor and miserable. It was also because they were too busy being an allegorical embodiment of the frustration and anguish of the first, second, and ultimate movements of Brahms's Symphony No. 4.

This is how one can account for the strangest thing about the people of the region, according to Buñuel. "In general, a people in permanent misery either emigrates en masse or their numbers are slowly depleted, until they finally disappear. In Las Hurdes exactly the opposite happens. Instead of decreasing, the number of inhabitants has grown annually, to the point of overpopulation today. How can such an anomaly be explained?" ("Land without Bread" 220). Whether this was factually accurate is beside the point. As Buñuel's fantasy, the answer is brutally obvious from the perspective of the film's Brahms score. When one listens to, or, like the people in the region, embodies Brahms's Symphony No. 4, frustration, awkwardness, and difficulty become things to be enjoyed. No one wanted to leave because it would have ruined their performance of Brahms.

Handel's *Messiah* Redeemed

For Buñuel, *Viridiana* (1961), which he returned from exile to film in Spain, was an intellectual sequel to *L'age d'or*. "*Viridiana* follows most closely my personal traditions in filmmaking since I made *L'age d'or* thirty years ago. In all my work, these are the films which I directed with the greatest feeling of freedom" (Buñuel, "On *Viridiana*" 216). Paradoxically, Buñuel's sense of creative freedom seems to have depended on the likely prospect of government censorship. *Viridiana* was not released in Spain until 1977, after Franco's death, and when the pope called it blasphemy, Buñuel's response was predictably mordant. "I didn't deliberately set out to be blasphemous, but then Pope John is a better judge of such things than I am" (quoted in Wood, "Viridiana: The Human Comedy").

The most obvious reasons to censor the film are its two most iconic images: a scatological reenactment of the Last Supper by homeless people (with Handel's Hallelujah Chorus's as a soundtrack) and a shot of a crucifix that is also a switchblade knife. Buñuel played down the subversive quality of the latter, noting that the knives were commonplace. "One finds them everywhere in Spain and I saw many of them in Albacete. I didn't invent them. It is the photography which stresses the malice and the surrealistic character of an object fabricated innocently and put into mass production" (Buñuel, "On Viridiana" 217).

This remark shows the basis for Buñuel's surrealism in a vision of everyday reality at once naive and critical. Buñuel's Last Supper set to the Hallelujah Chorus is also a product of this vision. In both cases, the point is not to blaspheme but to satirize Viridiana's (Silvia Pinal's) well-meaning charitable attitude. Like the crucifix knife, charity is surprisingly dangerous; it seems to protect but actually harms. Early in the film, her cousin Don Jorge (Francisco Rabal) tries to warn her that "helping a few beggars does nothing for the thousands of others." The film's climax corroborates his skepticism. The moment Viridiana leaves her homeless wards unsupervised, they take full advantage with a riotous banquet, finding guilty pleasure in betraying their saintly caretaker.

In this way, Buñuel's critique of charity goes further than Don Jorge's observation. Viridiana's charitable acts exemplify Oscar Wilde's observation that "charity degrades and demoralizes" (Wilde, "Soul of Man Under Socialism"). In assuming the best about her wards, Viridiana unconsciously dehumanizes them, making them lifeless objects for her good deeds. By contrast, in their drunken revelry, "these vile creatures," Andrew Sarris observes, "become gloriously human" ("The Nun and the Devil"). This is most true of the syphilitic beggar, the outcasts' outcast, abhorrent even to the other beggars, who has the idea to play a record of Handel's *Messiah* to accompany their debauchery.

At the beginning of their revelry, while the syphilitic is permitted inside, he is still relegated to a separate table during dinner. The others' attitude toward him is about more than his disease; as they try to warn Viridiana, he is evil as a matter of principle. During the bacchanal, his behavior manages to stand out for its indecency, no small feat given that the others are binge drinking, fighting, and abusing their children. When they pose for their mocking tableau of the Last Supper and one of the women mimes a photograph of it by exposing her vagina, the syphilitic beggar is finally welcomed to the table, as if the rest of them had now descended to his level of depravity. His next move is inspired: having found the record player, he decides on the Hallelujah Chorus. As soon as the music begins, a flash of insight leads him from the room. He returns wearing a wedding dress that belonged to Viridiana's aunt and begins dancing to the music.

His drag show is not simply ironic in reference to Handel's music, but also deeply fitting. For although today we see Handel's *Messiah* as a sacred work, for Handel it was a matter of commercial opportunism. Having dominated the opera scene in London for years, by the 1730s Handel faced intense competition and the prospect of financial ruin. "Handel and his competitors were near bankruptcy and Handel was forced out of the opera business. With his practically incredible business sense he divined a huge potential market in English oratorios: Biblical operas presented without staging" (Taruskin). Correspondingly, Buñuel used this music in a film that revived his own career as an international auteur.

There are further likenesses between Handel and Buñuel. Biographically, both were artists who thrived abroad. Artistically, as a result of the commercial pressures they faced, they were both extremely efficient producing new work. Handel wrote the music for the *Messiah* in fewer than three weeks (Taruskin). After years working with limited budgets in the Mexican film industry, Buñuel prided himself on being able to film efficiently, even as his budgets grew more generous in his golden years. And just as Buñuel was fond of borrowing classical music at decisive moments in his more radical films, so, too, Handel was known for his knack for borrowing, which by some accounts amounted to plagiarism.

Viridiana's critical and commercial success, and the resulting restoration of Buñuel's reputation, are fitting tributes to Handel's *Messiah*, as the piece had the same effect on Handel's fortunes. But it is a disturbing tribute nonetheless. The syphilitic beggar's drag show is only an overture to the evening's greater excesses of sex and violence, and the Hallelujah Chorus is the point where the escalation begins. Indeed, it is significant that even after the outcasts realize they have gone too far and flee, the music continues to play, as though the power of the sacred love of God were an illicit pleasure their destructive orgy cannot hope to match.

Viridiana is often thought of as the first part of a trilogy of Buñuel films that star Silvia Pinal and question the efficacy of Christianity for modern times; the others being *The Exterminating Angel* (1962) and *Simon of the Desert* (1965). *Viridiana*'s and *Simon*'s use of rock music offer some proof of this theory. At the end of *Simon*, the devil (played by Pinal) transports Simon (Claudio Brook) from his ascetic universe in the desert to a nightclub in New York, with the club's rock music standing for both the unrelenting drive of capitalist modernity to overcome all impediments (especially traditional values such as Simon's) and the secret compatibility between his pleasure in self-denial as a stoic and the consumerist hedonism he seamlessly converts to. Similarly, after the beggar's orgy forces Don Jorge to put an end to Viridiana's experiment in charity, in the final scene of the film she capitulates to his advances and comes to play cards in his room, where a modern rock song plays on the record player. Paradoxically, the subversive rock music accompanies her act of conforming to modern life, while Handel had been the soundtrack for the outcasts' glorious if fleeting rebellion. But these are both false outlets for the film. The homeless characters' superficial rebellion confirms the limits of the charitable political ideal, and the alternative—Viridiana's initiation into Don Jorge's sexual intrigues—is hardly any better. Similarly, the rock music continues rather than contradicts the *Messiah*'s modern, secular roots in commercial considerations. For the film, Handel's *Messiah* is commercial rock music dressed in religious garments, not unlike the film's syphilitic outcast disguised as a virginal bride.

Music and Time in Paradise

Stephen Jay Gould argues that the opposed but related metaphors of arrows and cycles are our foremost ideas for comprehending the unfolding of time (see *Time's Arrow, Time's Cycle*). The arrow of time suggests pushing forward into a contingent and indefinite future from which there is no going back. Time's cycle evokes traditions and customs, nature's seasons, even the market's cycle. Buñuel's mature films heighten the tension between the cycle and the arrow by taking the cyclical metaphor to a surreal extreme, so that, in Gould's epitome, "time has no direction" (11). Buñuel's use of time's cycle turns it against its usually reassuring effect to destabilize familiar everyday experiences and reframe them as compulsions. In this way, he suggests that capitalist modernity is maintained by strange, quasi-religious rituals.

But if Buñuel uses time's cycle to critique bourgeois culture, then he uses its arrow to overcome them. Such is the case in *The Exterminating Angel* (1962), where time's cycle is pierced by its arrow when the bourgeoisie inexplicably trapped in a drawing room after dinner temporarily escape their surreal prison by consciously repeating the moment that led to their imprisonment. That this moment involves classical music is significant if not surprising.

Allusions to classical music are subtle but important in *The Exterminating Angel*. The dinner takes place after a night at the opera; one of the guests is an aging conductor; and Silvia Pinal's character is dubbed "La Valkyrie" for her fierce persona and purported chastity. Most crucially, and to the delight of the other guests, Bianca (Patricia de Morelos) plays a sonata by Paradisi after dinner. After she finishes and, complaining of the lateness of the hour, refuses requests for more music, it seems as if they

Figure 2.3. The bourgeoisie entering paradise in *The Exterminating Angel* (Luis Buñuel, Producciones Gustavo Alatriste/Criterion Collection, 1962). Digital frame enlargement.

all will shortly depart. Yet, mysteriously, they do not, and then they realize that for some unknown reason they cannot. Trapped for days, barbarism sets in. The film suggests that their imprisonment has something to do with their class position. Only those of the highest social circles are in the room, with the exception of one loyal and dignified butler, while, ominously, the rest of the servants, with little planning or coordination, leave the house in fear as the guests arrive for dinner.

The Paradisi Sonata offers another explanation for why they do not leave. They stay because they have entered Paradise. But like many dreams come true, this one turns out to be a nightmare, for their paradise is an earthly one. They still need to eat, drink, and relieve their bowels; to shower and change their clothes—yet none of this is possible. Buñuel's heaven on earth becomes a living hell that brings on an awakening akin to madness. This makes the closest analogue in modern literature to *The Exterminating Angel* Jean-Paul Sartre's *No Exit*: "The connections between [the two] are numerous and significant. In both, the basic story is quite simple, the setting and the action equally symbolic . . . we are given a parable that points an accusing finger at the basic state of human life" (Estève 245).

But while *The Exterminating Angel* has certain existentialist traits, their expression is fundamentally different than in Sartre's famed drama. In their starvation, madness, and death, Buñuel's dinner guests are more real than Sartre's characters. These real depravations, while challenging their solidarity, ultimately strengthen it when they finally remember, organize, and set themselves free, a possibility foreclosed in *No Exit* when the end of the play restarts the cycle of the story. In the brief, euphoric moment of solidarity as they exit the salon, Buñuel's bourgeois characters embody the overcoming of their own social class. They embody the revolutionary leader Amilcar Cabral's imperative that the bourgeois intelligentsia "must be capable of committing suicide as a class in order to be reborn as revolutionary workers, completely identified with the deepest aspirations of the people to which they belong" (Cabral).

This key moment of cyclical time submitting to time's arrow begins when Edmundo (Enrique Rambal), the evening's host, is about to be murdered as a sacrifice, and his wife, Lucia (Lucy Gallardo), notices that they are, improbably, all back in the exact positions where they were during Bianca's initial performance of the Paradisi Sonata. "Don't you see? Don't you remember?" she cries. Soon she demands Bianca perform the piece again in the hope they might, through reenacting their earlier experience, break out of their prison. Bianca returns to the keyboard and begins to play. After she finishes, they rehearse the compliments they paid her, and she repeats her previous refusal to play more on account of the lateness of the hour. Suddenly no longer rehearsing their previous experience, they are repeating their past with new solidarity and enthusiasm. Deciding as one to leave the drawing room, they are finally able to cross the invisible barrier separating them from the rest of the world. The logic of using the Paradisi Sonata to first imprison and then release them is similar to Wagner's motto from *Parsifal*: "the wound can be healed only by the spear which smote it (*die Wunde schliesst der Speer nur, der sie schlug*)" (quoted in Žižek, "Why Is Wagner Worth Saving?"). The music turned the key that locked them in, and the same key also unlocks them.

In the film's last scene, they find themselves imprisoned again, and the stakes of the problem have been raised to connote full-scale political unrest. As the dinner guests are leaving the funeral of a friend who died during their ordeal, again, inexplicably, they are unable to leave the church. But this time there are many more people trapped, including members of the clergy, and the space itself is a more public one. A place of refuge for the oppressed and downtrodden becomes what Buñuel might wish it was: a prison for the privileged, where their suicide as a class and their rebirth as revolutionaries might begin. The church's new role relates to another key detail from the ending. The scene outside the gates of the church, where people have again congregated but are unable to enter the church, pits the military against ordinary citizens in a bout of chaotic street violence. This detail all but anticipates the Mexican authorities' brutal response to the student protest movement in the Tlatelolco massacre of October 2, 1968, when government troops opened fire on peaceful protestors, killing dozens by conservative estimates. In this final, resonate image of political unrest, Buñuel repurposes the Catholic Church for revolutionary ends and anticipates a real conflict brewing in Mexican society.

Robbing the Bourgeoisie of Their Convictions

As in *Viridiana*, the most scandalous scene in Buñuel's associative masterpiece, *The Phantom of Liberty* (1974), occurs at a dinner. In this case, guests sit on toilets around the dinner table and retreat to the bathroom in embarrassment when they want to eat. Naturally, the first thing they discuss at "dinner," before moving on to overpopulation, is the latest production of *Tristan and Isolde*. It was astonishing. The soprano was

Figure 2.4. The bourgeoisie at a public bathroom in *The Phantom of Liberty* (Luis Buñuel, Greenwich Film Productions/Criterion Collection, 1974). Digital frame enlargement.

moving and charismatic. The world is turned upside down in terms of its informal social organization of eating and defecating, but making superficial comments on the beauty of *Tristan* remains a constant for the bourgeoisie.

Buñuel wants one to hear the conversation about Wagner in the context of a total transgression of social mores to bring the superficiality of the dinner guests' conversation into sharper relief. And just as their conversation about Wagner is a superficial one, so too is their quasi-Malthusian economic debate that follows, as though the problems of political economy can be reduced to rational calculations about the removal of waste. Finally unstuck in terms of its ability to perform the simple act of meeting for the dinner that haunts them throughout *The Discreet Charm of the Bourgeoisie*, the bourgeoisie remain as stuck as ever in their obsessions with reducing politics to the dismal science of economic calculation and artistic expression to material for small talk.

The association of classical music with breaking a taboo recurs in the film's reference to Brahms's G minor Rhapsody, Opus 79, No. 2 (1879). While the police commissioner character who had related the toilet dinner party story waits for friends in a bar, he meets, by chance, a woman who bears an improbable resemblance to his dead sister. He loved his sister deeply and tells the woman who resembles her a story about a summer evening just before her death when his sister played the piano for him. Before he enters his sister's room, his mother reprimands him for skipping a meeting because of the heat. "You'll never amount to anything," she tells him. In keeping with his mother's infantilizing treatment, when he enters his sister's room and she is revealed to be naked at the piano, their mutual lack of embarrassment suggests early childhood's shameless comfort with the naked body. Her piano playing, not her nakedness, is what matters. Even when he drops his lighter during her performance and crawls under the piano to retrieve it, he simply does not notice her fully exposed genitals.

In both this scene and the toilet dinner one, Buñuel pairs an impossible overcoming of a basic taboo with an avowal of love for classical music. That, as the commissioner reports, his sister died from a spectacularly grotesque form of cholera (vomiting excrement from the mouth) within a matter of days thus seems like a divine punishment for violating a basic social taboo and also a fitting death in a film where the bourgeoisie are at one point no longer embarrassed to go to the bathroom.

After the freedom of narrative movement in *The Phantom of Liberty*, Buñuel's final film, *That Obscure Object of Desire* (1977), marks a return to the predominance of time's cycle, with the frustration of a simple desire again raised to an absolute. Mathieu (Fernando Rey) can never have

Conchita (Carole Bonquet/Ángela Molina); she remains both spiritually and sexually impenetrable to him. To heighten the inexplicability of the frustration, the film famously has her played by two different actresses, often within the same scene. And just as this theme of sexual frustration recalls *Un chien andalou*, so it has often been noted that the final sequence of *Obscure Object* recalls the first sequence of *Un chien andalou* and thus brings Buñuel's career full circle. In his first film's opening scene, a woman's eyeball is slit open; in the final scene of his last film, a shop girl repairs a tear in a piece of embroidery. The main difference is one of tone. Because it was no longer possible to shock the bourgeoisie, this last scene practices what he called "sweet subversion."

In the final minutes of *Obscure Object*, Mathieu and Conchita have reconciled and are out shopping when, as always, their relationship begins to deteriorate. Loudspeakers in the mall announce that far-left groups have joined forces under the umbrella of "The Revolutionary Army of the Baby Jesus" and that a series of attacks should be expected. To allay concerns, the mall's sound system begins to play Wagner while Mathieu and Conchita (played here by Carole Bonquet) approach a shop where a seamstress is repairing embroidery in the window. It is an excerpt from the duet between Siegmund and Sieglinde, the lovers who are brother and sister, from Act One of *Die Walküre*. As the music plays, Mathieu, spellbound by the seamstress's work, mutters to himself, and fondles

Figure 2.5. Window shopping to Wagner in *That Obscure Object of Desire* (Luis Buñuel, Greenwich Films/Criterion Collection, 1977). Digital frame enlargement.

Conchita's hand. Sensing for the first time in their relationship that she is an afterthought, an incensed Conchita storms off. He lingers and looks again, shaking his head in awe of the seamstress's work before finally catching up with Conchita (now played by Ángela Molina). When she rebuffs him, her habitual capriciousness acquires a new sincerity. He is, as usual, perplexed, but then the presaged terrorist bombing interrupts their spat and brings the film to a close with the credits rolling over an image of smoke billowing from the explosion. That an act of terrorism should punctuate Buñuel's films is deeply fitting. In its drive to create art that could transcend art, terrorism was the aesthetic ideal of surrealism.

The terrorist attack can be read in two ways that provide a culminating instance of the dialectic of the scared and the modern in Buñuel. In a secular context, of course it is only bad luck that Mathieu and Conchita happen to be in the mall when the bomb explodes. Unlucky contingencies plague Mathieu throughout the film, like the car bomb that trapped him in traffic at the beginning of the film or the gun fight outside his apartment that killed Conchita's mood and delayed the consummation of their love yet again. But from a neurotic, superstitious perspective, the bomb kills them as a punishment for Mathieu's first and only act of infidelity. It is an act of magical thinking on Conchita's part; she warned him earlier in the film that she would destroy him if he were ever unfaithful, and now politics helps her make good on her promise.

To combine both perspectives, the film ends with Conchita and Mathieu martyring themselves, heroically committing suicide as figures for bourgeois life. She leads him knowingly to their shared destruction in a droll, consumerist reimagining of *Die Walküre*, for Mathieu's sin—to have regressed sexually to a fixation on the partial objects—resembles Sieglinde and Siegmund's. Their duet convinces them their love is so important and authentic that they can violate the taboo on incest; and, like Mathieu, this regression leads to their destruction in the end. In both cases, their self-destruction is part of a larger political upheaval meant to destroy the status quo.

What is one to say by way of summary of Buñuel's use of classical music in these later films? That in *Viridiana*, *The Exterminating Angel*, *The Phantom of Liberty*, and *That Obscure Object of Desire* the experience of classical music is strongly associated with the bourgeoisie as they live out, cyclically, their moment of ascendancy on the historical stage. Troubled by nightmares, afraid of their own ideal of liberty, and terrorized by the far left, they are all but ready to committee suicide as a class. That Buñuel tried to expropriate classical music from the complacent bourgeoisie is obvious. That he tried to do so repeatedly says as much about how he views classical music as an ally in his attacks on philistine sensibilities as it does about his preoccupation with satirizing the complacent ruling class. As the last scene in *That Obscure Object of Desire* makes plain, Buñuel associated classical music with political violence. But it is also, in its crucial and timely appearances in his most provocative films, treated as something that should endure even after the existing social order he despised has dissolved.

If today such an overcoming of capitalism seems a romantic impossibility, this should be taken as a sad comment on the horizon of the political imagination in the early twenty-first century, when what is politically necessary for human survival is dismissed as impossible. Until a more just society is born from the ashes of the present, classical music in Buñuel's films behaves toward the bourgeoisie like the dead sister of the police commissioner in *The Phantom of Liberty*. He thinks she has died until he meets someone who looks just like her. Then the phone rings at the bar, and it *is* her, calling from the cemetery, demanding he meet her there. But when he walks into the family tomb for their rendezvous, he finds himself imprisoned inside, buried alive. The same is true of classical music in Buñuel's films. Like the police commissioner's dead sister, classical music is a beautiful ghost haunting bourgeois consciousness with memories of its glorious past that are waiting to be redeemed in an inchoate revolutionary future. And like the police commissioner's sister, Buñuel's classical music lures the bourgeoisie to their tomb by robbing them of their convictions, so that without knowing it, they commit suicide as a class and are reborn as harmless ghosts confined to the cemetery.

Coda: Inviting Chance

Although many regard it as the foremost adaptation of the novel, Buñuel's *Wuthering Heights* displeased him for an unexpected reason. The film's producers had added too much Wagner to the film's soundtrack for the final cut. "It's no good. A great book. In the old Paris days, it was the one we most admired," Buñuel reminisced in an interview in 1977. "But while I was away they overlaid a huge Wagnerian sound track on the print. Nobody can even say 'Thank you' without its sounding like the 'Liebestod' " (Gilliatt 57–58). This sentiment appears inconsistent with Buñuel's use of Wagner throughout his first two films. Why would it have become a problem for him later? But there is only the appearance of an inconsistency here. His comments show that Buñuel was mostly upset by the inappropriateness of the music for the story's details. The Liebestod should not accompany a mere "thank you."

This is in keeping with his earlier uses of Wagner and Brahms, where the films banked on their continuity with the music, not simply the incongruity so many perceive. But Buñuel's style also evolved over the course of his long career into one of detachment from his own lyricism. With music in the late films, the detachment from lyricism was extreme. Musical scoring was simply by-in-large totally absent from the films, and what music there is occurs in the films themselves. This was an aesthetic decision no doubt, but still it was also influenced by a contingent personal event. "I like natural sound," Buñuel confesses in the same interview. "A zipper, a glass on a table. I can't bear music put onto a film any longer. Perhaps it's because I am deaf" (70).

After confessing to his hearing loss, Buñuel relates an anecdote from his youth that becomes a parable with wider meaning for his artistry.

> One day at the Jesuit College, there was this undervest in my soup. "Please, sir, there's an undervest in my soup," I said. I was sent out of the room, but I said as I went, "But there is an undervest in my soup." I suppose some boy put it there. The same thing has often happened to me in my films. People don't believe it, but there *is* an undervest in my soup. (72)

The producers who added Wagner to his *Wuthering Heights* were like that boy who put the undervest in his soup. They had added something to the recipe that for Buñuel and his superego (the "sir" he pleads with in the anecdote) felt inappropriate. That the resulting film is still viewed as perhaps the best adaptation of the novel is a testament to both the original material's vitality and Buñuel's tradesmen-like mastery as a director.

The "undervest in the soup" story suggests a key disruptive element for the creative process: chance. How to temper it? How to insure against chance's more harmful effects for an artist aiming for perfection and control? In *The Phantom of Liberty*, Buñuel's most perfect film, the answer to is to embrace chance. "When Jean-Claude [Carriere, his screenwriting partner for his late films,] and I work together," Buñuel explains, "we work always from a key word. *The Milky Way* was 'heresy.' *Discreet Charm* was 'repetition.' *The Phantom of Liberty* was 'hazard'" (60). Turning a problem into a solution, to inoculate itself against the undervest in the soup problem, *The Phantom of Liberty* makes chance its governing principle.

This embrace of chance recalls Mallarmé's poem "A Throw of the Dice." Like Buñuel in *The Phantom of Liberty*, Mallarmé was embracing chance in this poem. The final line of the poem is justifiably famous—"All Thought utters Dice Thrown." There is, in other words, an element of chance in all thought. Mallarmé and Buñuel let in through the front door and treat as a dignified guest the indeterminacy that normally burglarizes the house of the creative process. *Phantom*'s use of chance is structural. It occurs in the associational logic that shifts by whim between scenarios. But in terms of the episodes themselves, the dice are loaded to favor Buñuel's political and psychological fixations: the hypocrisy of the bourgeoisie, the fascist tendencies of the police, the wish to be free of the guilt and anxiety of sexual desire. It is, after all, still a Buñuel film. And, like Mallarmé's masterpiece, in its abandonment of conventional storytelling and sense making, *The Phantom of Liberty* approaches the condition of music.

When asked after surrealism what film should do for our lives, Buñuel responded with an answer that also suggests music's condition. Cinema should "give us the ease of a quest for pleasure and inquiry which isn't followed by the pounding hooves of guilt. It should be possible. Imagination will do the work" (72). Creating a film that is not a guilty pleasure, but that is still somehow easily enjoyed is no small task. What such a film would be, besides an imitable one by Buñuel, is hard to say. Easier to say is that the pleasure derived from it would resemble the joy of listening to music, where the indeterminacy of the music's meaning both releases us from the sense of guilt in enjoying what in cinema are too often meretricious storylines, while also calling on our imaginations to go to work.

3

"A Film Should Be Like Music"

Stanley Kubrick and the Condition of Music

"Something Big That Comes to an End"

EMOTIONALLY RICH BUT IMPOVERISHED of concrete meaning, music is a paradoxical medium of signification. Charles Rosen illustrates this paradox of surplus and lack with a droll example: "you cannot . . . by purely musical means, ask your listeners to meet you tomorrow at Grand Central Station at 4 o'clock . . . however, language must seek out poetic methods even to approach at a distance the subtlety and emotional resonance of music" (*Music and Sentiment* 5–6). This indefiniteness of musical meaning, which makes it notoriously difficult to describe, is similar to the challenge awaiting interpreters of Stanley Kubrick's films, many of which are celebrated for their use of classical music. Kubrick himself noted this likeness of his movies to music. "A film is—or should be—more like music than like fiction. It should be a progression of moods and feelings. The theme, what's behind the emotion, the meaning, all that comes later" (quoted in Kagan 231).

Later, if it comes at all. For in Kubrick's films, more often than not, the indefinite and the definitive coincide, with key musical moments marking points where his films' historical theses—especially regarding the development of the modern psychological subject—come to the fore. In Kubrick's films that relate to historical shifts in modern psychology and Kubrick's sense of that history, classical music and the condition of music are central to scenes of indoctrination, scenes of recognition and reversal for protagonists, and most memorably, scenes of pseudo-evolutionary change in the human mind. This pattern occurs at crucial, often exceptional, moments in *2001: A Space Odyssey* (1968), *A Clockwork Orange* (1971), *Barry Lyndon* (1975), *Full Metal Jacket* (1987), and *Eyes Wide Shut* (1999).

As a case in point, consider Kubrick's iconic use of the "Sunrise" fanfare from Richard Strauss's tone poem *Also Sprach Zarathustra* (1896), based on Nietzsche's philosophical novel of the same name, to punctuate key scenes of psychological transformation in *2001*. The story behind the decision to use the opening illustrates the point that the indefinite and the definitive, the music and the turning point of recognition, coincide in Kubrick's films. Kubrick was unaware of the reference in Strauss's tone poem to Nietzsche's story of a new superman ("Übermensch") to overcome present humanity. He had simply asked that the music be "something big that comes to an end" (quoted in Gengaro 75).

At first glance, this story undermines the assumption that Kubrick was a master of detail who left nothing to chance, while also providing a cautionary tale for critics and scholars who work at reading intention into the musical selections on his soundtracks. But if the choice of the Strauss and the happy correspondence of its philosophical background with the film's story arc were a matter of good luck, this represents an extreme case of the indefinite and the definitive coinciding in Kubrick's films. A piece of music inspired by a similar philosophical point of view to the film becomes in Kubrick's request just "something big that comes to an end," and what was a tone poem with a specific ideological inspiration is rewritten as a leitmotif of more indefinite significance.

Furthermore, the dubious scientific assumptions behind the pseudo-evolutionary transition from prehuman to human in *2001* correspond to the extreme indefiniteness of the classical music Kubrick employs most extensively in the film: Györgi Ligeti's *Atmosphères* (1961) and the "Kyrie" from his *Requiem* (1965). Excerpts of both pieces support the process of evolution from prehuman to human and from human to "starchild" that are then punctuated by the Strauss fanfare. Ligeti's compositions are known for their micropolyphony, in which clusters of chromatic notes and semitones begin to sound like undifferentiated masses of sound moving in eerie melodic patterns. Ligeti's radically indefinite music provides a fitting rhetorical support for *2001*'s unsubstantiated, implicit scientific claim about mankind's evolution usually passed over in silence in the critical response to the film. As Stephen Jay Gould pointed out, *2001*'s transition from apelike pre-humans to modern humans is predicated on the false assumption that aggression and violence were key to human evolution. The first evolutionary breakthrough in the film involves pre-humans repurposing skeletal remains as weapons, and a femur bone thrown in the air match-cuts, famously, to a floating moon orbiter to indicate a direct causal link between our supposedly violent prehistory and the film's brilliant hi-tech future. But this bit of visual poetry is predicated on a thoroughly discredited interpretation of fossil remains that, like the rendering of pre-humans by Kubrick and his cowriter, Arthur C. Clarke, mistakenly reads our violent, modern present into the prehistorical past ("The Nonscience of Human Nature" 237–42).

2001 both conceals and reveals its own historical context in its primordial image of violence as key to our evolution. It is a troubling sign of its times, of the "resurgent biological determinism" that was a reaction against civil rights victories of the 1960s, and that has yet to abate (237). Needless to say, the right-wing political forces behind biological determinism's resurgence since the 1960s resonate sympathetically with the Nazi co-optation of Nietzsche's Übermensch concept, not to mention the aged Richard Strauss's own compromises and half-hearted collaborations with Hitler's regime. In light of such correspondences, Kubrick's much-hailed popularization of Ligeti's music begins to sound more like its reactionary co-optation.

One venerable way of understanding the correspondence of Kubrick's films' indefinite, musical condition to their definitive historicizations of the modern psyche is the idea that images and sounds are "sutured" in the spectator's consciousness, with classical music acting as the suturing closure that also leaves a scar in its indefiniteness (Žižek, *The Fright of Real Tears* 32). But Roland Barthes's related notion of "the grain of the voice," with its connection of a singer's body to his or her voice through diction and enunciation (271), provides a more salient analogy for understanding the key shift in the historical development of filmmaking prefigured by Kubrick: film sound's increased and increasingly immersive role in cinematic experience from the late 1960s onward. Kubrick's use of classical music is a prototype for modern sound design's paradoxical stabilization of a film's narrative world through destabilizing, unreal levels of auditory detail. If, as Barthes defines and develops it, "the 'grain' is the body in the singing voice, in the writing hand, in the performing limb" (276), then the grain in contemporary cinema is the way in which its soundscape embodies the filmic world, a development augured by Kubrick's use of classical music.

Classical music and the broader condition of music are then key to unlocking the historical significance of Kubrick's films in a double sense, both their arguments about psychological history and their place in film history. But music's indefinite meaning should also remind us that the search for singular, definite meanings in Kubrick's films, as in the interpretation of music, is ultimately misguided. Regarding the problem of music's indefiniteness for critical inquiry, Barthes suggests that one change the very object of musicological inquiry to solve this problem. "Rather than trying to change directly the language on music, it would be better to change the musical object itself, as it presents itself to discourse, better to alter its level of perception or intellection, to displace the fringe of contact between music and language" (269). Kubrick's films require a similar shift: an alteration in the object of his films to reflect the importance of classical music's indefiniteness at their most definitive moments.

What We Talk About When We Talk About Kubrick

In introducing the grain of the voice, Barthes perspicaciously notes language's habitual failure to do justice to music's significance. "If one looks at the normal practice of music criticism, it can readily be seen that a work is only ever translated into the poorest of linguistic categories: the adjective." Barthes continues, "Music is, by a natural inclination, what immediately receives an adjective. The adjective is inevitable: this music is *this*, that execution is *that*" (267). Something similar goes on in the critical response to Stanley Kubrick's films—with critics often reducing his films to a single adjective or epithet. At least in this pejorative way then, in the way many critics talk about them, Kubrick's films have attained the condition of music.

Kubrick's films are most often described as "cold," both in the sense of emotional detachment and in the implied sense of being "cool." The heritage of the former sense includes, perhaps most famously, Pauline Kael's attack on the lack of humanity in *2001*. "It isn't accidental," she noted acidly, "that we don't care if the characters live or die" (145). There is perhaps even more truth in the sense of Kubrick's coldness as coolness. He was an indifferent student who became a prodigious street photographer, jazz aficionado, and sidewalk chess hustler before he ever made a film. "Coldness" in this sense is the name squares gave to Kubrick's coolness, to the part of his art they did not get.

In an interesting attempt to use a Lacanian psychoanalytic perspective to rehabilitate Kubrick's "coldness" as something more like warmth, Todd McGowan equates the lack of affect in Kubrick with something often associated with affect: fantasy. "Kubrick strikes us as cold," McGowan argues, "precisely because his films so thoroughly immerse themselves in the realm of fantasy" (43). In McGowan's telling, there is a political dimension to Kubrick's cold fantasies. Kubrick uses "film's fantasmatic quality to bring to light the hidden obscene dimension of . . . authority" (44). But the larger lesson McGowan sees in this is overly optimistic about the effect of Kubrick's films on viewers—"by exposing . . . authority's illusion of neutrality, Kubrick's films work to break the hold that . . . power has over us" (44). In fact, Kubrick's cynical view of authority is more frequently enervating than empowering. His films often simply present corrupt authorities in action, with attempts to break their grip on power being generally futile. Nevertheless, McGowan's reading of Kubrick's "coldness" has the merit of attempting to convert what is often considered an aesthetic weakness of Kubrick's style into its chief ideological-critical merit.

Going further, James Naremore questions the validity of coldness altogether by emphasizing the simultaneously terrifying and comical nature of Kubrick's films. This makes the key word for describing Kubrick not "cold" but "grotesque" in John Ruskin's sense of both "ludicrous" and "fearful." So while, like others, he is preoccupied with reducing Kubrick to a single adjective, Naremore's choice is a complex signification with greater purchase than coldness. And up to a point his analysis is persuasive, especially when he locates the one scene in Kubrick's films where the word "grotesque" actually occurs.[9] This comes near the beginning of *Full Metal Jacket*, where the grotesque authority figure, Sergeant Hartman (R. Lee Ermey), verbally and physically abuses his new recruits, singling out Leonard Lawrence (Vincent D'Onofrio), whom he quickly baptizes "Private Gomer Pyle." Lawrence cannot help but naively smirk because of his fear of Hartman's obscene witticisms, which only further infuriates Hartman. With escalating anger, Hartman asks Lawrence, "Did your parents have any children that lived? . . . I bet they were grotesque. You're so ugly you look like a modern-art masterpiece!"

Naremore justifiably calls this scene a "meta-commentary" on Kubrick's films as a whole and their modernist aspirations, but he does not mention how the grammatical ambiguity in Hartman's speech complicates the meta-commentary's meaning. At the moment we hear the word "grotesque," it is both overdetermined and indefinite. The acting style and the language are grotesque, yet the grotesqueries Hartman's use of the word designates do not appear in the film. When one looks closely at the lines of dialogue, the referent of "grotesque" becomes even more indefinite. In "I bet they were grotesque," the antecedent of "they" could be Leonard's parents, his siblings, or both. Not only does one not see the "grotesque" referent, but the identity of the missing referent is also unclear. Thus what Naremore argues is the definitive moment in Kubrick's films aesthetically also approaches the condition of music. The grotesque is like music in this scene because it both lacks an unambiguous referent but also contains a wealth of visceral meanings. Naremore seems to have found the moment that completes the puzzling search for the grail-like epithet for Kubrick's aesthetic, but the very use of the term in *Full Metal Jacket* is indefinite regarding its own referent.

Figure 3.1. Private Lawrence and Sergeant Hartman in *Full Metal Jacket* (Stanley Kubrick, Warner Brothers, 1987). Digital frame enlargement.

This paradoxical coincidence of grammatical indefiniteness and aesthetic definitiveness corresponds to a historical shift in military indoctrination exemplified by the training of Lawrence and his fellow recruits. *Full Metal Jacket* depicts a fundamental and depressing change in the training practices of the US military following World War II. To the surprise of senior military commanders and strategists, Army lieutenant colonel S. L. A. Marshall's famous 1947 study, "Men Against Fire: The Problem of Battle Command in the Future," concluded that "only about fifteen percent of American riflemen in combat [during World War II] had fired at the enemy" (Baum). Marshall's report argued, "Fear of killing, rather than fear of being killed, was the most common cause of battle failure in the individual . . . At the vital point, he becomes a conscientious objector" (quoted in Baum). Marshall's findings led to significant changes in the way the military instructs recruits. "Within months, Army units were receiving a 'Revised Program of Instruction.'" The Army began teaching soldiers to shoot by downplaying "the fact that shooting equals killing . . . Soldiers now acquired the skill of 'massing fire' against riverbanks, trees, hillcrests, and other places where enemy soldiers might lurk . . . By the Vietnam War, according to internal Army estimates, as many as ninety per cent of soldiers were shooting back" (Baum).

The story lines in Kubrick's war films correlate to this change. In *Paths of Glory* (1957), the venal officer class executes a few scapegoated soldiers in an attempted cover-up of an entire division's refusal to fight in an unwinnable situation during World War I. *Full Metal Jacket* tells a story about the opposite problem. Rather than refusing to fight, the film's soldiers become uncontrollable killers. This is the fate not only of Lawrence, who has a psychotic break during boot camp and murders Hartmann before killing himself, but also of Matthew Modine's character, Private "Joker," who excels in boot camp and early in his Vietnam tour on account of his ironic detachment, but who in the film's climactic scene kills a Vietnamese child soldier as she lies wounded.

Full Metal Jacket's particular genius consists in its development of the chief insight of the novel on which it is based, Gustav Hasford's *The Short-Timers*. Among the many victims of the US military's new training program were the soldiers themselves. Like Hasford, Kubrick depicts what the "Revised Program of Instruction" only implied. To play down "the fact that shooting equals killing," Hartmann repeatedly equates shooting with sexual gratification and its generative power to create life. But as the film shows, the enjoyment of killing can itself become a problem for military discipline and fighting effectiveness. Above all, as with Barthes's emphasis on the grain of the voice, it is Hartmann's uniquely grotesque vocal performance that renders the transposition of libidinal investment from the recruits' families to the military convincing. And at the crucial grotesque moment, Hartmann's voice becomes music, historically and aesthetically definitive in its meaning, but indefinite in its referent.

Seeing with Your Ears

A key scene from Alex's (Malcolm McDowell) treatment to correct his sociopathic and sadistic tendencies in *A Clockwork Orange* is another definitive and indefinite moment in Kubrick's films. The "Ludovico treatment" forces Alex to watch scenes of sadistic violence while he feels the effects of a torture drug that simulates the feeling of dying. With enough repetition, his mind will connect the effects of the drug to the images and make him averse to his own sadistic impulses. The clips he watches are almost indistinguishable from earlier scenes of Alex's violent exploits. Kubrick once said the film was made purposely to resemble a dream (Naremore 155). The reeducation film is then not unlike "a dream within the dream," which Freud saw as unique moments of certainty in dreams *because* the unconscious depreciates them (*Interpretation of Dreams* 328). *Clockwork*'s "film within the film" and Alex's reaction to it are similarly definitive, for they critique psychology while anticipating, with dreamlike distortion, the future of cinema, all in a scene in which the film approaches self-parody, asking to be taken seriously and not.

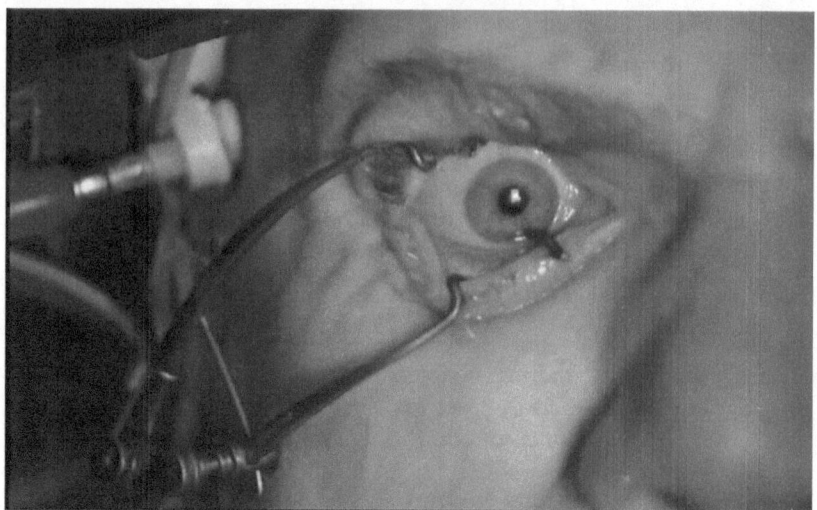

Figure 3.2. Alex reacts to Beethoven in *A Clockwork Orange* (Stanley Kubrick, Warner Brothers, 1971). Digital frame enlargement.

On the crucial second day of his treatment, Alex finds out why the treatment is named "Ludovico" after Ludwig van Beethoven. The scenes he watches are from Nazi newsreels and propaganda films, but this time there is a musical accompaniment: an arrangement for moog synthesizers and voice of the Turkish March section from the Finale of Beethoven's Symphony No. 9 (1824). "I noticed, in all my pains and sickness, what music it was that cracked and boomed," Alex notes in the film's voiceover. "It was Ludwig van, Ninth Symphony, Fourth Movement." His reaction is swift and unambiguous. " 'No! No! Stop it! Stop it, please! I beg you! This is sick! It's a sin! It's a sin! It's a sin!' " This is the only sequence in all of Kubrick's films where characters discuss the effect of background music, and Alex's reaction speaks to the power Kubrick saw in it. Indeed, because of the new soundtrack of his favorite music, the treatment starts to have its intended effect.

Alex's predicament during treatment epitomizes the descriptions of the viewer "sutured" to the "cinematic apparatus" from the film's contemporaneous heyday of psychoanalytic theory in film studies, when critics often likened filmgoers to the prisoners in Plato's cave. Like Plato's cave dwellers, Alex is immobilized and forced to stare at the images passing before him. But unlike Plato's prisoners, Alex knows full well that "the shadows of artifacts" he sees before him are just images from a "professional piece of sinny." Kubrick's version of suturing the viewer is thus seemingly fully conscious, not unconscious. Such a behaviorist method for transforming the test subject is more cynical than subtle. The subject knows full well he is being indoctrinated, yet the indoctrination works. It seems to create a picture of what suture would look like if one could bypass the need to manipulate the unconscious mind, the causal nexus of Alex's pathological fantasies.

This, however, is not Alex's psyche deprived of an unconscious, but his unconscious, as in a dream, rendered conscious. Crucial attributes of the Freudian unconscious are on full display, including the basic workings of perception and exemption from mutual contradiction (Freud, "The Unconscious" 584). His primary sensory responses are brutally reorganized with the help of the torture pill in a nightmarish realization of "total cinema" that doubts the existence of free will in a far less subtle way than Freud. For exemption from contradiction, note the almost expected irony of playing Beethoven's "Ode to Joy" alongside both images of Nazi violence and the exploitative machinations of Alex's Pavlovian reprogramming. Furthermore, in a sense he does not realize, Alex's comment that "it's a sin" is a fair summary of many critics response to the Turkish March variation. It is the point in the finale to the Ninth Symphony where the mood shifts from earnest to nearly farcical. In Žižek's reading, this variation is a necessary antidote to the banal earnestness of the variations that come before it ("'Ode to Joy,' Followed by Chaos and Despair").

The appearance of Alex's unconscious as fully conscious suggests that while the methodology of the Ludovico treatment is behavioral (albeit in an exaggerated form), the intended effect is closer to the domain of psychoanalysis: making the patient's unconscious fantasies conscious in order to change his way of relating to them. This strange mix of behavioral methods and psychoanalytic aims accounts for the failure of Alex's Ludovico treatment. It is not that the treatment is not radical enough; it is, instead, too radical—aiming at rewiring Alex's relationship to his fantasies rather than, as psychoanalysis would have it, helping him to acknowledge and understand them. Yet for a patient like Alex, the psychoanalytic setting is clearly not enough. Thus, in a final gesture toward historical reality, Alex presents a difficult question for modern clinical psychology. Not how, but should one treat a sociopath? Like the psychoanalytic community at large, the film assumes that psychoanalysis is ineffective in such cases, but the alternative of behaviorism seems capable only of remaking him as a broken man, not a free one.

The crucial shot as regards Alex's unconscious appearing fully conscious is the extreme close-up on his eye as he screams upon having recognized the Beethoven. For a proper sense of its place in the history of modernist cinema, this shot should be read alongside the close-up shot in Buñuel's *Un chien andalou* where a women's eyeball is sliced open, and the zoom out from Marion's lifeless eye in Hitchcock's Psycho (1960). Both of these definitive eye close-ups imply a certain depth—in the first case metaphorical, in the second case negative—behind the eye. In the Buñuel sequence, when the man (played by Buñuel) cuts open the women's eye, in a Freudian metaphor, he enacts his own unconscious belief in the primordial castration of women. *Psycho*'s eye shot escalates Buñuel shocking scene. Marion's death, which precedes the close-up on her eye, is not a surreal fantasy but a brutal murder. Similarly, the metaphorical relationship between the close-up on Marion's eye and the subsequent pan to the bathtub drain cannot be decoded by Freudian symbolism. Suggesting there is no soul behind the window of the eye, Hitchcock equates her lifeless eye with the emptiness of the drain.

Kubrick's shot of Alex's eye is the third part of this violent trilogy. But with its emphasis on the film's music instead of the visual implications of the eye, it anticipates contemporary cinema's move toward a phenomenology of immersion where overwhelming soundscapes render

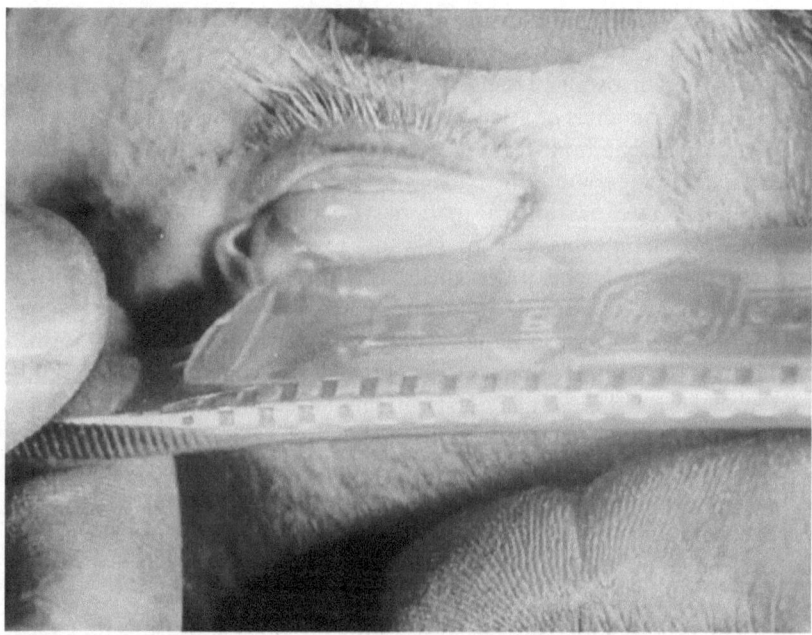

Figure 3.3. A razor cuts an eye in *Un chien andalou* (Luis Buñuel, Les Grands Films Classiques/Transflux Films, 1929). Digital frame enlargement.

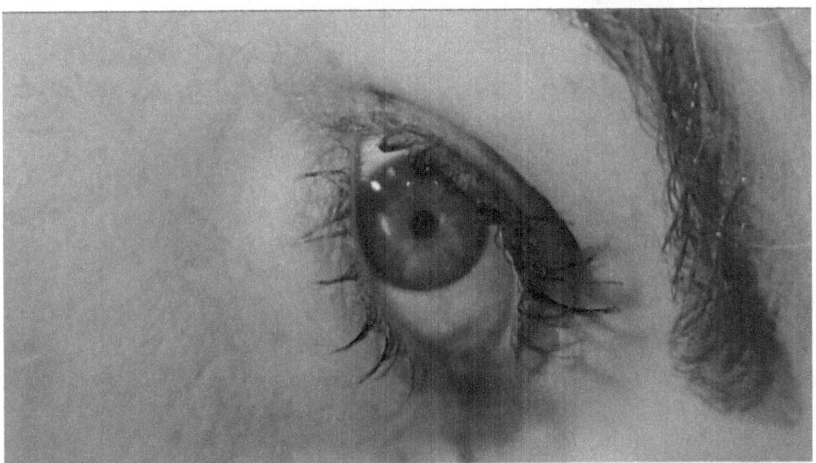

Figure 3.4. Marion's lifeless eye in *Psycho* (Alfred Hitchcock, Paramount Pictures, 1960). Digital frame enlargement.

the surface/depth dichotomy embodied by Buñuel and Hitchcock's shots passé. Missing from the close-up on Alex's eye in *Clockwork*, in other words, are exactly the implications of unconscious material or negativity in the sequences of Buñuel and Hitchcock. Instead, as suggested by the metal brackets holding it open, Alex's eye is reduced to its instrumental essence as a device for detecting and processing light. The irony is that although this extreme close-up is ostensibly the most intense shot in Alex's entire treatment sequence, as far as the logic of his treatment is concerned, the shot's focus is not exclusively visual. It resides in Alex's reaction not to the images he sees but in their combination with the Beethoven he hears and how the mixture is made to correspond to the torture drug.

The logic of the cut that follows his second day of treatment confirms this. After his vociferous complaints about Beethoven's inclusion in his course of treatment, the film jumps forward to Alex's publicity appearance to prove he is cured. As his doctor puts it, Beethoven is his most "rewarding association." But the hope of a cure is quickly dashed when his new, civilized mentality is shown to be little more than a state of learned helplessness that his previous victims mercilessly exploit for revenge. And when his treatment is finally reversed and he is allowed to be his sadistic self again, his incorrigible behavior is another case in point of the influence of fashionable, biological determinist theories of innate aggression on Kubrick. Alex's fate is an extreme form of that of the modern consumer; he is allowed to transgress and rebel so long as his transgression does nothing to disturb the larger relations of power.

Music as History

Like Barthes's argument for the relocation of the musical-critical object to the interaction between the musical sound and the body producing it, Annette Michelson argues that Kubrick's film "solicits . . . the relocation of the terrain upon which things happen" (204) to their special effects. That is, in their predominance on-screen, the very experience of them as "special" is lost, and their new normalcy compounds their illusory power. As in *Clockwork*, *2001*'s "relocation" anticipates cinema history, but in this case the film prefigures the dominance of computer-generated images in blockbuster spectacles. But Michelson is notably silent on the other relocation of events in *2001*—not just to its epochal visual effects, but to its musical score. Thus, what is conspicuously absent historically in the story of *2001* returns in the score's interaction with the film—namely, modern history itself, transfigured as a brief survey of modern classical music history. "The film neatly brackets the entire arc of twentieth-century musical history. It begins with Strauss's *Thus Spake Zarathustra* . . . in the final section, the movie is subsumed into Ligeti's alternate universe, spiraling through the outer limits of expression" (Ross, *The Rest Is Noise* 469).

The film's most cheerful scene—the space-docking sequence after the momentous match-cut from prehistory to the near future—diverges from this pattern in its anachronistic musical selection of Johan Strauss's *Blue Danube* (1866). The wry humor of the anachronism should not lure one into taking it lightly, however. To paraphrase Oscar Wilde, some things are far too important to talk seriously about them. In this case, indeed, "rather than supporting and/or coloring the visual images and narrative situations, the Strauss stands as an image in its own right" (Brown 240). As an image, the Strauss waltz represents nothing less than the Western cultural tradition prior to the modernist moment.

The Strauss waltz refashions space as a grand ballroom in which machines flirt and play in a cosmic, anthropomorphic dance. Like a real waltz, which traditionally begins slowly to allow the dancers time to find their partners and assemble, Kubrick's opening montage for this sequence introduces a few scattered and seemingly motionless spacecrafts with the Earth and the moon as a backdrop. Kubrick then focuses in on the two partners who will be the subject of the space-docking dance sequence:

Figure 3.5. The routine problems of space travel in *2001: A Space Odyssey* (Stanley Kubrick, Metro-Goldwyn-Mayer, 1968). Digital frame enlargement.

the space station and the shuttle. The station rotates in a deft allusion to the spiraling movement of the Viennese waltz itself while the shuttle appears just as the main melody is stated at a proper dance tempo rather than as an introductory atmospheric. A dance within the dance follows suit when an important bureaucrat sleeps during his commute, and a flight attendant struggles to secure his pen floating harmlessly in the aisle, showing how space travel transfigures even the most mundane tasks, transforming small steps into giant leaps.

Cézanne argued that painting should render the act of seeing itself rather than the thing seen. Similarly, this scene's iconic combination of images and music represents the psychological process of hearing itself rather than the thing heard. The images one sees are meant to replace the personal associations so frequently reported in a listener's reaction to music, so that in a way the film is listening for us. Viewers are not free to make their own associations, their own pictures of what the music reminds them of, but are practically compelled to accept the film's association of Strauss with space flight as their own. The historical substitution then is double: the missing cultural history of mankind that *2001* match-cuts passed is comically underrepresented with a light waltz, and then this waltz's historicity is supplanted in the viewer's associative faculty by sequences of images from the future. Finally, the suggestion the film is listening for us foreshadows its most iconic character, the sentient HAL 9000 computer that makes all our decisions for us, including whether we should live or die.

Schubert and Oedipus

Looking more closely at the relationship between Kubrick's use of music in his films from *2001* onward and the historical milieu implied by the films, instructive patterns emerge. There are films in which the music, comprising works composed in the time period of the film, participates in the same zeitgeist as the world of the film—*Barry Lyndon* and eighteenth-century classical music; *The Shining* and sonority-based, post-tonal music of the postwar period; and *Full Metal Jacket* and pop and rock of the 1960s. On the other hand, *2001*, *Eyes Wide Shut*, and *Clockwork Orange* each draws more loosely on musical sources of various periods and styles. One could also make a third category that combines films from both of these groupings based on the shared trait of a reliance on the music of György Ligeti: *2001*, *The Shining*, and *Eyes Wide Shut*.

Of the historically contemporaneous compilation scores, *Barry Lyndon*'s is probably the most easily recognizable as such. But the most significant piece of music for the film—the Andante con Moto from Schubert's Piano Trio No. 2 in E flat (1827)—does not correspond to the film's eighteenth-century period. The music of Schubert, who was born in 1797, is renowned for reflecting the difference between the pre-Revolutionary time period of *Barry Lyndon* and the period following the eruption of the French Revolution. "For Schubert's generation the unspoken faith in a preexisting theoretical order of experience from within was beginning to weaken. The rapid and confusing succession of events in contemporary life was not, as before, a surface manifestation of a simpler order and more fundamental laws, moral and divine, but the basis of history and of existence" (Rosen, *Frontiers of Meaning* 124–25).

In the film, the Andante is a sign of such things to come: of the new instability fundamental to modern history after the French Revolution, reflected in Schubert's musical language, characteristically, in his rapid alternations between parallel major and minor modes. And the Schubert's juxtaposition with the wrong historical period bears witness to the way in which a historical event, work of art, or person can occur at the wrong time, out of phase with its historical context, exemplified by Barry's failed attempt to gain admittance to the peerage of George III.

Schubert's Andante is an especially apt choice because of its relationship both to the French Revolution in general, and the Oedipal shadow Beethoven cast over Schubert's creative life in particular. Debuted at a concert to mark the first anniversary of Beethoven's death, it recalls the theme from the Funeral March from Beethoven's Symphony No. 3 (1804), the movement Beethoven wrote to express his disenchantment with Napoleon. Thus the Andante notes the passing of the ancien régime, the failures of the revolution that destroyed it, and, not least of all, Schubert's oedipal anxiety concerning Beethoven, all in a film set before the revolution actually occurred.

In its first appearance, the Andante plays continuously (though in an arranged/abridged form) through three scenes that present Barry's (Ryan O'Neil) desire for a good marriage (financially speaking), show his seduction of the rich and beautiful Lady Lyndon (Marisa Berenson), and explain that she is now, a little more than six hours after meeting him, fully in love. The music lends continuity and a sense of inevitability to these scenes, covering over the fact that although these events are of critical importance, little of what transpires in the film before prepares us for them. The piece's first theme's seriousness of purpose, embodied in its stately dotted-rhythm accompaniment and solemn main theme, help make Barry's conquest of Lady Lyndon seem not so much natural and convincing as all-but preordained.

Yet not despite, but because of, its seemingly artificial role in the film, the Andante is fundamental for understanding the film's moments of recognition and its historicization of the key event of childhood development: the Oedipus complex. In the film's oedipal rivalry, however, the roles of the rivals are reversed. The son, Lord Bullingdon (Leon Vatali), is older in a way: he belongs to the dying aristocratic class and sees his mother as part of his patrimony. His stepfather, Barry, is, as it were, younger: the entrepreneurial grifter from the impoverished Irish gentry belongs spiritually to his era's embryonic ruling-class fraction, the bourgeoisie. The resolution of the Oedipus complex is similarly inverted. Bullingdon wins the struggle with Barry for control of his mother, just as in the Andante, the violin's main purpose seems to be to prevent a duet between cello and piano.

The Andante can first be heard when an establishing shot introduces the castle where Barry will, in short order, secure the heart of Lady Lyndon. The narrator describes Barry's mental state after years of wandering with little to show for himself and the circumstance in which he finds Lady Lyndon:

> Five years in the army and some considerable experience of the world had by now dispelled any of those romantic notions regarding love with which Barry commenced life. And he began to have it in mind, as so many gentlemen have done before him, to marry a woman of fortune and condition. And as such things so often happen, these thoughts closely coincided with his setting first sight upon a lady who will henceforth play a considerable part in the drama of his life,

The Countess of Lyndon . . . a woman of vast wealth and great beauty. She was the wife of the right honorable Sir Charles Lyndon, Knight of the Bath, Minister to George III at several of the Courts of Europe, a cripple wheeled about in a chair, worn out by gout and a myriad of diseases. Her ladyship's Chaplain, Mr. Runt, acted as tutor to her son, the little Viscount Bullingdon, a melancholy little boy much attached to his mother.

When the narrator speaks about Barry, and the cello plays the main theme of the Andante, it is the film's first musical suggestion that Barry's attempt to reach the pinnacle of society is happening at the wrong historical moment. It is too soon, like hearing Schubert before the French Revolution. Then as the melody appears in the piano, the narrator introduces Lady Lyndon's burdens: her elderly and crippled husband and her melancholy son, whose Oedipal relation to his mother is dwelled on here and elsewhere. And while the narrator mentions Barry's motivations but not Lady Lyndon's, the structure of the music, with the melody played first on the cello (Barry) and then the piano (Lady Lyndon), presents both their desires and the implicit quid pro quo between them. (Recall that Lady Lyndon plays the piano several times in the film.) In exchange for access to her fortune and social sphere, Barry gives her both the immediate thrill of a love affair and eventually—when he begins to mistreat her—further justification for her habitual depression.

The Schubert serves as a sound bridge to the next scene. It is evening, and Lady Lyndon and Barry are seated across from each other at the card table, trading sums of money and amorous glances. The Andante has modulated to the relative major key of E flat and a new theme, but one that is based on developing a seemingly insignificant two-note motif from the conclusion of the principle theme. The music here is almost playful, approaching near to levity after the solemn first theme. Then, as they become more and more transfixed by one another, the Schubert returns to its first theme. The music seems to know before the characters do that they are late for an appointment with destiny on the balcony. In short order, Lady Lyndon absconds to the balcony, where she is met by Barry for a fateful first kiss.

For the film, the crucial element of the Andante is the definitive and indefinite role of the violin. Regarding the exposition of the first theme, the violin is a mere afterthought. While the cello plays the melody, it is accompanied only by the piano, and the structure of the music thereby supports the thesis that Barry will get on perfectly well with the support of his rich wife. But this is an illusion; there is a violin—a third party impeding their marriage's success and the rise of the social class Barry represents more generally. In the more public social sphere of the gaming parlor, when the music has moved to a new key and different, lighter material, the violin is much more prominent, as if to say their love must deal with society's objections to their attachment across class boundaries.

But unlike when the cello has the melody, when the piano plays it, both the violin and the cello play the accompaniment figure. In this case, the violin is Lord Bullingdon, Barry's Oedipal rival and class enemy. This musical structure suggests that although the violin cannot play the melody, it nevertheless prevents the music from being a sonata, a duet between Barry and Lady Lyndon. The film's judgment on the music is thus that the Andante, especially as it is arranged for the film, is not so much a piece for piano trio as it is a failed cello sonata, one where a violin keeps interrupting the duet. The same goes for Lord Bullingdon's relationship with his mother and his new stepfather. He cannot prevent her marriage to the meddling upstart from the poor Irish gentry. But he can through cunning and obstinacy thwart Barry's attempts to remain in his marriage and receive the title that would guarantee his family's aristocratic status for generations to come.

This interpretation is corroborated by the key moment of recognition and reversal in Part II of the film. After realizing that without an aristocratic title of his own he and his family will be penniless upon his wife's death, Barry sets out to buy a title by hosting lavish dinners, overpaying for lands and luxury goods, and administering bribes in high places. His efforts in the clientelist sphere yield a few well-connected allies and even a brief audience with George III before Bullingdon provokes a fateful misstep that dooms the enterprise.

The scene begins when Lord Bullingdon and Brian (David Morley), Barry's son by Lady Lyndon, interrupt Lady Lyndon's piano recital by parading into the recital hall with Lord Bullingdon having dressed Brian in his own oversized shoes so as to cause enough noise to drown out the music. Brian is very much his father's son, intruding on a social event and sphere where he does not belong. As he walks next to Bullingdon, the difference between these half-brothers could not be greater: Brian revels in the joke, Bullingdon in his sanctimony.

At the front of the hall, the music having stopped, Bullingdon makes a sarcastic bow in front of Barry and asks his mother, "Don't you think he fits my shoes very well, your ladyship?" This is followed by a medium shot of Bullingdon kneeling to speak to Brian with Lady Lyndon in the background. The shot is from the point of view of Barry, and its composition encapsulates his predicament. His stepson, the chief obstacle to securing his family's future, grabs hold of his son while standing between him and his wife. Continuing sardonically, Bullingdon addresses Brian, "Dear child, what a pity it is that I'm not dead for your sake. The Lyndons would then have a worthy representative and enjoy all the benefits of the illustrious blood of the Barrys of Barryville. Would they not, Mr. Redmond Barry?"

Lady Lyndon rises from the piano bench in disgust and seizes her younger child. "From the way I love this child, my lord, you ought to know how I would have loved his elder brother had he proved worthy of any mother's affection." As she flees the room, Bullingdon announces he will leave their home and never return as long as Barry is alive. No longer able to control his emotions, Barry horrifies his guests by assaulting Bullingdon, providing proof of Bullingdon's accusations for all to see and dooming his ascent to the peerage in a fit of pique.

This scene is another one where Kubrick's film is like music. Specifically, it resembles the Andante's central, development section, whose essence is its sense of violent struggle between the different instruments for control of the movement's direction and development. In this case, the film transforms the music's indefinite sense of struggle into the struggle between the aristocracy and the bourgeoisie on the cusp of the latter's ascendance to power in the proper era of Schubert.

When we next hear the Schubert, there is proof of this. It recurs in the film's denouement, and the part we hear is the end of the movement. So the central section of the piece never occurs, except by means of Kubrick's translation of the struggle between piano, violin, and cello into the struggle between Lady Lyndon, Lord Bullingdon, and Barry in the midst of the concert that marks the beginning of the end for Barry. The film represses the central section of the Schubert from the soundtrack only to have it return not in but *as* the film. This corresponds to the conflict because the music is appearing too soon in history, just as Barry, a figure for the coming era of the career open to talent, is trying to overtake his aristocratic predecessors too soon, before 1789. His attempt is doomed because it assumes the wrong historical form: marriage and bribery rather than birth, just as a piano trio is the wrong form for a cello sonata.

At the end of the film, the Andante begins as before, with the funeral march's dotted rhythm in the piano. Barry hobbles out of the inn, where he has recovered after the loss of his leg in a duel with Bullingdon, while once again the first theme sounds in the cello. But this time its funereal message has finally reached its sender; its prophecy of doom has come true. His marriage effectively over, Barry is impoverished, disfigured, and disgraced. "He never saw Lady Lyndon again." As these words are heard, there is a freeze frame on Barry as he enters the coach and exits the film. With a cut to the familiar establishing shot of the Lyndon Estate, the Trio moves to the second instance of the main melody, with the accompaniment shifted to the strings and the melody in the piano, again in parallel with a shift from Barry to Lady Lyndon.

The next shot shows the interior of the estate, with Lady Lyndon surrounded by her handlers, most notably, Lord Bullingdon. She is busy with the mundane task of signing checks, but the music, like a living memory of her lost love, transfigures this quotidian situation. At the third check she pauses. A shot from her point of view shows the date as 1789 and the name on the check. Of course it is Barry's.

The memory of Barry awakens something within her, and correspondingly the music is doing something new. The violin takes the lead in the coda to the Andante, just as Bullingdon has supplanted Barry in the Lyndon home, but the cello is still there. Barry is gone but not forgotten. The music is winding down; the melody is disintegrating into fragments of itself, and a medium shot shows a despondent Lady Lyndon. The cello plays a low trill, a brooding shadow of its former melodic glory, while the camera shows Bullingdon—his head lowered as though straining to hear the distant trill—waiting to proceed. He is clearly fearful of the passion the mere name of his rival has stirred in his mother's breast. He finally looks up only to find her still transfixed, her vacant gaze at once definitive and indefinite. Barry is so near and so far.

The Trio is not done yet either, as one last iteration of the melody occurs in the piano with the accompaniment played in a haunting pizzicato by the strings. If the cello can no longer play the theme, it is now up to the piano. The tempo is slower, this time with feeling, not mercenary interests. Her spell finally breaks, and as she looks down to continue her work, the melody switches—mid-phrase—to the cello and violin together, as if they were fighting for control of it. By implication she has recalled the horrible scene during her concert, the last time they were all together.

One last flourish in the piano leads directly to a cut to a final title card excerpted from the beginning of Thackeray's novel: "It was in the reign of George III that the aforesaid personages lived and quarreled; good or bad, handsome or ugly, rich or poor, they are all equal now." This last assertion can be read in two ways. They are all equal now in death and in the sense in which the Revolution would render everyone formally equal, even those who have already lived and died. And it is finally here that the Schubert regains its proper historical temporality, back to a future the film has, in the narrator's previous words, "not the means of representing"—except with the music of Schubert.

Figure 3.6. Lady Lyndon hears Schubert one last time in *Barry Lyndon* (Stanley Kubrick, Warner Brothers, 1975). Digital frame enlargement.

The Castrating Spirit of Music

For Beethoven aficionados, the category of late style refers not just to works from late in the composer's life, but to ones that entail new aesthetic contradictions. Beethoven's late music is both veritably avant-garde and somewhat old-fashioned in its choice of musical forms. Most famously, the Grosse Fugue for string quartet relies on a preclassical counterpoint form, but even today its dissonances sound modern. His preferences for such preclassical forms thus "are evidence not of a return to an idealized past . . . but of Beethoven's search for germinating influences and modes of expression that could aid him in the symbolization of new spheres of psychic and social experience" (Solomon 387).

In a similar sense, *Eyes Wide Shut* is a work of late style. It is a work of renewed purpose derived from some of Kubrick's earliest "germinating influences," including the films of Max Ophuls. Like Ophuls's *The Earrings of Madame de . . .* (1953), *Eyes* is renowned for its long takes, tracking shots, and story of erotic intrigue and marital infidelity. Correspondingly, its classical musical selections have an understated intensity. The compilation score's signature piece is the second movement from Ligeti's solo piano work *Musica Ricercata* (1953), "Mesto, rigido e cermoniale," which consists of only three notes. The film also has personal touches missing from other Kubrick films. His family members appear in the Christmas party scene, and the paintings hanging throughout the Harford's apartment are mostly by Kubrick's wife, Christiane. The apartment itself, which critics complained was unrealistically opulent for a Manhattan doctor, is thought to resemble the one the Kubricks lived in as a young couple. And although *Eyes* was filmed in the United Kingdom with locations chosen for their resemblance to New York, there is still a sense in which Kubrick was returning, Ulysses-like, to an initial muse for the first time since his noir classic, *The Killing* (1956).

Because of such personal touches and germinating influences, not despite them, the film's ambition is arguably greater than Kubrick's more acclaimed films. While *2001* envisions a new age and a new man to surpass us, *Eyes* is about something more mundane, but more significant—how to live in this world, the fallen world of the bourgeoisie, with its intrigues, affairs, and other banalities that pass for happiness. It is a story of love and marriage and their fraught relationship with one's innermost fantasies. For the film, fantasies are the secret core of an individual's identity, and for that reason, when they emerge in daily life, they appear as foreign intruders, disrupting the stability of Alice and Bill Harford's (Nicole Kidman and Tom Cruise's) relationship. When Alice confesses to wanting to cheat once years ago, she becomes like a stranger to her husband. Bill similarly becomes a different person when he pursues his vengeful quest for infidelity. Shirking his normal responsibilities, he wanders the night alone, forgoes his identity behind the mask he wears to the orgy, and begins to neglect his work to pursue his investigation following the orgy. For Alice, her fantasy is a source of power over Bill, and of women's power over men more generally. "If you men only knew!" she exclaims before her confession. Bill's fantasy odyssey, by contrast, turns into a debilitating series of failed sexual encounters, compulsively repeated, that lead him out of the domain of the pleasure principle and into the territory of the uncanny and its reference to infantile sexuality's castration complex.

But in a further and more mundane complication of late style, *Eyes* is an unfinished work. Kubrick died before post-production and the premiere, before being able to apply his customary finishing touches. James Naremore argues that although Kubrick "probably didn't supervise the final sound mixing, and he had no opportunity to fine-tune the editing after the initial release . . . *Eyes* is substantially what he aimed to accomplish and is a remarkable last testament" (222). For Michael Herr, Kubrick's friend and collaborator, the film is an example of the proverbial "unfinished masterpiece." "He would have fiddled and futzed with it right up to the moment of release and beyond if he thought he could tune it any finer" (91). Both of these arguments rely on the same metaphor—Kubrick's inability to "fine-tune" the movie given his untimely death—that should give us pause, because changes in music cues were often Kubrick's finishing touches. The best close analysis of *Eyes'* score and especially its classical elements overlooks this problem in its thesis that in *Eyes*, "music is deployed in perhaps the most carefully developed manner of all his films" (Gorbman, "Ears Wide Open" 11). But if the film and score are unfinished, the significance of both lies elsewhere. Because the final touches were not applied, *Eyes* is a more transparent variation on Kubrick's aesthetic and philosophical tendencies. Like Nicole Kidman in the film's first shot, it renders the mechanism of his classical music selections interaction with the narrative in a naked form. But this nakedness should not be mistaken for simplicity. The film's use of music is thoroughly dialectical, with aesthetic and psychological opposites coinciding.

This is especially true of Kubrick's use of Ligeti's "Mesto, rigido e ceremoniale" from *Musica Ricercata*, which Kubrick relies on repeatedly and nearly exclusively in the latter half of *Eyes*. This marks a return to a composer he used in *2001* and *The Shining*. But, symptomatic of the contradictory nature of Kubrick's late style, the Ligeti piece in question is an early work that relies on traditionally defined pitches and offers a mixture of transparency and depth in style and structure. In *2001*, Ligeti's music chiefly embodied the psychological turmoil of sudden, pseudoevolutionary progress. In *The Shining*, by contrast, his music furthers Jack Torrance's regressive transformation into a monstrous, primal father. In a synthesis and cancellation of these movements in opposite psychological directions, in *Eyes*, the "Mesto" represents Bill Harford *stuck* in a cycle of repetition.

Both the piece and the film deal in the uncanny, in the feeling of dread when something that was supposed to remain secret and hidden is brought to light (Freud, "The Uncanny" 199). Naremore also argues for the importance of the uncanny in the film by emphasizing the recurrence of figures of doubling (229–32). But as Freud makes clear, the "strangely familiar" quality of doubling is a poor substitute for the dread inspired by the uncanny's "return of the repressed" ("The Uncanny" 202). One has to look elsewhere in the film for a figure worthy of the uncanny— to the masked leader of the secret order at the orgy and his implied threats to castrate Bill. In *Eyes*, the uncanny occurs at moments when the primordial fear of castration reemerges in adulthood with the same weight it carried during childhood. This is the answer to the riddle of the film's title. Its "eyes wide shut" suggest fantasizing in general while also, as in the case of Oedipus gouging out his own eyes, symbolizing castration in particular.

Setting its main theme of the uncanny firmly in the milieu of bourgeois decadence, the film underscores the underappreciated historical character of Freud's sense of the concept. It is significant that Freud uses E. T. A. Hoffmann's story "The Sandman" to develop the uncanny's connection to castration anxiety. The story belongs to Romanticism—the founding movement of avant-garde, modernist literature. *Eyes Wide Shut*'s own milieu highlights how little has changed in bourgeois culture since the fin de siècle setting of both Freud's essay and Arthur Schnitzler's *Traumnovelle* on which Kubrick's film is based. The film suggests instead that we are stuck with the bourgeoisie's quiet desperation and their false escapes into fleeting transgressions. Kubrick's suggests it is not despite but *because* of its roots in the nineteenth-century Gothic that the uncanny *remains* a quintessentially modern concept. We still live in the same era as Hoffmann, the era of capitalist modernity and the bourgeoisie. Similarly, the film takes the old bourgeois maxim—the more things change, the more they stay the same—and turns it into a nightmarish regression to childhood sexuality, repeating Bill Harford's infantile longing for castration.

The key uncanny moment in *Eyes* occurs when Ligeti's piece plays for the first time as Harford is brought before the leader of the orgy for questioning. A haunting montage of masked partygoers accompanies the Ligeti, with the grotesque masks as ideal figures for the ambiguous structure of the film's notion of fantasy, in which "fantasy conceals horror, yet

Figure 3.7. Revealing masks in *Eyes Wide Shut* (Stanley Kubrick, Warner Brothers, 1999). Digital frame enlargement.

at the same time creates what it purports to conceal, its 'repressed' point of reference" (Žižek, *Plague of Fantasies* 7). Kubrick's masks hide the identities of the powerful people attending the rite, yet in their very appearance the masked figures generate the fear and dread they are meant to conceal. With a mocking tone, the orgy leader tells Bill, "Remove your mask. Now get undressed." Such commands are tantamount to castration. It may have come to that if not for the mysterious woman who appears and offers to "redeem" Bill with her sacrifice. And her sacrifice is also a figure for castration in Lacanian psychoanalysis, where the woman's body is a phallus.

Film music scholar Claudia Gorbman is partially correct when she suggests that the Ligeti is a "sign of something else." "It takes rigor to edit a three-minute film sequence to a musical piece with such a distinctive sound and such starkly contrasting dynamics," she argues. "Each scene with the music is meticulously choreographed to its formal and dynamic dictates. For each scene, for example, Kubrick had to identify a 'worst moment' hitting Bill with shock, which that hammered G-natural underscores" (Gorbman, "Ears Wide Open" 11). But Gorbman shies away from other crucial details of the Ligeti that would further her reading of its interaction with the film when, oddly, she invokes the figure of the "musically super-literate" viewer. "All but the musically super-literate doubtless experience [the Ligeti] as merely a collection of disconnected notes—aleatory, hardly music at all, primitive in its sparseness, and well suited to the stripping away of the protagonist's complacencies" (Gorbman, "Ears Wide Open" 11). Kubrick scholar Kate McQuiston's analysis of the Ligeti is similarly over before it has begun. "Ligeti's *Musica Ricercata*, and in particular the movement featured in *Eyes Wide Shut*," she argues, "stubbornly resists typical modes of musical description and classification" (61).

But rather than resisting typical modes of musical analysis, in fact, the Ligeti rewards them. In such an analysis, one would note that the movement's two thematic areas are of contrasting characters and that, as in the classical style, Ligeti eventually combines them in a polyphonic texture of melody and accompaniment. The first main thematic area is an elemental musical dialogue. Its first phrase starts on E-sharp, oscillates between E-sharp and F-sharp, and then arrives at a long-held F-sharp. Its second phrase oscillates between F-sharp and E-sharp and then returns to a sustained E-sharp. This two-bar idea comprises an elementary example of antecedent and consequent phrasing in melodic writing: the idea goes somewhere in its first phrase (from E-sharp to F-sharp) and then returns to its starting point in its second (back to E-sharp).

This dialogue between phrases repeats in a few variations and builds in volume before suddenly breaking off in mid-phrase. Instead of hearing the expected consequent response to the first measure's arrival at F-sharp, a forte G-natural sounds in a high register, repeating over and over and faster and faster. It is the second main thematic area, interrupting and contrasting with the first. The G is both far away and close to home, only another half-step up from F-sharp but then distinguished by its displacement to a higher octave. As the G continues, a synthesis of the two themes occurs when a polyphonic texture emerges with the E-sharp/F-sharp reappearing as an accompaniment to the G.

The Mesto's form resembles eighteenth-century Viennese classicism's preference for first opposing musical ideas that represent contradictory sentiments and then synthesizing them in a polyphonic texture (Rosen, *Music and Sentiment* 50–54). This is not surprising given Ligeti's intention. He wanted *Musica Ricercata* to be a "Cartesian" search for first principles, which in this movement leads to an idiosyncratic repetition of the classical preference for synthesizing ideas of contradictory emotional character (Rourke 532–35). This is the key element of continuity between the piece and the film. The classical aesthetic is the repressed returning in Ligeti's "Mesto," just as castration anxiety returns in Harford's odyssey.

The meaning of this elementary musical work is then both overdetermined and rendered uncertain by Kubrick's use of its contrasting themes to both reinforce and undermine the return of the repressed in the scenes it accompanies. In other words, the problem with this piece in the contexts provided by the film is that its meaning seems certain to the point of obviousness, where the suspense the piece is supposed to generate is also dissipated by it.

Each time the first theme occurs, it creates a mood of suspense that somewhat predictably but nevertheless convincingly pays off in an event timed to coincide with the "castrating" G. A brief account of the exact moments that the G-natural marks gives some idea of how predictable this structure is and how, although it took a lot of planning to coordinate the editing of these sequences to the music, its sheer predictability corroborates the unfinished status of the film. The dreaded G begins sounding at the following precise moments: first, when Bill admits that he has forgotten the second password to the uncanny orgy leader after enduring his withering questions; second, when Bill receives a letter with his name on it at the gate of the orgy mansion warning him to cease his inquiries, as if they knew he would return at that precise moment; third, when his pursuer emerges from around a street corner, confirming Bill's suspicion that he is being followed; and fourth, when, after his troubling conversation with Victor about the orgy, he finds a mask from the orgy menacingly placed beside his sleeping wife.

But in a closer analysis, it is misleading to call the antecedent-consequence E-sharp/F-sharp figure in the scenes leading up to the G suspenseful or the G itself particularly surprising within the film. This is because the suspense is all but over in these scenes before the suspenseful music really begins. Bill and the viewer both know he has been discovered at the orgy and that he is being followed on the street before the Ligeti begins. Similarly, although with a measure of dramatic irony, the threatening mask on Bill's pillow is already seen in a shot intercut with his entry into the house prior to his discovery of it. The emotional shock corresponding to the G occurs in the film before it occurs on the soundtrack, insofar as each of these scenes begins by revealing something dreadful to the viewer and then reveals it again when the G itself occurs. So while this repetitive structure confirms an axiom of Ligeti's "Mesto" and the film—that the repressed returns—the film also complicates and undermines this axiom by giving away the surprise of the return prior to the arrival of the "castrating" G.

This seeming flaw in the film's timing of its musical cues becomes intelligible when one views the film from the perspective of the structure of the Ligeti. In the context of the "Mesto," it is not the G, but the first theme of the oscillating E-sharp and F-sharp, that returns and, in a gesture of quasi-classical synthesis, becomes an accompaniment for the G as they continue together. Correspondingly, one can reject the intuitive reading that the G represents the "worst" moment in each of the sequences it accompanies. The G instead represents the intrusion of a contingent event that gives rise to the uncanny, as when Bill and Alice's argument leads Alice to confess her fantasy affair to Bill and sets him unconsciously on his castrating quest. Indeed, the brooding character, repetitive structure, and oscillating dynamics of the Ligeti's first thematic area are a better musical representation of a repressed sexual wish from childhood than the clarity of the G, which more readily symbolizes Alice's clearly articulated fantasy. And like the Ligeti's first theme, Bill's castration complex underscores and undermines Alice's fantasy when the themes form a polyphonic texture. It is as though his unconscious response to Alice's confession is to punish both himself and Alice by seeking out castration. That way she will never have sex with him again.

In a similar but broader reversal of perspective, and as a final contradiction that confirms Kubrick's late style, the end of the film more directly calls into question its axiom of the return of the repressed. When Alice and Bill agree to return to their normal sex life and stop worrying about their innermost desires, they seem to be agreeing to a repression that will inevitably explode again. But rather than reading the film's ending as merely a brief respite before another traumatic encounter with the objects both concealed and generated by fantasy, perhaps Kubrick was reading his film's preoccupation with the return of the repressed against the grain. When Alice says they need to "fuck" to get their marriage back on track in the film's final scene, this is not only amusing; it is also simply true. Neither cold, nor grotesque, nor haunted—and so close to Christmas— the final scene suggests Bill and Alice will let the dead bury the dead.

Similarly, Ligeti's *Musica Ricercata* attempts to start over without the whole burden of the history of Western classical music. Yet it gets caught in the logic of the return of the repressed when the classical opposition and synthesis of sentiments occurs in "Mesto, rigido e ceremoniale" and corroborates the film's meditation on this mechanism. But after this piece and his immigration to the West, Ligeti moved beyond the classical aesthetic, creating highly original music derived, like late Beethoven, from experiments with preclassical polyphonic techniques and forms foreshadowed in the distant echoes of classical polyphony in the "Mesto." Ligeti's happy biographical outcome is in a sense an avatar for the optimistic ending one might attribute to Bill and Alice's prospects for the future. Having come clean to each other and dug into the past, they are ready for the future. Consciousness now speaks where before their ids acted out.

Coda: "Give Up Your Inquiries"

To conclude, consider again Bill's return to the orgy mansion as the one truly suspenseful iteration of the Ligeti. The scene is also uncanny

Figure 3.8. Giving up your inquiries in *Eyes Wide Shut* (Stanley Kubrick, Warner Brothers, 1999). Digital frame enlargement.

in a unique way for the film, as the uncanny may involve the illusion that normal causality has been suspended and psychic forces are directly causing changes in physical reality. How could they have known he would come back? As of yet, Bill and the viewer are unaware of the lengths to which the cabal is going to limit his inquiry, and the encounter appears supernatural. "Give up your inquiries, which are completely useless, and consider these words a second warning," the letter cautions. "We hope, for your own good, this will be sufficient." Bill is shocked, and the prospective film critic should be as well. This message reads as if it were addressed to Kubrick's interpreters. It is as though Stanley Kubrick's ghost were standing there, silently admonishing the foolish critic he knew would dare to come this far. Behind his gates he keeps the definitive meanings of his films hidden in their indefinite musical selections. For your own good, he warns the film critic, give up your inquiries.

Two documentaries on Kubrick, *Stanley Kubrick's Boxes* (2008) and *Room 237* (2012), show to varying degrees the downside of failing to heed this warning and of looking too far into Kubrick's films. As a compendium of insane interpretations of *The Shining*, *Room 237* features commentaries by fringe academics and unabashed conspiracy theorists, with claims ranging from implausible to ludicrous. Ludicrously, Danny's Apollo 11 sweater and the haunted room 237's key chain indicate that, according to conspiracy theorist Jay Weidner, in *The Shining* Kubrick secretly admits he helped the US government fake the moon landing. The moon, you see, is approximately 237,000 miles from the earth, and with some imagination the letters on the key chain ("ROOM NO 237") become an anagram for "moon room." Of course Weidner does not doubt that NASA went to the moon (that would be ridiculous!); he believes that Kubrick filmed fake footage of the event for television. Less ridiculously, historian Geoffrey Cocks argues that a series of numerological coincidences across Kubrick's films point to another bizarre interpretation: all of Kubrick's films are allegories for the Holocaust.

Only a filmmaker with Kubrick's reputation for detailed craftsmanship could, in the first place, be assumed to have put so much thought into his films that the tiniest details—like a poster in the background or a number barely visible on a license plate—are part of a grand film á clef of world-historical implications. But the obsessive allegorical readings of Kubrick's films are more detrimental to his legacy (not to mention rational thought) than illuminating of anything in his films. In the final analysis, as with all conspiratorial interpretations, the problem resides in a lack of appreciation for indeterminacy and contingency. Kubrick wanted his movies to be like music, to have the feeling and the mood come first and the meaning come later if at all.

Stanley Kubrick's Boxes is a distant, more successful relative of *Room 237*. The film as a whole succeeds because filmmaker Jon Ronson has a contagious enthusiasm for his subject, but no overarching thesis like the commentators in *Room 237*. Ronson was invited by Kubrick's family to explore his archive when it was still housed at his estate, and the film is full of ephemera and trivia—from the bizarre to the hilarious—that would delight any Kubrick fan or student of genius. Kubrick often gave bizarre instructions, like the command that there never be fewer than three fresh melons in the house. His assistant compares the shell corporation Kubrick set up in the 1980s with readers preparing reports on novels he might adapt to the Soviet spy system, where no one knows who else works for his or her side. Best of all, Kubrick, the famous recluse, shopped at the Ryman's stationery store near his estate so frequently that he joked he could have opened a stationery nostalgia museum.

But near its end, when the boxes are taken for safekeeping to University of the Arts London (UAL) in 2007, Ronson makes the fateful and by now familiar mistake of so many fine commentators on Kubrick. He thinks he has happened upon the one item in the archive that can capture the essence of Kubrick's achievements. "All this time," Ronson confesses, "I suppose I've been searching for some kind of 'Rosebud,' some individual item in a box that contains the essence of Kubrick. And I think I've found it in a few lines from this acceptance speech." The speech in question was recorded when Kubrick accepted the D. W. Griffith Award from the Directors Guild of America. "Anyone who has ever had the privilege to direct a film," Kubrick reflects, "also knows that although it can be like trying to write *War and Peace* in a bumper car in an amusement park, when you finally get it right there are not many joys in life that can equal the feeling."

It is a nice sentiment, but Ronson fails to recognize its banality. One need not spend five years in an archive to infer that Kubrick enjoyed making movies more than almost anything else. The search for the unitary feature of Kubrick has, once again, come up short. But consciously or unconsciously, Ronson recognizes this when he ends on a different note. "I think Kubrick knew he had the ability to make films of genius. And to do that when most films are so bad there has to be a method. And the method for him was precision and detail. I think these boxes contain the rhythm of genius." As with the classical music he is known for excerpting, perhaps precision is the key to Kubrick. But what is clearer from the five years of investigation that went into this film, the lifetimes of crazed close analyses that inform the commentaries in *Room 237*, or the response from so many perceptive critics to reduce Kubrick to a single word, is that people love Kubrick's films to the point of obsession.

This makes the response to Kubrick like the response to music. In both cases, to break the spell of the enchantment, critics try to describe Kubrick or music definitively. But, like music, Kubrick's films cannot be definitively reduced to a key meaning. Music cannot be fully translated into language, and no theory of Kubrick's films will ever be totalizing. Like music, Kubrick's films have all the emotional and philosophical resonances that come from the technical precision of a virtuosic performer, but still leave open their meanings, especially in their most definitive moments. In this sense, masterpieces like Kubrick's, like the journeys of modern psychological subjects themselves, remain unfinished.

4

Too Soon, Too Late, and Still to Come

Jean-Luc Godard and the Ruins of Classical Music

The Intensified Meaning of Fragments

MANY ADMIRERS OF GODARD's *A Married Woman* (1964) and *Two or Three Things I Know About Her* (1967) are no doubt aware of his partiality for excerpting fragments of classical music for his films' soundtracks. *A Married Woman* pairs fragments from Beethoven string quartets (Opus 59, Nos. 1 and 3 [1806] most prominently) with a familiar melodramatic premise: Charlotte (Macha Méril) is pregnant and does not know who the father is. But thanks in part to the ascetic use of Beethoven, mordant attacks on consumerism, and oblique but pointed criticisms of France's legacy of Nazi collaboration, the film avoids melodrama in favor of a modernist, historical parable on the empty choices of consumerist individualism and the resulting alienation.

In the more essayistic and groundbreaking *Two or Three Things*, Godard reduces Beethoven's late String Quartet in F major, Opus 135 (1826) to a few haunting but recognizable shadows of its former self. Its first theme and phrases from the middle movements accompany the film's ruminations on conspicuous consumption, the Vietnam War, and its main subject of casual prostitution among housewives in the newly constructed housing projects on the periphery of Paris. In the film's concluding shot, the final bars of Opus 135 are juxtaposed with strangely familiar commodities as the shot zooms out from a single word ("ideas") to a pastoral landscape strewn with household consumer goods.

As this sardonic final audiovisual emblem indicates, for Godard, fragments of classical music are more than emotive refinements of narrative developments. In their very fragmentation, they are signs for the shattering of historical memory, for the challenge to connect with the past in the midst of a period in history that, thanks to rampant consumerism, "has forgotten how to think historically" (Jameson, *Postmodernism* i). Godard's films sift through the fragments from classical music and other cultural artifacts for traces of his two fixed ideas: left-wing political revolution and the history of cinema. At the same time, Godard's creative destruction of classical music reminds one of the avant-garde origins of the masterworks he borrows from. This is felt, above all, in the way classical music fragments in his films feel strange and out of place even while in some cases they still function like leitmotifs in traditional film music. Arnold Schoenberg once noted that musical novelty "always attracts attention, and its sound is considered unpleasant, although it is not" (*Theory of Harmony* 69). Godard's use of classical masterpieces helps them regain the mystery of their initial, misunderstood beauty, before their nearly universal appreciation became a cliché.

The venerable name for Godard's use of classical music to present historical understanding as lost yet persisting in fragments is allegory. "Allegories are, in the realm of thoughts," Walter Benjamin argues, "what ruins are in the realm of things" (*Origin* 178). Like ruins, Godard's allegorical fragments are repositories for historical meaning; indeed they embody the historical process itself to the extent that they appear decayed. "In the process of decay, and in its alone, the events of history shrivel up and become absorbed in the setting" (179).

Playing a version of himself in *First Name: Carmen* (1983), his film that incorporates classical music fragments most extensively, Godard reflected that "no matter where or when the classics always work." This is because, as Benjamin observes, the classical pieces Godard transforms into allegorical ruins "acquire a changed and intensified meaning in [their] fragments" (*Origin* 208). Godard's films exploit this intensification of fragmentary meaning to attempt to make whole again what consumer society has done to our sense of history. In this way, his goal is similar to Benjamin's, whose work is "marked by a painful straining toward psychic wholeness or unity of experience which the historical situation threatens to shatter at every turn" (Jameson, *Marxism and Form* 61).

Godard's main approaches to fragmenting classical music should be understood as fundamentally political. First, to a certain extent, he uses classical music fragments according to Wagner's leitmotif technique, where short musical ideas are repeatedly associated with particular events, ideas, or characters. But Godard departs from this tradition by taking it to an extreme, so that isolated motifs are often the only music heard. By contrast, for Wagner, a leitmotif never stands alone, but "is paralleled by the heroic dimensions of the composition as a whole" (Adorno and Eisler, *Composing for the Films* 2). Godard remakes Wagner's technique in the spirit of Brecht, depriving leitmotifs of their larger musical context to estrange them and awaken the viewer.

Second, Godard deploys musical fragments in ways that are analogous to his own more well-known visual innovations. *First Name: Carmen* (1983) features the auditory equivalent of Godard's signature jump-cuts, interrupting Beethoven quartets mid-phrase only to return to the same piece a few bars later. Similarly, in *Passion* (1982) and *Detective* (1985), Godard applies the logic of his extremely long tracking shots, made famous by the nine-minute-long traffic jam shot in *Weekend* (1967), to extended fragments of works by Ravel, Fauré, and Schubert. Like the infamous traffic jam shot, the alienating, disrupting auditory effects of these techniques mirror the alienation felt by the characters in these films and are meant to shock viewers out of their complacency.

Third, by depicting classical music performances within *Breathless* (1960), *Weekend*, *Every Man for Himself* (1980), and *For Ever Mozart* (1996), Godard creates allegorical, audiovisual emblems for classical music's significance that address both its leftist political implications and its relationship to the history of cinema. In *First Name: Carmen*, as well as in his films that feature pop and rock music extensively, *One Plus One* (1968) and *Keep Your Right Up!* (1987), one also finds a similar intertwining of interests in leftist politics and cinema history alongside extended, but still fragmentary, depictions of musical performances. In all these films, the musicians' creative struggle becomes an allegory for the special blend of hope and despair needed during revolutionary political struggles.

For Godard, the struggle to create is not a problem but a precondition for his cinema. Two months after the triumphant premiere of *Breathless* in 1960, he told a reporter at Cannes, "I have the impression of loving the cinema less than I did a year ago—simply because I have made a film, and that film has been well received, and so forth. So I hope that my second film will be received very badly and that this will make me want to make films again" (quoted in Brody, "An Exile in Paradise"). Without this sense of struggle, Godard undoubtedly would have felt he was only making commercial entertainment instead of connecting with traditions of modern art predicated on social disaffection.

Who better to evoke as archetypes for the struggling artist than Beethoven, whose degenerative hearing loss ended his performing career prematurely and made composing an arduous process, or Mozart, who died young and penniless, buried in a pauper's grave? In Godard's reimagining of the context for their music, these two composers become modernists of differing but related political sensibilities. Beethoven is often associated with the pessimism of Godard's historical intellect, while Mozart connotes the optimism of Godard's political will. There is something quite fitting in Godard's use of Beethoven and Mozart for political ends. The composers of *The Marriage of Figaro* (1786) and *Fidelio* (1805), two operas renowned for their defiance of the ruling class and their calls for a more just world, were no strangers to the political power of art. Godard's use of their music continues this aspect of their legacies by cinematic means right down to the present.

Allegorical Leitmotifs

Despite his films' avant-garde reputation, musicologist Miriam Sheer notes that "Godard embraces the traditional leitmotif technique, using Beethoven quartet-themes for signifying certain feelings . . . or a traumatic experience . . . grammatically abstracting [leitmotifs] . . . but employing them in the same manner as in more traditional movies for linking scenes distant in time" (188). Even Godard's interruptions of musical ideas mid-phrase can be convincingly described as mirroring the outcome of particular events, such as a lovers' quarrel in *A Married Woman*. In this account, the irony of the use of classical music in *A Married Women*, *The New World*, and *Two or Three Things* is that the music is not deployed ironically: "strangely enough . . . Godard . . . does not choose musical cues that ironically negate the visual character" (188).

But while it is true that the use of middle and late Beethoven quartets in these films does not undermine their visual character or story line, nonetheless the way in which the quartets are heard as fragments does ironically negate the quartets themselves. Furthermore, depriving Beethoven's masterworks of the entirety of their dramatic force is not just an aesthetic choice; it carries with it the effect of an accusation and a critique, as if consumerism, misguided urban renewal, fascism, and other modern and contemporary historical phenomena represented in the films had done this to Beethoven.

Walter Benjamin observes that "in the last analysis structure and detail are always historically charged" (*Origin* 182). This is a major premise in Godard's approach to film form in general and to his use of classical music in particular. The historical charge created by the use of Beethoven quartet fragments in Godard's films is, quite literally, worthy of the nuclear age. The premise of the first of his films to use Beethoven, the science fiction short film *The New World*, features a nuclear explosion in the atmosphere above Paris. Similarly, Godard's *King Lear* (1987) features the Scherzo from Opus 135 heard as a slowed-down, distorted leitmotif, while the film's characters repeatedly evoke the Chernobyl nuclear disaster of 1986. In *The New World*, the nuclear explosion is based on extrapolating pessimistically from possibilities implicit in world politics after World War II; in *King Lear*, the Chernobyl disaster is already a part of the historical record. In both cases, the effect of the fallout is felt more strongly in the soundtrack's fragmentation of Beethoven's quartets than in either film's visual character. Ripped from their larger musical context and often cut off mid-phrase, Godard's allegorized leitmotifs become critical commentaries, contaminating the dramatic situations they support.

To distinguish allegories from symbols, Walter Benjamin contrasts symbolism's logic of sacrifice with allegory's resistance to tropes of sacrifice and redemption: "Whereas in the symbol destruction is idealized and the transfigured face of nature is fleetingly revealed in the light of redemption, in allegory the observer is confronted with the *facies hippocratia* of history as a petrified, primordial landscape" (*Origin* 166). Benjamin's key phrase, *facies hippocratia*, refers to the change in the face when death is imminent but still pending, and imagines history as not quite dead but no longer able to recover and fully live again either. Unable to find a sacrificial payoff in death, Benjamin's history as an allegorical ruin becomes a deeply melancholy subject; neither absent nor fully present, lost nor found, the grieving cannot fully begin, nor can it end.

History is also on the verge of death but lingers on in Godard's use of Beethoven in *The New World*. At the beginning of the film, the nuclear explosion high in the atmosphere over Paris changes both everything and nothing. At first a state of emergency is declared, but then increasingly life goes on as before, except that everyone, with the exception of the film's hero, has forgotten how to love. In this context, brooding fragments from Beethoven's Great Fugue (1826) and Quartet in C-sharp minor, Opus 131 (1826) not only capture the inner turmoil of the hero, but also suggest, in the pieces' fragmentary diminution, how little mankind's greatest achievements matter now that no one can feel passionate intensity anymore. If the Beethoven fragments represent history, then in their fragmentary state history is too sick to recover but too bitter to finally die.

In Godard's *King Lear*, the Chernobyl disaster effects the very sound of the Scherzo from Opus 135. In its slowed-down rendering, it has been contaminated by nuclear radiation. This suits a *King Lear* similarly exposed to the Chernobyl disaster. Thus rendered, Opus 135's fateful motto—"It must be"—takes on a new, and far less amiable, significance. It foretells the dark fate of nuclear winter. This is deeply unfair to Beethoven, who in his late quartets like Opus 135 "ordered what he was so pitifully unable to order in any other aspect of his existence" (Kerman, *Beethoven Quartets* 350). In Godard's slow-down version, Beethoven's music sounds like it has been contaminated by the failures of his later personal life, especially his strained relationship with nephew Karl, whom Beethoven drove to attempt suicide as a young man. But if this rendering of the Scherzo is unfair to Beethoven himself, for Godard what matters is that it reflects the significance of Chernobyl, a ruin without historical precedent.

Music Becoming Cinema

In Godard's *First Name: Carmen*, Beethoven quartets appear both on the soundtrack and in the film, culminating in a scene featuring the Prat Quartet performing in a hotel lobby where Carmen and her anarchist comrades attempt and fail to kidnap a wealthy industrialist. Godard's

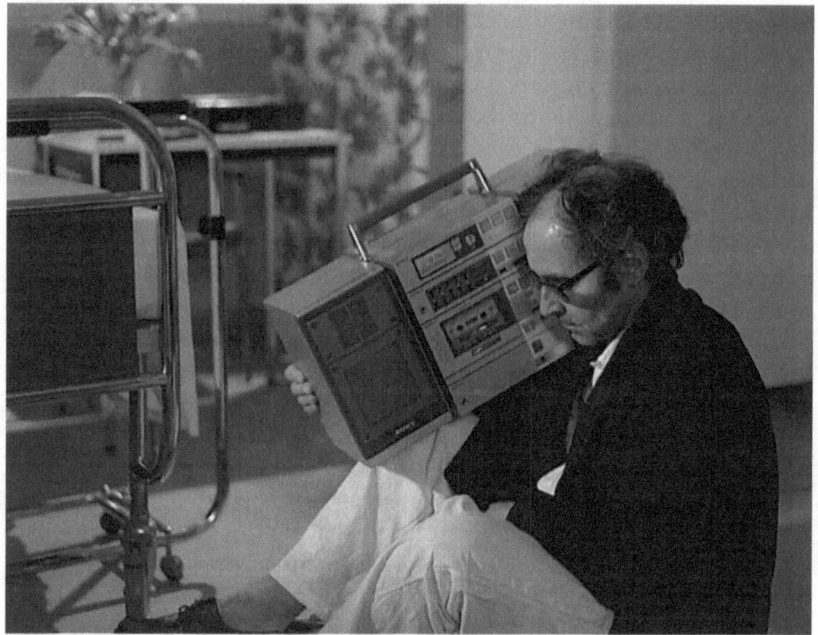

Figure 4.1. Godard listening to his new film in *Prénom Carmen* (Jean-Luc Godard, Sara Films, 1983). Digital frame enlargement.

Carmen also departs from his other Beethoven films in its use of significantly longer fragments, and especially in the way the fragments do not recur later in the film and therefore are not leitmotifs. The fragments from the quartets (including Opuses 59/3, 74, 131, 132, and 135) instead form a parallel musical narrative, with each occurring roughly in chronological order of composition and accompanying distinct parts of the film. If in his early Beethoven films Godard still treated the quartets, at least at a logical level, as one traditionally uses music in film (as a series of leitmotifs), in *First Name: Carmen*, he treats Beethoven's music as if it were cinematic material, subjecting it to discontinuous editing techniques analogous to jump-cutting, interrupting different quartets and then jumping forward in the same music to points only slightly ahead of where the music had left off.

But at the same time, Godard was also attempting to subordinate the film to the story of the quartets. "Here, it's Beethoven, he's telling me something . . . ," Godard commented on his creative process during filming. "Everything depends on the story that he's telling me" (quoted in Brody, *Everything Is Cinema* 453). Critics have rightly wondered, why Beethoven as an accompaniment for *Carmen*? Surely Godard's choice of Beethoven as the music for a loose adaptation of *Carmen* is more than an arbitrary one, but if one forgoes Bizet's score, why Beethoven in particular and not some other canonical composer or composers? Godard's thoughts on the matter are suggestive but not totally satisfying. The film needed "music that marked the history of music," he argues. "Music that is at the same time the practice and the theory of music" (quoted in Brody, *Everything Is Cinema* 447). But because Beethoven is not the only composer of such fundamental music, Godard's comments do not fully explain why Beethoven was chosen over other household names from classical or popular music.

A better clue resides in the way, at first glance, the musical genres of chamber music and opera interacting in *First Name: Carmen* seem opposed. Opera is classical music at its most public and collaborative. It is the genre that "from its inception has almost always been subsidized by the state," and the one where music unites with other arts to create what Wagner called the Gesamtkunstwerk, the total work of art composed of all other art forms (Rosen, *Romantic Generation* 600). By contrast, chamber music, as the name suggests, is more intimate and private. It could rightfully be called music for music and musicians' sake, music that does not depend on a large audience or major state support, but on musicians who are interested in playing it for themselves.

Godard further complicates matters in this pairing of opposed genres by choosing examples of each that transcend their respective genres. Beethoven's string quartets, especially the late ones, are music in its most esoteric, hermetic form. Frequently, "the emotions touched on . . . are so intimate," Joseph Kerman writes of the late quartets, "it hardly seems right to be allowed to witness them" (*Beethoven Quartets* 198). By contrast, *Carmen* is more recognizable to the public than almost any other opera. Its original musical and dramatic parts have full afterlives of their own. Its story is perhaps *the* central modern variation of the femme fatale trope. Indeed, despite many other differences in story and setting, Godard's version carries over the femme fatale trait most saliently. Meanwhile, because of its use in cartoons and other popular bastardizations that obscure the original operatic source, the music of *Carmen* is familiar to generations of casual listeners.

But upon closer inspection, the pairing of Beethoven's quartets with Carmen works not despite but because Godard intuits and further realizes the operatic dimension of Beethoven's chamber music. Beethoven's chamber works, especially the late ones, often implicitly and explicitly reference operatic form. One well-known example occurs in the late Piano Sonata in A flat major, Opus 110 (1821). After two movements in the expected sonata and minute-trio forms, the unique finale of the piece alternates between a haunting arioso ("aria-like") and a dramatic fugue. In the sonata's final movement, in other words, Beethoven places "pure" instrumental music (the fugue) alongside opera (the arioso) within a piece of instrumental chamber music. Godard, with assured intuition, arrives at what Beethoven intended when he pairs the operatic elements embedded in Beethoven's quartets with the story of Carmen.

Like *First Name: Carmen*, Beethoven's late quartets also have egalitarian political connotations. For all the private and esoteric qualities usually attributed to the late quartets, "an equally strong 'public' impulse accompanies the 'private' one: a striking new directness of emotional appeal, a determination to touch common mankind as nakedly as possible" (194). This public impulse takes the form above all of melodies written with the voice in mind, tuneful melodies, easily sung. All the late quartets were indeed written in the wake of the Beethoven's most populist melody of all, the "Ode to Joy" from the Ninth Symphony. "The voices sing about man-to-man fellowship, and they are not delicate about exploiting the naïve *élan* of a military rally and the naïve awe of a churchly rite in order to force their point" (194). The tune is "half folk-like, blinding in its demagogic innocence, torn from the womb of recitative without a shred of accompaniment clothing" (194).

First Name: Carmen also politicizes the late quartets, and in a way that corresponds to Beethoven's one extant opera, *Fidelio*. *Fidelio* is the story of the heroine Leonora impersonating a boy (Fidelio) to free her husband, Florestan, an unjustly persecuted political prisoner. In the opera's most famous number, "O What a Joy," known as the Prisoners' Chorus, the entire prison population sings a hymn to freedom. Similarly, Godard reimagines *Carmen* as a modernist, leftist political drama. Carmen (Maruschka Vetmers) is part of leftist anarchist cell that robs a bank early in the film to finance the kidnapping of a prominent manufacturer and his family. In a close echo of the original *Carmen*, during the robbery she falls in love almost instantly with an inept security guard, Joseph (Jacques Bonnaffé). The two have a brief love affair before Carmen breaks his heart and abandons him. Godard borrows her signature line from Otto Preminger's *Carmen Jones* (1954). "If I love you," she tells him as their affair deteriorates, "that's the end of you." In fact, it is the end of her. Joseph revenges himself by informing the police of the plot and shooting Carmen as the police close in. "What's it called when everyone is dead but something remains?" she asks with her dying words. A minor character responds, "It is called dawn."

The note of promise here in the film's last exchange corresponds to the film's allegorical use of the quartets to describe Godard's own recovery from an apparent artistic crisis. Carmen is the niece of a film director character named Jean played by Godard himself. When she visits him at the beginning of the film he is living in a sanitarium, but the doctors are keen to expel him because they can find nothing wrong. "It's difficult," he tells her, "I have to get sick every week." His true problem is artistic; he has lost interest in filmmaking. "It is better to close your eyes than to open them," he tells her. Carmen comes to see him because she wants to use his apartment to make a film, but the film project is just a ruse that will allow them to get close to the manufacturer at his hotel. Ultimately Godard's character leaves the sanitarium and, against Carmen's wishes, is brought in on the kidnapping plot as the fake film's director. But their plot is doomed from the start; Carmen and company are clearly disorganized amateurs. And in killing them off, Godard is allegorically killing off his filmmaking's own amateurish, revolutionary pretenses.

The crucial part of the film for Godard's artistic reawakening occurs during Carmen's brief and tempestuous love affair with Joseph. These twin stories of Godard's and Carmen's renewals are accompanied by the third movement of Beethoven's String Quartet in A minor, Opus 132 (1826). This famously biographical and programmatic movement is a good match for the film here, as Beethoven wrote this movement after recovering from a nearly fatal illness in 1825. The names for its two alternating sections say it all: the A section is titled "Holy Song of Thanksgiving of a Convalescent to the Deity" and is purposely archaic in its early-modern counterpoint's Lydian mode and its painfully slow tempo; the B section is called simply "feeling new strength" and features brighter, more energetic music. In parallel with the music, Carmen convalesces by feeding on Joseph's love before inevitably abandoning him. Godard's character's convalescence is never shown on camera; he simply emerges from the sanitarium ready to work after Opus 132 occurs.

The use of the piece during a film where the main character and a director figure convalesce to rejoin the radical left brings out the unconscious political dimension of Beethoven's deeply personal piece. In particular, the sense in which the recurrence of the "feeling new strength" section in the piece is one of almost exact repetition speaks volumes for Godard's political interpretation of the music. Kerman describes the relationship between the two sections as one where, "instead of surprise or revelation, the alternation makes for relief and inevitability" (257). The left's underdog cause is similarly a recurrent one in Godard's work, a fixed idea, not a surprise. So a piece whose transition to new strength feels inevitable, even repetitive, suits Godard's wish for the inevitable victory of the radical left, even if that victory is foreclosed in this particular film.

The key feature of the third movement of Opus 132 that points towards the way in which the music is straining towards something greater than its current form, towards something like a fuller realization of itself in the cinematic context, is the unnaturally slow tempo of the "Thanksgiving Song" section. "Forty strings could sustain the hymn at this speed with comfort," Kerman notes, "but four can bear it only with a sense of strain" (256). The strain is not a bug but a feature of the music, fittingly reflecting Beethoven's difficult recovery from illness. For Godard, this straining towards what a larger ensemble could accomplish with ease perfectly suits an anarchist cadre short on numbers, long on odds, and straining to keep their cause alive.

More generally, *First Name: Carmen* suggests that the idiom Beethoven invented with his chamber music happened too soon in the history of art. It needed the technology of cinema and the intuition of an auteur of Godard's caliber to realize its dramatic potential more concretely. This is part of a pattern in the history of music where, as Charles Rosen puts it, "the processes of invention and exploitation are out of phase." Musical systems, Rosen argues, are relatively independent from their historical contexts.

> A musical system appears to have a logic of its own that can be inflected but not completely controlled by social pressures; it can act as an inspiration to composers, who often felt as if

they were discovering rather than inventing ... Works like Beethoven's Great Fugue for String Quartet appear principally as a response to possibilities of the musical system of the time, possibilities that are irrelevant to any kind of contemporary social conditions. ("From the Troubadours to Frank Sinatra")

Godard's achievement, in this light, is twofold. First, *First Name: Carmen* helps further realize the operatic dimension of the Beethoven quartets. Second, by subsuming Beethoven's quartets into his own forward looking artistic practice, Godard guarantees that Beethoven's quartets will continue to be part of the unique, modernist tradition of art that has been created in relative independence from its social conditions. In Godard's film Beethoven remains ahead of his time. But in a more melancholy detail, Godard politicizes the quartets for the left at a moment in history when the leftist mobilizations of the 1960s had decidedly waned, so that Carmen and her anarchist militant comrades come across as anachronistic political amateurs. If Beethoven's operatic late quartets occurred too soon; at a political level, Godard's *Carmen* is too late.

Nonmusical Interlude: Love, Politics, and Cinema Out of Phase

The two fixed ideas of Godard's films—left-wing political revolution and the history of the cinema itself—also exist relatively independently from their social context, so that Godard's political and cinematic revolutions are out of phase with their realization. For Godard, both the cinema and revolutionary leftism are over before they have ever properly begun, and yet the desire for them remains. The cinema is both ahead of its time, a potential yet to be fully realized, and also, in its mainstream Hollywood manifestations, aesthetically obsolete, politically backward, and economically and culturally overmatched by television, video, and contemporary digital media. Godard most famously announces the obsolescence of the cinema at the end of *Weekend* with texts that read first "End of Film" and then "End of Cinema."

But Godard has gone on making radical films ever since, in no small part because of his commitment to his attenuated leftist politics. And his films' sense of political history is also predicated on the non-coincidence of invention and realization. For Godard, leftist politics are an invention whose full utilization, due to prominent failed attempts, has yet to arrive in history. But, at the same time, at least since 1968, Godard's enthusiasm for leftist politics has been counterbalanced by an increasingly bitter resignation to the consensus that there is no imminent alternative to liberal capitalism. The left in Godard's films then too has not yet properly existed, and it is already obsolete.

Godard's vision of romantic love also adheres to this melancholy temporality where it is over before it has properly begun. So that, fittingly, the film that most clearly represents the disjunctive temporality of Godard's fixed ideas is the short film *Love: Departure and Return of the Prodigal Children* (1967). *Love* fluctuates between two distinct but overlapping scenarios, both of which feature a couple comprised of an Italian-speaking man and a French-speaking woman. In the first scene, a world-weary couple, the spectators (Catherine Jourdan and Paolo Pozzesi), leisurely read the paper, smoke, and display passing interest in another couple nearby on the roof of their apartment building. The other couple, the actress (Christine Guého) and the director (Nino Castelnuovo), are younger and less cynical when they discuss their love and the tumultuous leftist politics of the 1960s in the film within the film. The spectators are conscious of the fact that the actress and the director are from a film, and their lack of interest in the actress and the director's film prompts a debate about their general dissatisfaction with both current cinema and its larger political context, where the problem is that obsolete leaders and economic systems still dominate. While the spectators have this debate, the actress and the director dramatize it.

The debate about the disjunctive temporality of cinema and politics coincides with the spectators' attempt to speak to the actress and the director. "What are you doing?" they ask. Not receiving an answer, the spectators then begin to speculate about the film they are watching.

> WOMAN SPECTATOR (hereafter W): What are they talking about?
>
> MAN SPECTATOR (hereafter M): Considering the images, probably love.
>
> W: But sometimes, images lie.
>
> M: No, images never lie.
>
> W: Yes, images often lie. In fact, cinema is a world of lies. [Man laughs.] Why are you laughing?
>
> M: I've got the right to laugh.

W: Yes, but why?

M: I'm laughing because of what you said . . . that cinema is the art of lying.

W: So, why is that funny?

M: Why's that funny? Because you're of a certain age but you're speaking about something that's very young.

W: I'm not that old, I'm just 20. But the cinema is not so young. It has the age of Roosevelt, Churchill . . . Stalin after the war.

M: Yes, cinema has the age of Stalin, Churchill and Roosevelt, but they were old and that's why everything's going wrong today.

W: Is everything wrong "because they were old?" Why?

M: Because they were old people who led a new world without knowing it was new.

W: Like Kosygin, de Gaulle or Johnson today. Old men who don't know they are leading a new world.

M: Yes.

For Godard, these old leaders represent forms of political economy that have exhausted their usefulness for human needs but nevertheless still dominate civilization. Conversely, new-left ideas about political economy exist but are not yet fully exploited.

As the conversation continues, it transitions to thoughts about the place of cinema in a world where obsolete political and economic systems continue to dominate.

W: Yeah, alright, but what's the relationship between cinema and me?

M: What's the relationship between you and cinema? It's that you talk about something you don't know.

W: I talk about things I don't know? That's not true. I go to the cinema very often.

M: Perhaps you often go to the cinema, but you see very few films . . . or, on the contrary, you see lots of films, but you see little cinema.

W: How can you say I see little cinema if I watch lots of films?

M: [Looking directly into the camera] Because cinema doesn't exist yet, or films either.

Taken literally, the claim that the cinema does not yet exist in 1967 is absurd. But one can easily account for its spirit from the point of view of the noncoincidence of invention and exploitation. The cinema exists, but the idea of it has yet to be fully exploited.

The woman spectator then draws a comparison with the history of mathematics:

W: Cinema doesn't exist yet? So it's like mathematics before Euclid, and before Einstein. It's stuttering . . . It's clumsy.

M: It's like mathematics before Euclid and Einstein. It's a stuttering, clumsy science.

W: And the things we see, what are they?

M: Nothing.

W: Really nothing?

M: (The screen goes dark here) Sometimes . . . in an old Murnau film, or . . . a young Bertolucci film . . . you see something happening.

W: Yes, it's true . . . sometimes in a young Dreyer film . . . or in an old Rouche film . . . you can see something different . . . like a flash . . . that is the truth of cinema.

M: Like a bolt of lightning, that represents the truth of cinema.

The spectators' examples oscillate between young and old films and filmmakers, supporting the idea that for Godard the invention of the cinema is not being fully utilized, that the idea of it and its realization are out of phase with each other. These two stages of mankind's development, the "not yet" of youth and the "too late" of old age, correspond to the cinema's inability to fully realize itself. The cinema has not yet happened, and it is too late and practically over with. The latter point, that the cinema is no longer useful, is emphasized, presented as its "truth" in the concluding section of the film, where the relationship between the actress and the director cannot continue because of their political differences. He is a revolutionary; she is more moderate. He leaves for Cuba; she stays in Paris. Correspondingly, Godard's cinema, as it had existed so far—as an uneasy compromise between the radicalism needed for innovation and the moderation needed for commercial viability—cannot continue either. The director's choice reflects Godard's circumstance at the time. He was about to step away from the institutions of commercial film to make more doctrinally pure and communally produced films with the Dziga Vertov Group.

The end of *Love* foreshadows the limitations of Godard's radical period. The director character makes the possibility of avant-garde art conditional on militant-left politics. "Without an armed struggle," he argues, "there is no avant-garde." If the armed struggle is the precondition for avant-garde art, then another key phrase toward the end of the film suggests the goal of a life devoted to such rigorous art: "I met a being who fought all humanity to live only for what fascinates us." The first of these statements, that the avant-garde needs a militant wing, perfectly captures the problem confronting Godard at this moment in his career. The existing conventions of commercial cinema were the aesthetic corollaries of a capitalist political economy he wanted to overthrow. The unthinking Romanticism of the second statement, that one should fight everything to live a life of fascination, foreshadows the failure of his movement away from the film industry and gives a reason for his eventual return to it in the early 1980s. Without an actual revolution, you need money to live for what fascinates you, let alone to make movies about it.

The price Godard paid for his militancy was a decade of obscurity making films that for all their fervor are often politically dilettantish (*Tout Va Bien* [1972] being an exception), a decade from which his reputation and his films have never fully recovered. The films he made upon his return do not mark a return to the 1960s style but its radical reinvention, with the compulsion to allegorize as the now central feature along with the themes of the left's and the cinema's ongoing obsolescence and persistence.

Mozart the Hopeful Monster

With cinema and the revolution (not to mention love) already over before they have had a chance to begin in Godard's films, it would be easy to conclude that a profound sense of melancholy—where mourning never properly begins or ends—is the cosmological constant of the Godardian universe. But as Godard said of Murnau and others, in certain scenes, "sometimes you see something happening." These somethings are not "the truth of cinema" so much as, to borrow biologist's Richard Goldschmidt's famous phrase, "hopeful monsters," which for Goldschmidt were organisms that had evolved dramatically within a brief period of geological time with the metaphorical "hope" that a fortuitous environmental change would retroactively render their mutation beneficial (Gould, "Return of the Hopeful Monster," 186–94).

Similarly in Godard's films, there are brief episodes that come close to a cinematic form of this sudden, monstrously hopeful change from his otherwise ubiquitous melancholy. These are moments of lyricism that cannot be fully maintained throughout an entire film and that, along with a levity of tone, in certain significant cases feature the music of Mozart. The monstrosity in such moments is there in what, in her review of *Weekend*, Renata Adler called "the raw right now": the way in which such moments draw attention to Godard's immediate political preoccupations or to the experimental form of the film. As with Goldschmidt's mutations, a fortuitous shift in the social environment's political or aesthetic climate may yet render Godard's hopeful monsters meaningful and relevant.

Perhaps the most straightforward instance of such a "hopeful monster" of a scene involving Mozart occurs at the end of Godard's half-forgotten, highly allegorical and antirealist film *For Ever Mozart* (1996). In the final scene, the film's main character and avatar for Godard, a film director named Vicky Vitalis (played by Vicky Messica), seeks refuge at a concert of a Mozart piano concerto. Prior to this, the film has been a tragicomedy of errors in which Vitalis joined his daughter and nephew on an artistic pilgrimage to Sarajevo, where they wanted to put on a play only to see Vitalis's young relatives captured and killed by paramilitaries. After their deaths, Vitalis is able to overcome his creative crisis and finish his film (in part by including their burial in it), but his film is a commercial failure. Realizing this, Vitalis retreats from a theater screening it to a concert hall.

The self-possession of the young musicians and the convivial atmosphere in the hall are a welcome change from the film's otherwise brooding tone. In fact, it is really more of an open rehearsal than a concert, as the conductor talks to the musicians about phrasing while curious people wander into the room. Some in the audience seem to be coming because of habit, but others arrive as if for the first time to some alien, enchanted place, in one case even approaching the orchestra in wonder only to be asked by the pianist to turn the pages of his concerto part. In this playful moment between musician and audience member, Godard asks us to see Mozart and the culture that surrounds it anew; to, by turning pages, participate as listeners more fully in the performance. Throughout late Godard, such "scenes of rehearsal," Godard scholar Daniel Morgan argues, "are examples of collaborative activity based on democratic foundations" (95).

A particularly egalitarian and democratic detail in this final sequence is that the dictatorial Vitalis never makes it into the recital hall. He reaches the top of the stairs and sits down outside the hall to rest. Godard's restraint in this detail implies an indictment of himself, as if the mere presence of the antidemocratic figure of the film director within the hall would corrupt the egalitarian, utopian enclave. It is as if the Mozart performance space represents a realm of horizontal collaboration possible for musicians but not filmmakers. Alone outside, listening and conducting to himself in jest, he maintains the gap between classical music and the cinema at the very moment when they seem united within.

The gap separating cinema and Mozart is also maintained in the film's sound design by the competing interests of the Mozart heard in the film and the new-age music on the soundtrack. The soundtrack's signature legato cello figures keeps interrupting the Mozart until Vitalis finally reaches the top of the stairs and lights a cigarette, at which point Mozart wins out. The final image of the film is also an unorthodox coincidence of music and cinema that emphasizes their distance over their proximity. After Vitalis manages to make his way to the top of the stairs for a smoke, the film cuts to a close-up point-of-view shot of what is presumably the score for the concerto heard within. Someone is casually leafing through it with a carefree indifference to whether the music heard corresponds to the notes they are perusing. The film then cuts to the credits, but the sound of the turning pages remains, as if the ideas for a new movie and its series of musical fragments were already in the works. And with that, we have seen "something happening"; fleetingly a hopeful monster has emerged.

Breathless Lenin

During an interview with Daniel Cohn-Bendit before a hostile audience confused by a screening of *For Ever Mozart*, Cohn-Bendit mentioned *Breathless* to try to calm the crowd by reminding them of Godard's genius.

In response, "Godard went on a rampage and yelled that he wished that [*Breathless*] didn't exist, that it was the worst, most awful film that he had ever shot, and that if he had the power to do so, he would destroy every single print of it, so that nobody could bother him about it anymore" (quoted in Brody, "Breather from 'Breathless' "). It is unwise to take such pronouncements from the ever provocative Godard literally. Still, his frustration is understandable; it must be exasperating for someone who has reinvented his filmmaking so many times to hear himself described as a one-hit wonder.

But had Godard been in a less passionate, more analytic mood, he might have noted how *Breathless* also features Mozart within the film in a way that presages the politicized allegories of *For Ever Mozart*. The scene in question occurs as the authorities close in on Michel (Jean-Paul Belmondo), and he and Patricia (Jean Seberg) take refuge in a hideout that also serves as a set for a photo shoot. While they wait, by chance Patricia puts on a record of Mozart's Clarinet Concerto, and Michel informs her it is the most meaningful piece of music in his life. His father was a clarinetist, he tells her, and a good one, a genius—and the piece seems to stir not just his pride but his ethical sensibility. This is reinforced by the text shown on-screen as the music continues; it is an aphorism attributed to Lenin—"We are dead men on leave." The paradox in the Lenin aphorism obviously appeals to Godard because of its disjunctive temporality—we are already dead but not just yet—which, for all its existential and political implications to seize the day, also describes Michel's predicament as the cops close in. This point is reinforced by the Mozart fragment. The Clarinet Concerto was one of the last works Mozart completed. But, unlike his more famous, unfinished Requiem, the concerto is a serene piece.

When mixed with Mozart's serenity, Michel embodies Lenin's aphorism's air of resignation, not its call to seize the day. Michel does not rage against the dying of the light; his leave merely ends. Lenin was famous for having denounced the pastime of playing and listening to music as an enervating distraction in the midst of revolutionary activity—"It affects your nerves, makes you want to say stupid nice things, and stroke the heads of people who could create such beauty while living in this vile hell" (quoted in Ross, *The Rest Is Noise* 218). Godard's invocation of him in *Breathless*, with its correspondence to Mozart, alters Lenin's opinion here, rendering him a gentler if not a more hopeful monster.

Stanley Cavell's criticism of Godard's films turns on instances like this, where Michel is not so much a full human being, but zombie-like and dehumanized, a dead man on leave. By draining the life from his characters, Cavell argues, Godard unwittingly furthers consumerism's life-draining dehumanization. "How do you distinguish the world's dehumanizing of its inhabitants from your depersonalizing of them?" Cavell asks rhetorically. "Without such knowledge," he answers, "[Godard's] disapproval of the world's pleasures, such as they are, is not criticism (the negation of advertising) but censoriousness (negative advertising)" (99).

But as this audiovisual emblem from *Breathless* suggests, the accent of Godard's social criticism began to fall in a more specific place than Cavell suggests. Godard also imagines cinema as an allegory that brings together fragments of culture and politics to shape a more meaningful future. If we are all dead men on leave, then what do we have to lose? When Lenin and Mozart meet in *Breathless*, the film rises to "the negation of advertising." He may burn the rest of the print, but Godard should not disown the moment in *Breathless* when Mozart meets Lenin after both their deaths, but before those of Michel and the cinema.

Mozart for Farmworkers

If any film of Godard's as a whole deserves the designation hopeful monster, it is *Weekend*. The film was at the forefront of contemporary cinema when it was released, and it remains there fifty years later. And it is certainly monstrous at a more literal level, with violence of every kind visited on the characters on-screen and on the sensibility of the viewer, as though such shocks to the system of filmgoers could precipitate political revolution. This monstrosity is also the source of the film's hope, its wish that an armed revolutionary conflict would sweep across Europe. Known as his "last first film," Godard thought he could go no further with commercial film after he had led viewers through a world in which the social order of 1960s France descends into barbarism.

But in a temporary stay of execution, the film's Mozart scene belongs to a series of tonally contrasting interludes that interrupt the main plot, where a money-hungry Parisian couple, Roland (Jean Yanne) and Corinne (Mireille Darc), try to reach the provincial town of Oinville to write themselves into Corinne's father's will before he dies. At the end of the film, after they arrive too late and murder her mother in anger, they are captured by cannibals, who allow Corinne to join them in devouring Roland.

Although it seems very different at first, in a closer analysis the Mozart scene is deeply related to the interlude that follows it, where militant sanitation workers (Omar Diop and László Szabó) hold forth on the Algerian and Kenyan struggles for independence from colonial rule.

Figure 4.2. Mozart for farmworkers in *Weekend* (Jean-Luc Godard, Comacico/Criterion Collection, 1967). Digital frame enlargement.

This more outwardly revolutionary scene offers the proper perspective from which to understand the significance of Mozart in *Weekend* and Godard's hopeful monster aesthetic more generally.

Three key differences between the two scenes underscore their similarities. First, where the Mozart recital and impromptu lecture bore Roland and Corrine, the radical workers terrify them. But boredom is, in a way, the beginning of terror for people like Roland and Corrine who will do anything to escape thought and reflection. Second, the Mozart scene is shot in a way that reflects their boredom, with one long, circular panning shot from a middle distance that pauses only briefly on the performance. The revolutionary speeches, filmed as long-take close-ups, are tonally opposite, as though the working-class people under surveillance in the Mozart scene were suddenly returning the gaze. But in both cases, the long take asks for sustained attention from the viewer. The third and most critical similarity underlying the difference is that while both the pianist and the radical sanitation workers tour the countryside for different reasons, they both give Roland and Corinne a ride for part of their journey and thereby precipitate their demise as allegorical figures for the bourgeoisie.

Although the Mozart scene precedes the radical workers' scene in the film in terms of its larger historical temporality, it is from after the revolution they demand, and after a Godardian cultural revolution has taken place. The radical workers are fighting for a world where the classical pianist (Paul Gégauff) from the Mozart scene is sent "down to the countryside." And indeed, the Mozart sonata is a moment of worker education on an otherwise mundane day. In an entirely realistic detail, the farm laborers seem at best only mildly interested. But this is understandable; how could they be interested in Mozart's music when it is performed by a patronizing stranger of mediocre ability?

Indeed, the pianist's talent at the piano corresponds to his mediocrity as a lecturer, evident in his haphazard litany of clichés about Mozart. "Mozart," he says, "is too easy for beginners and too difficult for virtuosi." Mozart is "music one listens to," and what he calls "modern 'serious' music" is "music one doesn't listen to": "No one goes to the concerts. Real modern music, paradoxically, is based on Mozart's harmonies, you hear bits of Mozart in the Beatles, the Rolling Stones or whatever. Fundamentally, they use Mozart's harmonies. Modern 'serious' music looked for others, resulting in what is probably the biggest disaster in the history of art." In fact, there is no substantive economic or aesthetic distinction between Mozart and modern "serious" music. Much of Mozart's music was considered challenging and "serious" in his day. And not enough people go to see classical music performances of any composer's music, including Mozart, to allow for major orchestras and opera companies to survive without state subsidies and philanthropic aid.

A better barometer of the reputation or legacy of a composer is not how many people listen to his or her music, but how many musicians continue to play it. By this measure, "serious" music is doing well enough, with a significant number of professional and amateur groups devoting their time and talents to its performance. If it is played less often than works by Mozart, this has more to do with the considerable difficulties involved in mastering such music than with the complaints of real or perceived audiences. "My music is not modern," Schoenberg once quipped, "it is only badly played."

The irony of the pianist's disparagement of "serious" music is that most of Godard's own films, especially in the years since *Weekend*, are the cinematic equivalent of the "serious" music derided in this monologue as an art-historical "disaster." If there are films to be watched and those not to be watched, then post-*Weekend* Godard mostly belongs to the latter category, with filmgoers staying away even when they are aware that Godard has a new film out in the first place. Before his modest resurgence in the mid-2000s, "the last time a Godard film received a regular commercial release in a first-run theatre in New York was in 1988, when *King Lear* played for three weeks at the Quad Cinema. According to *Variety*, it took in $61,821 at the box office in all of North America" (Brody, *Exile in Paradise*). But like "serious" modernist music, Godard's films, even the most obscure ones, do have a following among the most important film audience: established and aspiring auteurs and cineastes. If his films lack a more general audience, this is the result of a conscious decision on Godard's part to walk away from the film establishment both financially and aesthetically.

Thus, by invoking the crisis of modern music, Gégauff allegorically touches upon *Weekend*'s theme of the crisis in contemporary cinema. Godard's answer to this crisis in *Weekend* involves an escalation, where, as one character early in the film puts it, "the horror of the bourgeoisie can only be overcome with more horror." This helps one understand the film's ending. After Corrine joins up with the cannibals and they have devoured Roland, there is no heroic working class waiting in the wings at the end of the film, only more horror, only competing class fractions devolving into marauding barbarian tribes.

By contrast, the Mozart and revolutionary workers' scenes offer a happier depiction of ordinary people taking a break from their work to gain an appreciation of music and profess their faith in their revolutionary destiny. In this light, recall what transpires after Gégauff's recital and impromptu lecture. He is seen dropping off Roland and Corinne, shaking hands, and politely going on his way. This moment is a fitting emblem for the end of Godard's first period of filmmaking. He leaves the hopeless bourgeoisie behind and sets off with his piano for undiscovered cinematic country. One has to add only a few details to this image for it to be a complete emblem for Godard's work since *Weekend*. The back of the truck should contain both that piano and other fragmentary ruins from cultural history, while the radicalized sanitation workers ought to ride shotgun in the cab. This picture would be a comprehensive portrait of Godard in his own cinema as a hopeful monster. And it should be both painted as graffiti in the streets of Paris, à la 1968, and hung on a wall in the Pompidou to honor Godard's melancholic sense of history as both too soon and too late.

Godard's revolution is still just a prophecy written on the metro walls, and it has already occurred, failed, and been relegated to the museum. But, happily, Godard has managed to resolve these contradictions. If the world cannot be revolutionized, at least his own cinema can, which he has accomplished in the paradoxical way of all modernists—by clinging to the art-historical past, most frequently in his use of classical music, and using the cinematic stage to restore such music to the glory of its revolutionary origins, even if it is now audible only as fragmentary ruins.

Coda: Despair and Hope

Godard's two recent feature films, *Film Socialisme* (2012) and *Goodbye to Language* (2014), distill, to a remarkable degree, the dialectic of despair and hope outlined in this chapter. Critics praised the 3-D innovations and levity of *Goodbye to Language*; *Film Socialisme* was widely panned, with even supporters of Godard calling the latter film "castrating," "bad tempered and mean" (MacCabe, "Godard at Cannes, Part Two"). In this sense, *Film Socialisme* is the culmination of the censorious streak that runs through most of Godard's films. But it is no longer simply what Cavell criticizes as Godard's "negative advertising." The technique has evolved without having progressed; it is predicated on a determination to "deny you any pleasure" (MacCabe).

The first part of *Film Socialisme*, "Such Things," features a cruise ship full of passengers pursuing affairs and intrigues to the extent that they pursue anything at all. Patti Smith makes a cameo with her guitar; the Marxist philosopher Alain Badiou seems to have forgotten his. How this is socialism is unclear to your average socialist. The second part of the film, "Our Europe," focuses on a family, especially a young girl named Flo (Marine Battaggia). There are some poignant moments, including a scene where she brushes her teeth and discusses with her mother the lack of a program for the French Left while the Adagio Cantabile from Beethoven's *Sonata Pathétique* sounds in the background. The music is coming from the next room, as though it were history itself, here but distant, so near and so far. The dizzying array of references in the final part of the film, "Our Humanities," resembles Godard's forbidding documentary series *Histoire(s) du Cinema* (1988–1998). It repeats some of that series' main themes, including the suggestion that cinema has failed to adequately represent the Holocaust.

Given the often encyclopedic range of references throughout Godard films, it is understandable that a major critical tactic that has emerged is to catalogue and comment on the references, as Alfred Guzzetti did decades ago in his pioneering study of *Two or Three Things I Know about Her*. The most sublime example of this approach is Céline Scemana's web-based, shot-by-shot breakdown of all eight hours of *Histoire(s) du Cinema*. But as Colin MacCabe points out, there are limitations to the game of "hunt the reference." "Fascinating as such studies are," MacCabe argues, "they risk obscuring the extraordinary force" of Godard's montage style (*Godard* 299). For MacCabe, the problem is that such work forgets that "each sound and image is only incidentally a quotation or reference; their real function is as the direct material of the story Godard is telling" (299). Godard's montages create new meanings.

The tension here is a venerable one for the appreciation of art: the give and take between our understanding and enjoyment of a work. Inspired by music, it was Mallarmé who issued modernism's first challenge to the primacy of understanding over enjoyment. "Music inspired Mallarmé, as it did so many of the Romantics because the role of the message in it . . . is so substantially reduced" (Rosen, "Mallarmé and the Transfiguration of Poetry" 362). Mallarmé argued that his poetry was not difficult, but that "with the modernist tradition of poetry . . . understanding is temporarily postponed until we have savored and enjoyed the poetic art" (361). These are instructive comments for viewing Godard as well. Even for the critics and commentators busying themselves with understanding the film's works cited page, some degree of enjoyment comes first, while the understanding is deferred because of how unlikely it is that one will know all the references in a Godard film on a first viewing.

The most enjoyable part of *Goodbye to Language* (for this viewer anyway) involves a final hopeful monster—Godard's own dog Roxy—and the Allegretto second movement from Beethoven's Symphony No. 7, opus 92 (1812). As Godard's synopsis makes clear, the dog is central to the film:

> The idea is simple / a married woman and a single man meet / they love, they argue, fists fly / a dog strays between town and country / the seasons pass / the man and woman meet again / the dog finds itself between them / the other is in one / the one is in the other / and they are three / the former husband shatters everything / a second film begins / the same as the first / and yet not from the human race we pass to metaphor / this ends in barking / and a baby's cries.

That the dog's perambulations occur to fragments of Beethoven's Allegretto from Symphony No. 7 is both fitting and ironic. Ironic because what can a dog understand of music so profound? And yet fitting because a dog enjoying Beethoven is not entirely out of the question either, especially one answering to the last name Godard. The similarities between the music and the dog bear this out. The principal theme of the Allegretto matches Roxy's introspective poses, its countermelody her livelier moments. Its main theme is funereal, no doubt, but the countermelody is not. Its passion is unsubdued, especially by the time it occurs in the violins. The overall tempo marking of allegretto (fairly brisk) is, similarly, a bit of a contradiction thanks to Beethoven's famous comment that he regretted not marking the tempo andante (moderately slow) (Tovey 59).

More generally, these key tensions—a contrasting melody and countermelody; a brisk and slow tempo—make the Allegretto a fitting musical analogue for interpreting Godard. The opening of the Allegretto is easily played too slowly and, like Godard, misinterpreted as mainly melancholy. You have to get the tempo right to bring out the countermelody's persistent strains of hope. Godard's main theme has always been that politics and cinema (and love) are too soon and too late, that he awaits their arrival while also mourning their loss. But as Beethoven's Allegretto's presence alongside the intrepid Roxy in *Goodbye to Language* reminds us, there is also a countermelody in which the rumors of the cinema's and the left's demises have been greatly exaggerated. In this way, *Goodbye to Language* reveals that it is not only Roxy who is a hopeful monster, but also Godard himself, the enfant terrible of modern cinema.

Finally, if late Godard is one day perceived as essential and no longer neglected, such a rehabilitation would have one of its few precedents in the reception history of Beethoven's late quartets. In the twenty-five years after Beethoven's death, a total of only seven performances of his last five quartets took place (Kerman, *Beethoven Quartets* 192). The famous Great Fugue's second performance was twenty-seven years after

Figure 4.3. Roxy looks on in *Goodbye to Language* (Jean-Luc Godard, Wild Bunch/Kino Lorber, 2014). Digital frame enlargement.

the first. After such inauspicious beginnings, that these would become the most venerated of Beethoven's quartets should strike us not as inevitable but as contingent because "the history of musical taste affords few more striking phenomena than the subsequent change of attitude toward this body of music. It has to do with the main line of musical evolution into the twentieth century and new ways of comprehending new music" (192). In a hopeful mood, one can imagine a similar fate for Godard's late work. New developments in the undiscovered futures of cinema and society will make his late films essential viewing for not only for auteurs and cineastes, but also for the everyday filmgoing public. It goes without saying that these new developments would have to be radical. It befits Godard that this happy fate would have one of its few precedents in the reception history of Beethoven.

5

Before a Winter's Journey

Michael Haneke's Critique of Film Music in *The Piano Teacher*

The Origin of Film Music

"ONE CAN UNDERSTAND *The Piano Teacher* [2002] without access to *Winterreise*," Robin Wood observes of Michael Haneke's harrowing film, "but one cannot understand it completely" (59). Wood's idea can be taken a step further: for its heroine, the film *provides* access to Schubert's famed song-cycle *Winterreise* ("Winter's Journey"). When Erika (Isabelle Huppert) hits bottom after her affair with her student Walter (Benoit Magimel), the film ends when she is finally ready to depart on her winter's journey. Like the singer in Schubert's cycle and the speaker in Wilhelm Müller's monodrama, she has failed at love and abandoned the other defining characteristics of her life for an uncertain future of longing, isolation, and acceptance of death. In this way, the film is an anachronistic prequel to *Winterreise*, cycling back to the origins of film music in Schubert's songs and their "tone painting" accompaniments.

The music of Schubert, especially *Winterreise*, is crucial both to understanding the film overall and to grasping details of the film that, because of their violent or shocking content, defy or frustrate explanation. Haneke's controversial films are infamous for their depictions of violence, which critics complain he sanctimoniously exploits while nominally condemning. But one must distinguish between types of violence in his films.

Haneke's most important contribution to contemporary cinema resides in his films' overcoming their own fascination with lurid and sensationalized violence to foster a sensibility for crucial modes of aesthetic and economic violence.

Overall, there are three fundamental aspects to Haneke's work: one, his critique of cinema's essential elements, including genres; two, his films' exploration of modes of violence; and, three, his films' estranging use of film form to explore sociopolitical questions. Together these three aspects form a dialectical progression. First, the cinema of critique interrogates contemporary cinema practices and subject matter: from distinctive shots and media forms to genre conventions and fashionable culture-war issues. But this process of critique generates an ambiguous remainder: a fascination with violence. The redemption of this remainder in turn becomes possible through an examination of the way violence is central not just to his films' stories but to their estranging use of film form and their references to late capitalism's increasingly unjustifiable inequities. Common features of his films—alienated, miserable characters, long takes, abrupt cuts, estranging framing, and austere musical scoring—all connote a palpable disenchantment with the post-1989 political and economic order.

Within this framework, *The Piano Teacher* is both typical and exceptional. Haneke's early films critique essential elements of film form, while the majority of his more recent films critique particular genres. *The Piano Teacher* does both. Its critique questions both a fundamental element of film form—film music—and its related film genre—melodrama. It is also Haneke's only film that implicitly, but in a sustained manner, reflects on the construction and dissolution of sexual identity and sexual desire. What do the two, music and sex, have to do with one another? *The Piano Teacher* answers, bleakly, that while classical music advances courtship and love, its method of interpreting texts, when applied by Erika and Walter to the realization of Erika's sexual desires, causes one of the most dreadful sexual encounters in the history of cinema. More generally, after Haneke's films explored a variety of modes of sound design as *musique concrete*, featured limited appearances of music by Berg and Bach, and referenced musical silence in *Code Unknown* (2000), *The Piano Teacher*'s sustained use of Schubert's music is like George Eliot's "roar on the other side of silence," the invisible, emotional fabric of cinema that, after his film's previous musical asceticism, overwhelms our senses (162).

The Piano Teacher's paradox is that Erika abandons her musical career to more fully embody the condition of music in her identification with the protagonist of *Winterreise*. In this sense, her masochism is not a fixed identity, but, like a difficult musical score, a text to be interpreted as she performs her transition to a more indefinite identity and fate. She evolves from Masoch's modern, neurotic archetype back to Müller's hero's heartbroken abjection, and with it to a major origin of the Romantic sensibility. Similarly, Haneke's film moves modernist cinema's relationship to classical music forward by taking it back to Schubert, the pioneering master of "tone painting" background music and the "endless melodies" that film music inherited from Wagner.

The Critique of Cinematic Reason

In *The Critique of Pure Reason*, Immanuel Kant describes the task of critique as a call to set up a tribunal to question the nature and limits of abstract reasoning. "It is a call to reason to take up once again the most difficult of all its tasks—that of self-cognition—and to set up a tribunal that will make reason secure in its rightful claims and that will dismiss all baseless pretensions, not by fiat but in accordance with reason's eternal and immutable laws" (8). An adaptation of these and subsequent lines from Kant would create something near to the implicit artistic manifesto of Haneke's films. His films are a call to cinema to take up once again the most difficult of all its tasks—that of self-cognition—and to set up a tribunal that will make cinema secure in its rightful claims and will dismiss all baseless pretensions and propagandistic distortions, not by fiat but in accordance with cinema's eternal and immutable laws. This tribunal is none other than the critique of cinema itself. By critique of cinema, however, one does not mean a critique of books about cinema and systems of cinema aesthetics, but the critique of the power of cinema as such. Hence one means by it the decision as to whether a cinema as such is possible or impossible, and the determination of its sources as well as its range and bounds.

In other words, Haneke's films are a form of film criticism that interrogates the interconnection between the form and content of film to establish the aesthetic and ethical limits of cinema. Haneke's first three feature films in the so-called "Glaciation Trilogy" are representative cases for how his critique proceeds. Inspired by real events, each film critiques a dominant visual media trope alongside a recognized topic in the culture wars. *The Seventh Continent* (1989) critiques ideologies of happiness and wellness using medium-distance shots. Haneke uses this innocuous shot type against the grain to document a family's inexplicable collective suicide. *Benny's Video* (1992) is a tale of a troubled adolescent boy that uses amateur and surveillance camera footage to document his brutal and senseless murder of a young girl. *71 Fragment of a Chronicle of Chance* (1994) critiques both a mass shooting carried out by an alienated young man and the television news broadcast format by which we learn of such incidents.

Since these disturbing, early films, Haneke's critique has focused primarily on particular film genres: literary adaptations in *The Castle* (1997), exploitation films in *Funny Games* (1997), multinarrative films like Altman's *Shortcuts* (1993) in *Code Unknown*, melodramas in *The Piano Teacher*, disaster films in *Time of the Wolf* (2003), thrillers (and arguably noirs) in *Caché* (2005), and historical-period films in *The White Ribbon* (2009). Walter Benjamin's idea that great works create new, or destroy old, genres, while perfect works do both is a relevant remark for understanding Haneke's critique of genre and the greatness of these films (*Origin* 44). In questioning and undermining the expectations of each genre, these films all but destroy their respective genres. *Amour* (2012), Haneke's film about the difficulty of the end of life, is arguably his one perfect film in Benjamin's sense of both founding and destroying a genre.

Code Unknown is notable among the genre films because it critiques both the least established of any genre in cinema—the decentered multinarrative genre form—and Haneke's own previous contribution to the genre, *71 Fragments*. A prominent feature of *71 Fragments* and other well-known multinarrative films is a climax bringing together the different stories, as in the earthquake experienced by all the characters in *Shortcuts* or the eponymous crash in *Crash* (2004). By contrast, in *Code Unknown*, the lives of the characters converge in the second scene of the film and only tangentially thereafter. The absence of the typical, convergent climax suggests that this genre, and perhaps cinema itself, is an insufficient medium for representing the contradictions of contemporary life. The art form that could provide such a representation is the film's code unknown.

Because most of his films reject musical scoring entirely, Haneke's overall verdict on film music is decidedly negative.

> Fundamentally, I'm of the opinion that film music has no place in movies because ninety-nine percent of its function is to compensate for a deficit in the suspense or excitement. Emotions which are not created through the plot or action, the cinematography or by the actors, is then produced with a musical sauce underneath everything. That's why there's no music in my films except when it appears in the story. Of course, *The Piano Teacher* provided an opportunity to use music a bit more indulgently. ("*Piano Teacher* Interview")

In this verdict, the extended use of musical selections in a film is justified only when the film features music directly, as in *The Piano Teacher*'s story about music and musicians. This organic approach to film music resembles the Dogma 95 movement's limits on musical scoring in their "Vow of Chastity." Like Haneke, the Dogma directors Lars von Trier and Thomas Vinterberg maintain that "music must not be used unless it occurs where the scene is being shot" ("Vow of Chastity").

But such rules were meant to be broken, and indeed Haneke's use of Schubert's music in the film surpasses his own censorious view of film music in general. Like other films renowned for their musical scoring, *The Piano Teacher* shows that the thoughtful deployment of music in films can do more than compensate for a film's shortcomings. It can also intensify and broaden a film's meaning. Indeed, in *The Piano Teacher*, the reliance on music is that much more extreme than in most films. Schubert's music is the precondition for the story, the cause of its development, and its end goal or final cause.

The main argument against Haneke's critique of cinematic reason is that his films are complicit with the visual media tropes and "ripped-from-the-headlines" topics they supposedly interrogate. "*The Seventh Continent* and *Benny's Video* both gained passionate defenders," Robin Wood observes, "but many thought the films went too far, were too concerned with 'extreme' cases (did Haneke really endorse family suicide, did he really believe teenagers would commit casual murder because they watched violent videos?)" (55). His infamous torture film *Funny Games* is a less ambiguous case. For Wood, its grim and mocking depictions of sadism gave Haneke's critics "the ammunition they wanted" (55).

Nonetheless, critics of Haneke's sensationalized violence are missing what Kant would call the "contest of assertions" over the concept of violence in his work. For there are less visible, structural modes of violence asserted by Haneke's films. Such "objective violence" takes place at two interrelated levels in Haneke's films: both in the way his films draw attention to their social contexts and in the ways they highlight their use of film form. First, Haneke's films refer to "invisible" economic violence in a variety of ways. *Code Unknown* follows the often perilous lives of legal and illegal immigrants in Paris. *71 Fragments* excerpts news footage of the struggle for survival in the third world's failed states, and features as a central character a child refugee. *Caché* offers a case study in the blowback from colonialism. Structural violence also occurs in the very way Haneke attempts to make viewers conscious of film form in precise and consistent ways—through long takes, abrupt cuts, disorienting framing, and rhetorical tropes like paraprosdokian (where the end of a scene changes its entire meaning) and parataxis (where there is no transition between scenes).

The Piano Teacher's predominant modes of objective violence pertain not to the deterioration of social life in the increasingly unequal global order of late capitalism, but to the violence needed to define one's libidinal identity and the extreme degree of alienation that seems fundamental to the film's vision of an artistic career.[10] The sacrifice and discipline needed to become a musical artist are Erika's fixed ideas with her students, and she is living proof of the danger of following her instructions too closely.

Erika also takes the processes through which one learns sexual desire to an extreme. She is a very late bloomer and slow learner with corresponding appetites for incest and masochism. Through the use of these extremes in the context of a failed artistic career, *The Piano Teacher*'s indictment of the sexual revolution transcends the film's sensational sexual violence. "Erika's behavior . . ." as Wood notes, "can in fact only be understood within the context of our sexual history over the past hundred years, our 'progress' from neurosis-breeding repression to what some have hopefully regarded as sexual liberation, which has proven, in practice, to be simply another form of imprisonment" (55).

Misquoting Adorno

Erika and Walter's first conversation at a recital becomes unusually personal. "Look at them," Walter remarks of the concertgoers. "Do they give a fig about the benefits of illness?" She answers his question with her own: "Have you read Adorno on Schumann's C major Fantasy?" "No," replies Walter. "He talks of his twilight," she tells him, "it's not Schumann bereft of reason but just before, a fraction before. He knows he's losing his mind. It torments him but he clings on, one last time. It's being aware of what it means to lose oneself before being completely abandoned." Taken by her interpretation, Walter compliments what he assumes must be her exemplary teaching. To which she replies, again with undue seriousness, "Schubert and Schumann are my favorites, that's all. Since my father died completely mad in Steinhof asylum, I can talk easily about the twilight of the mind, can't I?" In fact, Adorno, a key influence on Haneke, never made such an argument about Schumann's C major Fantasy (see Tunbridge, "Schumann as Manfred"). Such a nervous lie signals that Erika does not yet know how to respond to someone like Walter, a talented and confident young man aware of how handsome he is. For his part, Walter struggles to reply to her confession of her father's illness. He changes the subject and looks for an excuse to get away: "Perhaps you'd care for something to drink?"

Erika's attraction to Walter truly sinks in after this exchange when she hears him play the *Scherzo* from Schubert's Sonata in A major, D. 959. "It is through the medium of music (specifically Schubert) that Erika and Walter fall in love," Robin Wood notes, "and the film is absolutely clear on this in the twinning of the two crucial sequences in the piano recital" (Wood 60). But these sequences are fraternal, not identical, twins; they have significant differences in their effect and their formal realization. When Erika plays and Walter listens, his gaze is unrestrained, the object of it unambiguous. But while he plays, Erika fights the urge to look at him before giving in. This pointed moment suggests three interlocking meanings. First, as the film clearly shows, she is looking away only until her jealous mother (Annie Girardot) stops watching her. Second, for her own sake, she fights the urge to look at this mercurial young man. These motives are mutually reinforcing; Erika knows that mommy knows best. A third meaning cancels and preserves them both: when Erika's gaze finally resettles on Walter, she sees past him to *Winterreise*.

The sound design in the second cut to her watching him is crucial for this third reading. As she looks directly at him while he plays, a voice-over sound bridge to the next scene begins with Erika reciting lines from "In the Village," the song from *Winterreise* that recurs throughout the film. "Dreaming of what they do not have, / Replenished of good and bad. / And next morning, all flown away." Here the poem's distraught speaker contrasts himself with the ordinary villagers asleep in their beds. While they sleep peacefully, he wanders the night alone, menaced by guard dogs, unable to rest. Like the villagers, Erika is dreaming of what she does not have, of Walter. For now, the dream is only there to replenish her of the good and bad of this fantasy, not to become reality. But

Figure 5.1. Sensing a rival in *The Piano Teacher* (Michael Haneke, Arte France Cinema/Criterion Collection, 2002). Digital frame enlargement.

at the same time, as the sound design suggests, she already sees past her Walter fantasy to her true goal of a winter's journey.

In the next scene, the film follows its sound bridge, and we find Erika in her studio explaining the relationship between the poem and Schubert's piano accompaniment to her ill-fated student Anna (Anna Sigalevitch). Erika's commentary on the piano score is apt but a little bit behind the film's tempo. "And here," she says, "the mood switches to irony." But in fact the film switched to irony when Walter's Schubert performance, unbeknownst to him, causes Erika and the film to move past him. As Anna's lesson continues, Erika continues to emphasize the satirical tone of the song while Anna struggles to keep up. The repeated high D-natural in the accompaniment must be emphasized because it is "the obstinacy of the complacent middle class." By identifying the mocking D in the accompaniment with the sleeping villagers, Erika shows where her sympathies lie. Like the song's protagonist, soon enough Erika, the master interpreter of the song, will not be one of the complacent bourgeoisie anymore.

A Schubertiad in a Sex Shop

The use of Schubert's "Andante con Moto" from his Piano Trio No. 2 in *The Piano Teacher* is the most prominent example in Haneke's films of background music. The Andante's presence in the film begins when it is part of Erika's rehearsal just prior to its appearance on the soundtrack. The sequence opens with an uncomfortable phone call where Erika's mother insists she come home directly after her rehearsal. Returning to her rehearsal after a pause to discuss a mistake, when the musicians begin the Andante again it becomes another sound bridge to the next scene, where it accompanies Erika on a visit to a sex shop at the mall.

Schubert's trio subtly parallels salient details from the ensuing sequence. Just as at first Erika walks anonymously through the mall, so too the piano, her instrument, remains in the background of the trio, accompanying the cello. Just as a random passerby bumps into Erika as she navigates the crowd, so too the accompaniment figure in the piano features a jagged dotted rhythm. And just as she walks purposefully toward her destination, so too the tempo marking of the music, "Andante con Moto," conforms to her pace.

The change of setting is also paralleled by the music. When Erika enters the sex shop, this coincides with the restatement of the principal theme in the piano, so that just as she takes the lead in the piece, she stands out among the male customers. And just as she knows the melody, she also seems to know this place, moving assuredly from the

Figure 5.2. The origin of film music in *The Piano Teacher* (Michael Haneke, Arte France Cinema/Criterion Collection, 2002). Digital frame enlargement.

register, where she obtains tokens, to the nearest viewing booth. Just as she was asked to start again by the cellist because of her error during her rehearsal, here too she meets with a problem: all the viewing booths are currently occupied. As she waits among the intrigued male customers, the Schubert leaves its somber principal theme for a relative major key and a new melodic idea derived from a simple, two-note motif in the principal theme. (Kubrick also exploits this contrast in the Andante in the gaming parlor scene in *Barry Lyndon*.) Although the situation may appear awkward for her, in fact it is the male customers who struggle with her presence, while Erika, unfazed, stares blankly, as if she were waiting for the metro. This scenario is reflected in the music as well. Just as she calmly waits her turn for a booth while the male customers exchange uncomfortable glances, so too in the trio here the piano plays an unexceptional ostinato figure while the strings struggle between themselves for control of the new theme.

When Erika finally enters a booth, the music continues until the moment she puts her coins into the machine and selects a film. This is the film's first substitution of a sexual encounter for music, and pointedly it involves both in their everyday forms of commodified alienation: as recorded background music and pornography. The unusual scene Erika selects underscores the alienation. A woman performs fellatio lying on her back with her head hanging upside down off the end of the table. She appears less like as a complete person and more as a conglomeration

Figure 5.3. Waiting her turn in *The Piano Teacher* (Michael Haneke, Arte France Cinema/Criterion Collection, 2002). Digital frame enlargement.

of disparate parts: a partial torso, flailing arms, a chin and mouth. The sounds of her muted moaning and his rapid breathing coming from the film are rendered equally strange by the deafening silence that has replaced the Schubert as the musical score.

In the reverse shot, Erika scrutinizes the movie before reaching into the wastebasket for a used tissue that she begins to sniff almost clinically, with no outward sign of enjoyment or disgust. Here, at this scene's point of maximum sexual exploration, "In the Village" returns on the soundtrack, again as a sound bridge to the next scene. It is the end of the song, and this time the last stanza of the poem is not recited but sung: "Bark me on my way you wakeful dogs, / Let me not rest in these hours of slumber! / All my dreaming is at an end, / Why would I linger among the sleeping?" Schubert's music and Müller's lines transfigure Erika's sexual experiment while her experiment contaminates the music. Paradoxically, the lyrics here ("All my dreaming is at an end") reconceive her pornographic research as a reengagement with reality apart from the illusionary dreams of the poem's sleepers. Indeed, the smell of that tissue ought to wake her up.

Despite the litany of matching correspondences and the final negation of the Andante, in several key ways, this sequence surpasses both the customary role of film music and its ironic standard deviation. Above all, showing the rehearsal of the piece before it appears as a soundtrack emphasizes the music to a degree that surpasses the typical scoring aesthetic in which a musical remains out of sight and, to a degree, out of mind. This emphasis on the background music, Haneke's bringing it to consciousness, is corroborated by three key details of the Andante and this specific performance: first, the use of chamber music and the distinct timbres of a piano trio in particular contrasts with the more indistinct, atmospheric possibilities of large ensemble scoring of most film music in the classical tradition; second, the length of the excerpt contrasts with the brevity of musical ideas in the leitmotif paradigm; and, third, the apparent rehearsal quality of the performance contrasts with the usual caliber of film score recordings.

With the choice of Schubert for background music, Haneke locates the preconditions for Wagnerism. In his late works like the Andante, Schubert refined the more theatrical style of his earliest compositions "to an economy that presages late Romanticism." "Schubert's declamation achieves what Wagner would later formulate as the ideal of musical art: 'endless melody' in which each note is expressive, eloquent, and meaningful" (Gibbs 103). Haneke's choice of Schubert's chamber music is therefore only apparently in contradiction with Wagnerism's preference for lush orchestration, for the chamber music selected is a key ancestor of the main Wagnerian style of film music. But in this dissipated context, Haneke's accent in this choice for background music also has a disapproving tone. In its juxtaposition of Schubert's pioneering music with the pornographic dead end of the sexual revolution, this sequence is a sardonic epitome of film music history, from its prehistory in Schubert to its debauched finale as a kitsch accompaniment for pornography.

Schubert in the Background

The rehearsal quality of the performance is an especially subtle, and probably unconscious, reference to the origins of film music. It recalls the early cinemagoing experience of hearing imperfect, live background music provided by pianists or ensembles. In an enthusiastic short text, Adorno surprisingly celebrated such live background music at cafés. "The fiddler does not make the noble melody ordinary with his soloistic intrusiveness," Adorno comments ("Music in the Background" 508). "It has already lost its noble character and therefore abandons itself to the fiddler." In this fallen state, famous opera melodies have a unique charm, the musical equivalent of the café's "bouquets of dead flowers":

> The joints between the brittle sounds into which they are layered are not firmly bonded. Through them shimmers the mysterious allegorical appearance that arises whenever fragments

of the past come together in an uncertain surface . . . The cafés are the site of potpourris. The latter are constructed out of the fragments of the work, its best-loved melodies. But they awaken the ruins to new, ghostly life. If our art music lingers in the comforting realm of Orpheus—here its echo sounds from Eurydice's mournful region. Its glow is netherworldly. It can remain unnoticed because it is unreal. But it is not a black shadow, rather a bright one, like milk glass. One can, as it were, hear vaguely through the music, through to the next room. This is why it shines. (508–09)

One might have expected Adorno to dismiss the idea of arranging and performing the classics in cafés as a corruption of art music. Instead, he acknowledges that the informal context awakens these ruins to "new, ghostly life." These ghosts are not uncanny specters; they shine beneficently, casting oxymoronic bright shadows. For Adorno, as in Benjamin's theory of allegory, the melodies' shadows are bright for a paradoxical reason: their very fragmentation from the larger work intensifies their meaning. In the choice of Schubert for background music, however, Haneke is willing to go further than Adorno. Some classics are ideal for the background according to Adorno: "One could think that Bohème, Butterfly, and Tosca were created with the thought of imaginary potpourri" (509). But Adorno singles out Schubert as blasphemous in the café setting: "Faced with Schubert, café music becomes blasphemous" (509).

But at a more fundamental level, Schubert is *the* composer of background music. This is true above all in Schubert's use of "tone painting" techniques in the accompaniments to his songs, which by adding rigor and complexity to the piano accompaniment elevated the lied from a minor musical genre to a major one. Charles Rosen compares Schubert's "tone painting" accompaniments in his song cycles to the new ways in which natural landscapes were perceived in late eighteenth century European and British literature and painting. What was new to both the landscape painters and Schubert was the attempt to record both the immediate and the historical aspect of the landscape, what Rosen calls "the double time scale" of Romantic landscapes, which combine two radically divergent senses of time: the immediate apprehension of the moment and the dawning comprehension of the immensity of "deep time" (*Romantic Generation* 139).

The shift in sensibility from the classicist historical landscape to the Romanticist natural landscape is best captured by the famous anecdote in which Goethe reproached his guide for detailing how Hannibal had waged war in an area near Palermo, while the guide was puzzled by

Goethe's scrupulous collecting of small and seemingly worthless stones from their path (156–57). Goethe was only interested in his own immediate impression and in the geological prehistory of the area. Trivia from the classical history disturbed both.

Schubert's contribution to this new sensibility of combining the deep past with the immediate present is most apparent in his music's economy of means. "It was Schubert's genius," Rosen comments, "to find a way to represent both past and present with the same motif." Rosen's example is the opening song of *Winterreise*, "Good Night": "The opening song of *Winter's Journey* is a walking song, as are many of the successive ones. From the first bars of 'Good Night,' the sense of walking combines with the anguish of memory." "The sense of grief and regret," Rosen adds, "is in the harmonies, in the way the melody opens by expressively outlining a ninth, and above all in the accents that break up the even surface, disturbing the regular movement without impeding it" (123–24).

Like "Good Night," the Andante from the Second Piano Trio reproduces the combination of present experience and memory with a walking tempo and jarring rhythmic accents that disturb without impeding the tempo. The memory Schubert had in mind in the Andante is a quite specific musical one. As was mentioned in discussing Kubrick's *Barry Lyndon*, the Andante is widely recognized as an elegy for Beethoven that reinvents the funeral march from the *Eroica* Symphony (Gibbs 159). The Andante's melody represents both the heroic past of the *Eroica* and the musical present of Schubert's own distinctive voice finally emerging from Beethoven's shadow. Beethoven's legacy disturbs but does not impede Schubert's own musical path.

Schubert's connection to background music also extends into his biography and his music's afterlife. Schubert lived much of his life in the musical background of Vienna due to his inability to stage a successful opera, the sine qua non of a financially remunerative career for a composer of his era. In the history of music, Schubert remains in the background, but powerfully so. He was not part of the classical generation that ended with Beethoven, yet he was too old to be considered part of "The Romantic Generation" (born around 1810), who were profoundly influenced by him and helped create his place in music history with their critical writings and performances devoted to his music. Neither exclusively classical nor entirely Romantic, Schubert was the link between the two sensibilities.

Furthermore, he was in a sense forced to wait in the background of music history throughout the first century after his death, as many of his masterworks were discovered and performed for the first time long after his demise. Nineteenth-century critic Eduard Hanslick described the gradual reception of Schubert in terms that made it seem supernatural: "If Schubert's contemporaries justly gazed in astonishment at his creative power, what indeed must we, who come after him, say, as we incessantly discover new works of his? For thirty years the master has been dead, and in spite of this it seems as if he goes on composing invisibly—it is impossible to keep up with him" (quoted in Gibbs 170).

Thus, Haneke's selection of Schubert's Trio in E-flat as a background for Erika's trip to the sex shop is, pace Adorno, not blasphemy but heresy. Haneke does to Schubert what Schubert does to Beethoven: Haneke remembers Schubert and his music not with slavish dogmatism, but by reinventing Schubert in his own distinct cinematic idiom, and with a critical eye to that medium's meretricious effect on virtually everything it touches, especially in this case love and music. Like Schubert before him, Haneke uses the Andante to represent a "double-time scale" in Erika's life. Erika's and music's pasts, both represented by Schubert, coincide with her increasingly unstable present as she ventures into the sex shop. As the accompaniment of Schubert to the sex shop shows, she draws inspiration from her musical life as her sexual experiments grow ever bolder, culminating in her disastrous affair with Walter. This leads her past Walter and toward the abject state of *Winterreise*'s singer. The film's ultimate example of Romanticism's double-time scale is that Erika's future belongs to music's past.

The Show Must Not Go On

"In the Village" is partially heard three times in the first thirty minutes of the film and a final time in the film's second hour. Each iteration of the song grows more complete and correlates with new revelations about Erika. In the first instance, the next scene shows Erika climbing into bed next to her mother at the end of the day as if this were perfectly normal. The second instance comes after she meets Walter at the fateful recital. The third instance punctuates her visit to a sex shop, and the fourth and final time the song is heard the film presents its fullest rendition of it, but this version occurs in a sequence that also renders a conventional performance of the piece impossible going forward.

In the fourth instance, her student Anna arrives late to her dress rehearsal of *Winterreise*, and Walter escorts her to the piano and soothes her nerves with a joke. Unfortunately for Anna, Erika takes notice of these attentions from Walter. The first line of the poem—"The dogs bark, their chains rattle"—is wonderfully illustrated by Schubert's accompaniment as it oscillates between chromatic neighbor tones in the base voice and half-bar rests. The rhythm is hard to place at first, as if the alternation of sound and silence were by chance, like the irregular barking of dogs and the rattling of their chains in an otherwise sleeping village. Until the song begins, Erika does not seem visibly upset. But when the music starts, as though inspired by it, her expression changes to one of jealous rage over Walter's attention to Anna. She quietly exits the hall for the backstage area, where, after failing to calm herself down, she grabs a glass, wraps it in a handkerchief, steps on it, and deposits the shards into Anna's coat pocket.

As she walks back into the concert hall unnoticed, *Winterreise* occupies center stage for the last time in the film. For the first time, one hears a significant portion of a song other than "In the Village." The song is "The Signpost," one of the cycle's most foreboding. The song has just begun as Erika reenters. Its words both describe and diverge from her recent activity:

> Why then do I shun the roads
> Walked by other travelers,
> Seeking out hidden paths
> Through snowbound rocky heights?
>
> I've done nothing wrong
> That I should avoid mankind,
> What foolish longing
> Drives me into the wilderness? (1–8)

Erika's singularly distressing life resembles the first stanza's Frostian "road less travelled." After all, how many grown people still share a bed with their mother? The Frostian "road less travelled" also foreshadows Erika's sexual desires that emerge during her affair. But after her shenanigans at the sex shop and elsewhere, including urinating while she watches a couple have sex in a car and mutilating her own genitals, having an unpaid sexual encounter with Walter is arguably a step toward the path of other travelers, not away from it.

The second stanza has a more complicated relationship to Erika's current predicament. While the poem's speaker "has done nothing wrong," Erika most certainly has. Or has she? While obviously cruel, Erika's act can also be understood as an unconscious effort to liberate Anna from her own miserable fate. Indeed, Anna's mediocre talent and weak nerves make for a worse fate than the one Erika is trying to escape. By injuring Anna, she tries to keep her away from the path shunned by other travelers, the path toward the deprivation required for mastery of *Winterreise*.

"Schubert Was Quite Ugly"

Erika and Walter's first sexual encounter is like a chaotic sight reading of a difficult piece. It occurs just after Anna's hand is wounded by the glass shards and Walter realizes that Erika has attacked Anna out of jealousy. He follows her into a public restroom in the recital hall and begins to undress her. She stops him and attempts to turn the encounter into one played by her rules. He must stand still, remain silent, and refrain from touching her while she performs fellatio. Here Erika attempts to continue her role as Walter's teacher, but she also is beginning to relinquish it for the uncertainties of a lover. When he refuses to comply, she stops, telling him she will write down everything he can do to her. She then allows him to masturbate, but only if he looks at her the whole time. They finally reach a compromise when she opens the bathroom door to heighten the danger of the scenario and so that Bach can be heard in the background. Then she finishes him herself. "You will receive my instructions," she tells him before leaving. He goes along with her demands throughout the scene, but as they part, he begins to laugh and joke with her. "How about a little smile?" he asks her mockingly on his way out. She is losing her grip over him already.

At Walter's next piano lesson, he plays the Andantino from the same Schubert Sonata in A major, D. 959 (1828).[11] Erika has makeup on and wears her hair down for the first time in the film, but the effect is the opposite of her intention: it heightens her awkward nervousness. She manages a minor victory when she admonishes Walter for the lack of dynamic range in his interpretation, but she is losing the larger war, having finally agreed to let him play Schubert. Fittingly, the fragment of the Andantino Walter plays—the part leading up to and including the recapitulation—is essentially a song without words. It borrows its form from an operatic recitative. It is a duet on one instrument in which the sparse accompaniment in the base mimics an orchestra during a recitative and contrasts with the speech-like moving line in the upper voice.[12]

In returning to the sonata that began their relationship at a song-like moment, it is as though Haneke is not doing away with music altogether, but gradually reducing the voice and piano parts of *Winterreise* to solo piano. Walter originally expressed his love for Erika by changing his recital program to include the Scherzo from this same sonata, and now the film has returned to this piece for its final instance of music. With music behind them, it is as though love too is being left behind and something else is at stake in Erika's affair with Walter. Indeed, their fragile love nearly collapses when Erika harshly criticizes Walter's inattention to the dynamics of the piece and attributes his indelicate playing to his good looks. "Schubert was quite ugly. Did you know? With your looks nothing can ever hurt you." His response shows a dawning awareness that this is about more than love for Erika, "Why destroy what could bring us together?" When he asks if he can kiss her neck after her harsh criticism, she has a grotesque coughing fit instead. She hands him her promised letter of instructions and asks him to read it alone before they proceed.

"You Really Are Shameless"

The specter of musical performance haunts Erika's letter to Walter about her masochistic desires. Like a difficult and unfamiliar musical score, on a first reading, Walter is unable to interpret it successfully. Halfway through the letter, when she requests he punch her stomach to force her tongue into his anus, he looks up and asks in confusion, "Is this supposed to be serious? Are you making fun of me? Do you want a slap?"

When he has read the entire letter and is visibly shaken by her masochistic desires, she shows him her collection of sex toys and tools and then asks, "Are you upset with me?" Her guard is truly down; she is no longer the authority in their relationship. "If you want to hit me, hit me," she implores him. "I don't want to soil my hands. No one should touch your sort, even with gloves on," is his response. In this exchange, a fundamental uncertainty emerges that will haunt the rest of their encounters. Is Walter now consciously playing his assigned role of dominant sadist, or is his anger spontaneous and real? Similarly, is Erika's new vulnerability in this scene and thereafter part of her submissive role or something more dynamic and authentic? In these ways, as the film shifts from problems of musical performance to those of sexual performance, it remains focused on the gap separating a fantasized ideal from its realization that haunts both sorts of performances. Her letter tells them how the sex is supposed to happen, but, like a piece of music beyond the abilities of the performers, it presents a script too difficult for them to execute properly.

As the scene continues, Erika's regression to the Oedipal stage creates the film's key allegorical tableau for the relationship between classical music and cinema. Having read the letter, Walter abruptly leaves, and Erika meets with more abuse than usual when she gets in bed next to her mother. "You really are shameless," she tell Erika. "All the sacrifice for this? You can set up a little bordello." Erika responds by attempting to have sex with her. After her mother has successfully rebuffed her advances, Erika tells her, "I saw the hairs on your sex" and then cuddles like a ravished lover in the crook of her mother's arm.

This shot is *the* allegorical emblem for the relationship between classical music and modernist cinema in the film, and the film's ultimate insight about the genealogical relationship between modernist cinema and classical music. Erika is modernist cinema; her mother is classical music. Modernist cinema is classical music's daughter; and like Erika, despite its age and hard work, it remains immature. But it has its overbearing mother to thank for much of its stunted development. Like Erika, modernist cinema loves its mother but wants to be free from her grasp. Like Erika's mother, classical music is getting older and but remains capable of making impossible demands upon the daughter that it should have let go of long ago. When they embrace, they have never been further apart.

The next sequence ends with a similarly allegorical image, but one that is more specific to Erika's impending winter's journey. After she tells Walter to think it over and get in touch with her only if he feels comfortable with what her letter asks him to do, she shows up at his hockey practice the next day anyway. "Forgive me for the letter," she says, as if it were the wrong musical piece to start with, one that, like Schubert, is too difficult for someone as unfamiliar with ugliness as Walter. They should began with something less ambitious, like the aggressive sex that ensues in the equipment room. Perhaps because Walter does not too strictly perform the role Erika asks of him in her letter, this rehearsal goes better than the performance later that night. He is cruel, but only after they are finished. As she tries to kiss him, something she has hitherto scrupulously avoided, he responds, "You know, you really stink. You should leave town until you don't stink so much." After these words, he opens the equipment room's door and Erika spills out onto the ice and into another allegorical emblem: Erika departing on her winter's journey.

Figure 5.4. Departing on her winter's journey in *The Piano Teacher* (Michael Haneke, Arte France Cinema/ Criterion Collection, 2002). Digital frame enlargement.

"Love Isn't Everything"

Walter and Erika's final sexual encounter is a harrowing, failed sadomasochistic performance that devolves into rape. Walter enters Erika's apartment in anger, and while abusing both her and her mother asks Erika if this is how she imagined it. She says no, and he grows both more confused and, tragically, more determined to bring her letter to life, to realize it like an untalented musician approaching a difficult musical score. Locking her mother in a room, he quotes the letter and asks for clarification as though she were still his teacher: "'As for my mother, pay no attention to her.' Am I quoting you exactly?" Erika is upset and does not reply. He quotes her again, "Give me lots of slaps, darling. Hit me around the face and hit me hard.'" Here he pauses seemingly to gather strength, and mockingly says, "At your service, madam." Then he hits her hard enough to knock her down and kicks her in the face for good measure. Her mother cries out continually from the next room as a morbid inversion of the Freudian primal scene plays out with her mother witnessing Erika's deflowering.

Switching out of his sadistic role, he tells her he does not always want to play by her rules, and then he gets on top of her as she begs him to stop. As they copulate, Walter repeatedly scolds her for being cold. "Love me, please," he says to her at one point. The expression on her face throughout this sexual act is one of total anguish. She has had her fantasy realized, and the result is a nightmare. When he has finished, Walter insists that for her own good Erika tell no one what has happened. She does not answer him, and in parting he adds, "You know, love isn't everything." This is a more revealing remark than he knows. Her love for him is just a step on a longer, more perilous journey.

The final minutes of the film confirm that Erika is planning a more radical version of *Winterreise*. Before she leaves for her recital, Erika takes a knife from the kitchen; and after Walter arrives late with friends and greets her in the lobby without bothering to stop, she waits in the lobby until it is empty, and then she stabs herself. The location of the wound, in the chest above her heart, is ambiguous. If she wanted to kill herself, she could have done better, and if she wanted to end her career, she would have stabbed her hand. In the original novel, Erika's injury is not life-threatening, and after leaving the building, she decides to return home (280). In Haneke's version, is it unclear that the wound is harmless, and there is no indication where Erika is headed when she leaves. The film's final shot of her exiting the building is from a great distance, and the closest human beings are in a few passing cars. When the credits roll, her new interpretation of *Winterreise* has already begun.

Because Adorno believed Central Europe's musical tradition was self-destructing like Erika in this final sequence, it feels appropriate to conclude with his actual commentary on Schumann's C major Fantasy, not the one Erika invented when she first met Walter. Adorno doesn't refer, as Erika suggests, to Schumann's impending madness but to how the end of the piece's resistance to closure prefigures Alban Berg's unique brand of modernism. "The way the end of the C major Fantasy opens into infinity, yet without transfiguring itself to the point of redemption, indeed, even without reference to itself: that anticipates the innermost essence of Berg's tone" (*Alban Berg* 5). This description of an end that is infinite without transcendence or redemption, that ceases not to be, but to refer to itself, is perhaps the most succinct formula for the state that Erika has entered at the end of the film. She has reached the end of her life as a stern teacher, oppressed daughter, and masochistic lover. Similarly, here Haneke's cinema of critique leaves off in its inquiry into film music and sexuality. *The Piano Teacher* reaches its limit when it becomes an impossible performance of *Winterreise* with the pianist in place of the singer and the accompaniment played by no one.

Coda: Music's Vanishing Evocations

Haneke's *Amour* continues and develops *The Piano Teacher*'s preoccupations with music and the dark extremes of love. The main characters, an elderly couple, are pianists and teachers, and when the film begins they are, even late in life, still in love. But when a series of strokes leaves Anne (Emmanuelle Riva) incapacitated and her husband George (Jean-Louis Trintignant) struggling to care for her, the everyday certainty of their love is put to the test. Their struggle to maintain their love contrasts with the illicit, disastrous affair of *The Piano Teacher*. If Erika's suffering in *The Piano Teacher* is neurotic and self-inflicted, George and Anne's suffering is real and inescapable.

Music figures in five key moments in the film. First, near the beginning of the film, Georges and Anne attend a concert of Anne's former student Alexandre that opens with Schubert's Impromptu No. 1, Opus 90 (played by pianist Alexandre Theroux). The Impromptu continues as background music in the two subsequent scenes that show them journeying home from the concert. Second, after her strokes, Anne and Georges are visited unannounced by Alexandre, who discovers to his alarm that Anne is in a wheelchair. She asks him not to inquire about her condition, and he obliges her in this and in her request that he play Beethoven. Third, as Anne's illness progresses, Georges sits at the piano and plays Bach, but then breaks off mid-phrase from a lapse of memory, startling

Anne. Fourth, having finally obtained Alexandre's new CD, they put it on only to have Anne almost immediately request that it be shut off. And fifth, and most poignantly of all, in a sequence that begins in a dreamlike flashback, Anne sits at the piano and plays another Schubert Impromptu (No. 3), but then, as the camera cuts to Georges, he turns around and shuts off the CD from which the music really emanates.

In the most direct connection with *The Piano Teacher*, *Amour*'s first musical selection, Schubert's Impromptu No. 1, reproduces the impossible performance that takes place at the end of *The Piano Teacher*. The beginning of the Impromptu can fairly be described as a song with the pianist in place of the singer and the accompaniment played by no one. The first few statements of the theme occur in a call and response. First one hears only a single voice, like an a capella singer, in the right hand of the piano. This is followed in each case by a variation on the a capella idea in a three-part texture that responds to the initial phrase. But it would be wrong to call the added voices accompaniments; they are more like equals. Though they differ in pitch and register, all three voices are homophonic: played in rhythmic unison with the melody. Eventually the piece moves on to more varied and diverse rhythmic textures with true accompanying figures, but Haneke's film only makes use of the opening: when the pianist is the singer, and there is no independent accompaniment except the melody's rhythmic pattern.

The film's subsequent representations of music dwell on its connection to the character's memories. In each case, music conjures a memory that proves powerful, so that the disturbing memory means the music must cease. To dwell too long in the realms of music and memory, it seems, invites despair, regret, and, in Georges's case, eventually madness. At the end of the film, after he has euthanized Anne, Georges leaves the apartment lost in a memory of their life together. Georges is mesmerized by his hallucination of Anne, and in an affecting detail she gently scolds him for forgetting his coat. This scene and several others mark a new development for Haneke in which shadows of a surrealism reminiscent of late Buñuel fall over the film. Such surreal traces correspond to the film's musical elements. Dreamlike scenes and music are both rich with meaning but ambiguous as to their message.

The last scene to feature music (Schubert's Impromptu No. 3, Opus 90) brings one to the limits of the film's musical framing of memories, but without entering the abyss of Georges's final, hallucinatory state. In the first shot, a still vital Anne sits at the piano as Schubert sounds. It is all we know of her former glory as a musician. In the reverse shot, Georges looks on, entranced. The moment recalls James Baldwin's famous comment about the effect of listening to music. What we hear is not the music, but "personal, private, vanishing evocations" (45). So much so in this case that the memory evoked seems literally present. But then Georges turns off the CD, so that, as in late Buñuel, only retrospectively is one aware the moment was hallucinatory and dreamlike.

The mastery of this moment speaks to the ethic of Haneke's art. Go to the limit; find the edge of film's form and of the corresponding human experience. But then leave it to the exigencies of the story to determine whether or not or for how long to cross over the limit. This search for limits is similar to what Immanuel Kant was after in his *Critique of Pure Reason*. For Kant, there are certain points at which abstract reasoning becomes entangled in contradictions, what he calls antinomies, where it is wise to set limits on the use of pure reasoning in the absence of evidence from the senses. As in Kant's antinomies, Haneke's films, and *Funny Games* above all, can cross over the limit for too long and fall into a self-defeating contradiction, hypocritically exploiting the violence they ostensibly condemn.

But the joke is on no one in *Amour*, especially in the scene where George turns off the CD. Haneke's film cares deeply for Georges and Anne, and so do we. To invoke a cliché, where words fail, music speaks. In Georges's hallucinatory memory of Anne at the piano, Haneke breathes new life into this cliché by adding an addendum: where music speaks, memory awakens. And when Georges decides to return to the present, to honor Anne's memory by accepting (for now) that the past is past, Haneke finds another limit for music's role in the cinema. When Georges shuts off the recording, Haneke shows us something both extraordinary and commonplace—that sometimes one wants music to signify something, and when it does the effect is too much for good taste or our own well-being. The repressed returns, and it is not uncanny, but overwhelmingly nostalgic. The past should stay in the past, for if it returns to life, as in Georges's final hallucination after he has euthanized Anne, we are in danger of vanishing into the past ourselves. Music then is for Haneke not finally just the code of unknown meaning, but the code whose meaning sometimes becomes so personal that it passes out of the realm of knowledge and into narcotizing fantasies and speculations.

Finally, there is a correspondence between the scene where George switches off the CD and Haneke's own biography. As a teenager, Haneke had planned a career as a pianist before his stepfather told him that he did not have the talent for it. "I wanted to be a pianist . . . My stepfather was a composer and a conductor, and, thank God, he realized early on that I wasn't talented enough" (quoted in Lane, "Happy Haneke"). When Georges switches off the CD, allegorically Haneke's other life as an obscure, failed musician ends and a vital new development in modernist cinema begins again.

Conclusion

Modernist Cinema's Family Tree

Clarification and Astonishment

THIS BOOK HAS OFFERED NUMEROUS metaphors or unlikely resemblances. Wagner sounds like helicopters. Buñuel, like Handel, resorted to the Messiah oratorio in a bid to revive his career. The slow movement of Ligeti's early piano work is reminiscent of Viennese classicism and Freudian castration anxiety. Kubrick's late style is a lot like Beethoven's, pushing forward by returning to germinating influences. The melancholy and hope of Godard's aesthetic resembles Beethoven's Allegretto from Symphony No. 7. Schubert's chamber music is an appropriate soundtrack for a visit to the sex shop. Taken together, such connections show that modernist cinema and classical music share a family resemblance. Like Erika and her mother, they sleep in the same bed.

Such family resemblances have philosophical significance. It is a cliché to say that philosophy begins in wonder or in doubt. Yet clichés like these are maddening because they are not untrue. Wonder was the ancient path to philosophical wisdom, doubt the modern route. Thinking people still walk both paths in their everyday lives. Indeed, the filmgoer's attempt to make sense of a modernist film very likely involves walking one of these paths. Their question—"What is this?"—depending on the tone of voice is either wondering, doubtful, or both. What comes after the doubt and wonder of the first encounter is equally important. For many of us, the way to understand new and difficult art is by comparison to something more familiar, and naturally to the construction of metaphors. The beauty of the process of constructing new metaphors is that it can lead, as Ludwig Wittgenstein suggests, to clarification, but the irony of the new metaphors, as Walter Benjamin suggests, is that they lead to a new, higher form of wonder, astonishment.

Wittgenstein thought such "new similes" formed the core of his philosophical enterprise. "I don't believe I have ever invented a line of thinking," he argued. "I have always taken one over from someone else. I have simply straightaway seized on it with enthusiasm for my work of clarification . . . What I invent are new *similes*" (*Culture and Value* 19). These thoughts speak to the form and content of his late masterpiece, *Philosophical Investigations*, which begins with a line of thought taken over from Augustine's *Confessions* about how language is learned heuristically. From this Wittgenstein derives a series of deceptively simple thought experiments, his famed "language games," to illustrate how we come to learn and use language. These "games" lead to powerful metaphors and similes on the nature of language. The varying definitions of a word have a family resemblance. Our languages are like ancient cities. Words are encircled by coronas of varying meanings.

We need such metaphors to clarify something as abstract as how we come to know and use language, or to grasp something as new and difficult as modernist cinema. Classical music helps clarify modernist cinema; the directors of the films considered in these pages implicitly acknowledge this. Here, they say, in the esoteric language of music is the material from which to create your own metaphors and similes. Listen to this unfamiliar context, but do not be easily seduced into thinking the only relationship to be found is irony or incongruity. Hear its likeness to the film as well.

At the same time, such metaphors and similes can be more than clarifying in Wittgenstein's sense. Walter Benjamin proposed that insights from metaphors ("dialectical images" in his terminology) lead to astonishment. For Benjamin, in his argument with Adorno about the proper critical attitude, Adorno had things backward: astonishment does not lead to insight; insight leads to astonishment. "You [Adorno] write in your Kierkegaard [book] that 'astonishment' reveals 'the profoundest insight into the relationship between dialectics, myth, and image.' I might feel tempted to invoke this passage here. But instead I propose an amendment to it. . . . I think one should say that the astonishment is an outstanding object of such an insight" (Adorno and Benjamin, *The Complete Correspondence* 292). Often for Benjamin the insights giving rise to astonishment take the form of metaphors and analogies. The work of art is a burning funeral pyre. Ideas are to facts as constellations are to stars. The storm blowing civilization away from paradise is called progress.

Conclusion

The foregoing analyses have sought both to astonish in Benjamin's sense and clarify in Wittgenstein's. Taken in total, the frequency of family resemblances between so much of the classical music and the modernist films that excerpt and repurpose it is astonishing. The general significance of these resemblances has a clarifying effect for our understanding of the artistic genealogy of modernist cinema. This book might have been called the birth of modernist cinema from the spirit of classical music.

With Wagner's presence in *Apocalypse Now* and in Herzog's documentary films, all these films share Wagner's sensibility for mixing the personal with the political, the intimate with the apocalyptic. Alex Ross remarks that the "usual way" of proceeding at "the world historical level" of analysis of Wagner, while engaging, is fundamentally a misreading of his music dramas. In fact, they are composed of mostly intimate moments, including his largest work of all, *The Ring*. Yet Ross's own reading of *The Valkyrie* (part two of the cycle's tetralogy) ends up musing on the world historical level when he emphasizes the opera's feminist critique of authoritarianism. The world historical level is then unavoidable in discussing Wagner. The miniature in Wagner has a way of becoming gigantic. Wagner's *Ring* is a tour de force at linking the two: its characters' secret inner torments seed revolutionary paroxysms in the social order.

Herzog's use of the Vorspiel from *Das Rheingold* in his recent documentary, *Lo and Behold* (2016), is similarly both intimate and of larger significance. It accompanies the professor who witnessed the first message sent on the Internet ("lo") as he introduces us to the computer that sent it. Wagner's auspicious, world-building music is entirely appropriate for the moment when the film introduces the birth of the Internet. In such cases, Herzog repeats Wagner by translating modernity into historically inflected myth. He does so by returning to Wagner's musical connective tissue of leitmotifs—an original source of narrative cinema's organizational coherence—and beginning again in new ways, while also giving credit where it is due.

In his early masterpieces, *Un chien andalou* and *L'age d'or*, Buñuel not only credits Wagner's *Tristan* but also corrects an error that Liszt began when he mistakenly called Isolde's final aria her Liebestod. In fact, Wagner labeled it her transfiguration. How fitting then, how like Wagner Buñuel is in his transfiguration of this music, especially in *Un chien andalou*. That early masterpiece borrows the music's dramatic structure for its two climaxes. Buñuel adds to Wagner the logic of dreams, where death is not an end but a point where the cycle of desire starts over again and again. There is a subtle and perhaps more astonishing resemblance Buñuel sensed between the villagers of Las Hurdes and the music of Brahms's Symphony No. 4. Brahms and the villagers share an awkwardness, a sense of struggle, and a fundamental difficulty that must be overcome without the reward of appearing brilliant. So while the relationship between Brahms and Wagner has too often been presented as one of opposites, Buñuel sensed their common ambition to renovate the tradition and made it part of his own heretical vision.

Kubrick sensed that his films and Ligeti's music shared an affinity, and for Ligeti, the feeling was mutual: "In Kubrick, Ligeti recognized a willingness to explore and take risks, a tireless concern for detail and an obsessive pursuit of perfection similar to his own" (Steinitz 164). Indeed, Todd McGowan's idea that Kubrick's films undermine authority by showing its corruption is truer of Ligeti's music's than it is of Kubrick's films. Ligeti's music breaks with consumerism's constant pressure on us to enjoy, representing an extreme instance of modern music's break with music's traditional function as an act of supplication to authority (Žižek, *Plague of Fantasies* 192). Like other post-tonal composers, Ligeti accomplished this by undermining the primacy of the fixed values of musical pitches with his revolutionary technique of micropolyphony, where dense clusters of notes create musical ideas of intensified expressive power.

It is thus both ironic and fitting that Kubrick chose Ligeti's micropolyphonic works for *2001*. Fittingly, Ligeti's indefinite music supports *2001*'s false premises that a higher power and natural human aggression are the keys to both evolution and contemporary progress. Ironically, the very indefiniteness of Ligeti's music is the film's unconscious critique of its ideological vision of authority. The way Ligeti undermines the authority of the fixity of pitch both supports and negates the film's monolith. The emblem for their dialectical interaction occurs when the apes discover the monolith to the Kyrie from Ligeti's Requiem. Kyrie is God in Greek, and here, the film says, is your modernist God: not a human form at all, but a black slab, an empty placeholder, a signifier in search of a signified. Ligeti's music is the monolith's signified to the extent that it both intensifies the monolith's significance with its expressive power and dilutes it with its indefinite plurality of meanings.

But what will replace authority when it is gone? Ligeti's music has an answer that *2001* is at most only unconsciously aware of: replace God with music; not music to persuade and inspire, but music to note the terrifying absence of any higher power; not a requiem to console but one that leaves us in a state of anxiety. As people are unlikely to accept such a bitter truth, a more comforting solution comes at the end of *Eyes Wide Shut*. After Ligeti's music has helped reveal that the fantasies of Bill and Alice are little more than infantile, destructive wishes, when Alice tells Bill that to get their relationship back on track they need to fuck, this is Kubrick's sardonic, heretical way of stating the traditional view that God is love.

Where *2001* renders the bourgeoisie's aggressive pursuit of self-interest as second nature, Godard shows the quiet desperation of their intrigues and affairs denaturalized by agitprop aesthetics. That his most famous film to use Beethoven's quartets, *Two of Three Things I Know about Her*, is also his first attempt at something like a film essay on the perils of consumerism speaks volumes. It says that for Godard the cinema could overcome its role in capitalist domination in part by co-opting the artistic past for new, radical purposes while also reminding us of the canon's original radicalism.

Classical music shows the scars of consumerism's historical impact in its fragmentary form within Godard's films. As fragments, he wagers, its meaning is intensified; the fragment's "less" is the meaning's "more." So that, not very often, but often enough there is hope in his use of classical music, even in his pessimistic and censorious late films with their dizzying array of references. Exemplary here is *Goodbye to Language*. This film makes clear that Godard still loves making films, at least if they involve his dog, Beethoven, and the capacity to push at the medium's boundaries as his use of 3-D does. Beethoven and his dog are witnesses to what is ever Godard's story: a tale of fleeting love in a fallen world—a world where the possibilities for cinematic art and for leftist political struggle are, as in Godard's view of romantic love, both over before they have begun and yet somehow still to come.

But abandon all hope those who enter into the theater to view a Michael Haneke film. Class is beginning at Haneke's school of suffering, and you are late. The censorious streak in Godard; the dispassionate gaze in Kubrick—together they amount to a summary of Haneke's severe pedagogy. Unlike almost all other Haneke films, in *The Piano Teacher* no one dies in gruesome and pitiless ways. Instead, the film entertains the possibility of love, albeit in a neurotic form, in its critique of the melodrama genre. The film is also not especially representative of film music. Most films, even those with compilation scores, do not motivate the use of music in the film's story, do not make the movie about working musicians and their lives. And despite his influence on Wagner and tone painting generally, most film music does not suggest Schubert's lieder as a direct or even indirect antecedent to the lush scoring that those who love Hollywood describes as "film music."

Haneke's *Amour* picks up where *The Piano Teacher* left off. The previous film had sought the origins of film music by excerpting Schubert's *Winterreise* song cycle and by leading its hero, Erika, to the heartbroken state of the singer performing Schubert's cycle. Erika becomes the singer, and the accompaniment is played by no one. *Amour*'s first musical selection, Schubert's Impromptu No. 1, Opus 90, also fits this description. The Impromptu begins with a single, unaccompanied voice in what would be the mezzo-soprano register. It is as though Haneke were following through on the restriction on music that the ending of *The Piano Teacher* imposed. Indeed, throughout Haneke's films, music's role is restricted: the film has to be about musicians to expect to hear much music, and what music there is appears in the film itself. It is a good thing hardly anyone making films listens to such austere implicit precepts; we would have very little music in film otherwise.

In all Haneke's films there is an elegant austerity that mixes with a violent disenchantment with the bourgeoisie and their milieu. Together these traits demand something beyond the status quo. The venerable name for part of this demanding sensibility is Romanticism. The other part is called modernism. In an escalation of the ideals of the Enlightenment, they both make certain core demands on the shifting and cycling fluctuations of the modern social order. They demand reciprocity between self and other and between the individual and society. They demand comprehension of the natural world. And most impossibly of all, they demand comprehension of the stranger within us all.

One key path to progress on these demands from the avant-garde days of Romanticism some two centuries ago is to go back. Return to the past but honor both the uncertainty and the creativity of memory, and use them to make the past new. Correspondingly, while the Romantics plumbed the depths of the mind's origins by communing with nature, the scientific community was also discovering the scale of deep time in the natural world. The earth was much older than previously realized, not thousands but billions of years old.

The comprehension of these two sublime objects, the natural world and the human mind, were coterminous processes for the Romantics. This is what Charles Rosen calls Romanticism's double-time scale: at the same time that the Romantics were cultivating the mind through their immediate apprehension of its impressions, they were also returning to the mind's origins in their comprehension, however inchoate, of the vast quantity of time needed to create something as complex as the human mind. Terrence Malick's *The Tree of Life* captures this dual process of the immediate apprehension of the mystery of existence and the comprehension of its precondition in geologic time's immensity. The film's largely classical soundtrack is the key to rendering its presentation of its venerable Romantic philosophy persuasive and affecting.

Nothingness Has Killed Itself

According to Coppola's brilliant tirade on the subject, auteurs are directors who say "fuck it" to being regarded as pretentious. No one working in modern Hollywood represents this attitude better than Terrence Malick. Because of their perceived pretensions, Malick's films have generally met with a mixed critical reception upon their release, with a favorable consensus building slowly over time. But the accusation of pretentiousness is also symptomatic of their achievement: part of Malick's signature as a filmmaker has been to capture Rosen's double-time scale of Romanticism in all its ephemerality and eternity. Malick's prominent landscape images recalling nineteenth-century paintings are the most obvious example of this—arresting images that seem at once superfluous and deep, unnecessary for advancing the story but necessary for the film to be recognized as Malick's. By capturing the double-time scale of Romanticism more explicitly and incorporating classical music more extensively than in previous films, no Malick film represents him saying "fuck it" to being perceived as pretentious better than *The Tree of Life*.

The Tree of Life represents an extreme example of modernism's return to origins for new paths forward in both art and life. The film returns to childhood for clues to a suicide; returns to the beginning of the universe in its most pretentious sequence; and returns to the beginnings of modernist music for its soundtrack to both. The main story returns to the protagonist's (played by Sean Penn) childhood in search of the cause of his younger brother's suicide. This marks a personal return to origins for Malick: like the troubled brother in the film, Malick's own brother was a gifted classical guitarist who committed suicide as a young man (Biskind, *Gods and Monsters* 259). Musically, *The Tree of Life* is a return to the origins of modernism in a compilation score ranging from Bach to Smetana to, crucially, the opening bars of Mahler's Symphony No. 1 and concert music by film composer Zbigniew Preisner. Preisner is best known for his collaborations with Krzysztof Kieślowski, and fittingly the Preisner piece used by Malick in the film is his *Requiem for a Friend*, dedicated to the late, great Polish director.

In its most discussed sequence, the film returns to the origin of the universe and the beginning of life on earth. This cosmological sequence occurs at the beginning of what turns out to be a flashback sequence. The mother (Jessica Chastain) and the older brother both try to recall where it all went wrong for the middle child, and the mother does so by questioning God himself. "Where were you?" she asks. The film answers by showing her how busy God was in the 13.7 billion years before her problem, flashing all the way back to the origins of the universe, through to the origins of our solar system, the formation of the earth, and the dawn of life. Finally, it refers to the extraterrestrial impact that destroyed most life on earth some 65 million years ago and paved the way for us before arriving in Waco, Texas, where she raised her family in the 1950s.

The film refers to the modern history of the universe and life on earth to affirm a very traditional text—the Book of Job, from which the film draws its epigraph and to which it refers during a pastor's oration at a funeral service for another child. When calamities befall Job, he rejects the wisdom that everything happens for a reason. God, he observes, "destroys blameless and wicked alike" (Job 9:22). *The Tree of Life*'s epigraph is the beginning of God's response to Job's inquiry into the significance of his suffering: "Where were you when I laid the foundations of the earth . . . when the morning stars sang together and all the sons of God shouted for joy?" (38:4–7). In other words, God asks Job, "Who are you to ask?" By answering a question with a question, God suggests that we cannot know in any satisfying, comforting way why the film's middle child commits suicide or why, more generally, there is so much other suffering in the world. In this way, the God of Job resembles the modern, secular universe depicted in the film: both are unfathomable on a human scale. In such a universe, where we are essentially an afterthought, the film suggests that grace is a matter of luck as well as devotion.

In his commentary on *The Tree of Life* soundtrack, Alex Ross argues that the film's use of the finale from Brahms's Symphony No. 4 is its most thoughtful musical moment, both for how it enhances the film's characterization of the stern father (Brad Pitt)—a mediocre businessman whose real passion is music—and for its connection to the Book of Job. When the father puts on a record of the finale of the Brahms during a family dinner, Ross finds it compelling because it goes beyond the cliché of classical music as emotionally cold. "We sense," while he listens to the symphony's finale, "that the father's unhappiness is rooted in the abandonment of his early musical aspirations" ("Music in The Tree of Life"). Ross argues the Fourth Symphony's finale, like "an exercise in philosophical negation," is a musical representation of *The Tree of Life*'s epigraph: "Where were you when I laid the foundations of the earth?" (*Listen to This* 324). Pity then, in a way, that Malick did not deploy Brahms's Fourth's finale as the accompaniment for *The Tree of Life*'s cosmological sequences. It is a musical analogue for God's indignant response to both Job and the mother character in the film.

But Malick's choice of the Lacrimosa ("weeping" in Latin) movement from Preisner's Requiem for his take on the creation of the universe is a more unexpected and interesting choice than the Brahms would have been. The film's use of Preisner's Requiem as background music for the birth of the universe is at first puzzling; this is a birth, not a funeral. But as has been shown throughout this book, there is no real contradiction here. Although it falls outside the realm of the natural sciences, something has definitely died with the creation of the universe. That something is nothingness itself. "Nothingness has killed itself, creation is its wound," the revolutionary German dramatist Georg Büchner once wrote. "We are the drops of its blood, the world the grave in which it slowly rots" (58). Like Büchner, Malick attempts to tell the secular story of the creation of the universe. And Malick's use of Preisner's music points to a humanist interpretation of cosmology beyond the limits of empiricism but well within the limits of philosophical dialectics, where the negation of negation, where nothingness committing suicide, "describes the direction given to history because complex systems cannot revert exactly to a previous state" (Gould, "Nurturing Nature" 154).

Preisner's music is easily recognizable for aficionados of film music or Kieślowski's films. His scores' austere instrumentation, lyrical melodies for voice and choir, and canny uses of silence steer a course toward intensity without becoming maudlin. Preisner's piece in memory of Kieślowski recalls their most famous collaborations: *Dekalog* (1988) and *Three Colors* (1993–94). Like *The Tree of Life*, Kieślowski's *Dekalog* (1988) is an attempt to modernize biblical wisdom. His *Three Colors* trilogy (1993–94) addresses the Enlightenment-era ideals of the French Revolution—Liberty, Equality, and Fraternity. Just when artists from Eastern bloc countries were supposed to be embracing the West, Kieślowski made a trilogy of films arguing that the struggle for the ideals of the French Revolution had only just begun. Today it is hard to overstate Kieślowski's prescience. The far right is in power or ascendant in many countries, including the United States, and the Enlightenment's universal project of human emancipation seems increasingly at risk of failure.

The cynical recurring quip in *White* (1994), the film in the trilogy about equality, says it all, "You can buy anything these days." This is the only equal right guaranteed to all in the post-1989 era: the right to extract wealth from anything and anyone. Throughout the trilogy, it is Preisner's music, with its austere but impassioned sincerity—its sense of moral purpose, really—that provides the counterpoint to the alienation and cynicism depicted on-screen, and that represents most consistently the ideals of the Enlightenment and the French Revolution.

Adorno, had he survived the 1960s and 1989, would be here today to say of late capitalism run amok, "You see? I told you so." But Adorno might have appreciated *The Tree of Life*'s use of the opening bars of Mahler's Symphony No. 1 as its leitmotif for the death of children and their lost innocence. Among modern composers, it was in Mahler and Berg that Adorno heard the kind of protest music he could march to. The opening bars of Mahler's First used in the film are a counterpoint to Wagner's Vorspiel from *Das Rheingold*. Both pieces famously open with a pedal point, a single sustained note. But where Wagner's opening pedal connotes a mythic beginning, Mahler's prominent harmonics in the strings are meant to sound, as in Malick's film's depictions of nature, realistically like a natural setting. But for Adorno, there is also an industrial quality to Mahler's pedal. "Reaching to the highest A of the violins, it is an unpleasant whistling sound like that emitted by old-fashioned steam engines" (*Mahler* 4). He switches from aural to visual metaphor for the pedal's musical texture. "A thin curtain, threadbare but densely woven, it hangs from the sky like a pale gray cloud layer, similarly painful to sensitive eyes" (*Mahler* 4).

The tone of these comments should not be mistaken for Adorno's usually unforgiving, critical posture. His book on Mahler appeared at a crucial time in the 1960s when Mahler's reputation was growing and performances of his music were becoming more frequent. But Mahler remained then an underground, subversive figure, a quality that, despite his canonical status today, his music still retains. It is this subversive quality that Adorno wanted us not to forget. What Mahler's music bears witness to is a truth that has become more apparent since the 1960s: that, as Adorno summarizes it, "the utopian identity of art and reality has foundered" (11). But, he continues, "[i]t is to this failure that Mahler's music henceforth addresses itself, no less earnestly in its technical progress than in its disenchanting experience" (11). Mahler's music is disenchanting, for Adorno, for a paradoxical reason. The more it achieves, the weaker its capacity for transcendence. "The more achieved the work," he writes, "the poorer grows hope, for hope seeks to transcend the finitude of the harmoniously self-sufficient work" (12). Adorno calls the self-sufficiency of Mahler's music its maturity, but warns that "unqualified praise" of maturity "is always corruptible by resignation" (12).

This last thought rings true of Malick's *Tree of Life*. It is fundamentally a film about maturing without resigning. The film thinks the key to understanding the brother's suicide decades after it occurs resides not in resignation but in recapitulation—return to the origins of the universe and of life on earth, and to mankind's improbable evolution; all as a prelude to the greatest and most terrifying return of all—the return to childhood.

According to Adorno, Mahler's music also features traces of the return to childhood. "Mahler's music holds fast to Utopia in the memory traces from childhood, which appear as if it were only for their sake that it would be worth living. But no less authentic for him is the consciousness that this happiness is lost, and only in being lost becomes the happiness it itself never was" (*Mahler* 145). Above all, for Mahler, childhood happiness never was except in retrospect for a tragic but all too common reason in his day: he was the second oldest of twelve children, only six of whom survived infancy. In this light, Malick's use of Mahler's First as a leitmotif for the death of children is entirely appropriate. In both Malick's film and Mahler's music there is the suggestion of a utopia, but one that exists only as an illusion, only after the death of a beloved sibling. For both Malick and Mahler, the lost possibilities of young lives cut short are the fleeting utopias that never were, except in conjectural hindsight.

But Mahler as a leitmotif for death in childhood does not get the final word in *The Tree of Life*'s musical score. That honor is reserved for Hector Berlioz's Requiem. Malick's film overcomes the losses of its illusory childhood utopia when it arrives at a real utopia in its concluding vision of heaven and eternity set to Berlioz. At the end of the extended flashback to childhood, Brad Pitt's father is forced to transfer jobs, and the family leaves its Edenic life in Texas. The film then cuts from the end of the family's life in Waco to the end of the world in a sequence in which the expanding sun destroys the earth, as astrophysicists have determined it will in another five billion years. After this, the film arrives in eternity, where all is forgiven, not by God, but by us. Indeed, about five billion years from now is when you can expect most mothers to be able to forgive God for the death of a beloved child.

The famously reclusive Malick commented in one of his only interviews that clichéd sentiments like Chastain's mother's final words to God, "I give him to you. I give you my son," are touching for a contradictory reason. "When people express what is most important to them, it often comes out in clichés," he notes. "That doesn't make them laughable; it's something tender about them. As though in struggling to reach what's more personal about them they could only come up with what's most public" (quoted in Michaels 104). Another word for such clichés at their most tender and public is simply wisdom. In resorting to such clichés, Malick and really all modernists seek not to repeat them as dogma but to renew and reactivate the dissident core of our collective wisdom. Malick's mother's cliché on mourning and moving on, "I give you my son," is a case in point. For most believers, it is God who giveth and taketh away, not us.

Walter Benjamin's Thesis VI from his "Theses on the Philosophy of History," referenced at the beginning of this book, makes a similar point about reclaiming wisdom from insipid conformism through dissident interpretations. To avoid the fate of *Apocalypse Now* and its co-optation of Wagner, which today has become "a tool of the ruling class," an attempt must newly be made "in every era," Benjamin argues, "to wrest tradition away from a conformism that is about to overpower it" (255). Modernist cinema is such an attempt. It wrests classical music away from such conformism, excerpting it for new heretical purposes that renew its revolutionary energy.

But at the same time, real cultures of musical training and cinemagoing must be maintained if modernity's ongoing project of Enlightenment is to succeed in the long run in returning control of tradition and wisdom to ordinary people. True, it is the vanguard artists who, as Buñuel suggests, "keep an essential margin of nonconformity alive." But their work matters little unless the public is educated to appreciate the modernist artists' reinvention of tradition freed from its service to conformity.

Notes

1. See Duncan, *Charms that Soothe*; Stilwell and Powrie, *Changing Tunes*; Goldmark et al., *Beyond the Soundtrack*, Buhler et al., *Music and Cinema*, Donnelly, *Film Music: Critical Approaches.*
2. See Joe, *Opera as Soundtrack*; Citron, *When Opera Meets Film*; Joe and Gilman, *Wagner and Cinema*; Grover-Friedlander, *Vocal Apparitions.*
3. Flinn, *The New German Cinema: Music, History, and the Matter of Style*; Hillman, *Unsettling Scores: German Film, Music, and Ideology.*
4. That is, "the specimen designated to bear the name of the species" (Gould, *Wonderful Life* 287).
5. The mythological component of Coppola's speech is symptomatic of the limitations of the film's critique of US imperialism. The latter part of the film mythologizes the history of the Vietnam War by substituting the sacrificial killing of Kurtz (Marlon Brando) for the actual confrontation over political ideology and resource extraction that motivated the conflict. In this way, the film makes a substitution common to much of modernist literature's depiction of imperialism's logic. The struggle to subdue the oppressed in order to take their resources is relegated to the background, and the narrative's center of attention becomes the struggle to save the empire's soul by sacrificing Kurtz (Jameson, "Modernism and Imperialism").
6. I rely here on Karl Deutsch's definition of a nation, "A nation is a group of people united by a mistaken view about their past and a hatred of their neighbors" (quoted in MacMillan, *Dangerous Games* 81–82).
7. In Milius's screenplay's original ending, Willard joins Kurtz in a futile attempt to repel an attack on Kurtz's compound by the Vietcong.
8. The text of the synopsis reads as follows:

This film, which begins with an extended and searching documentary on the life and manners of the scorpion, plus several fine sequences of the great outdoors and of rugged rocks passes directly to the misadventures of one of those excitable types unhinged by modern life. Believing himself mandated to do good, he takes it into his excited and sick mind not to do so; on the contrary, through his improbable attitude he contrives to upset a fashionable soiree. A very fine number by a classical orchestra of fifty musicians is present during the course of the soiree. Then, victim of a banal accident which further excites his thoughts and his fragmentary visions, and which the author has not ceased indicting throughout the film, he disappears following a series of incomprehensible acts.

The film redeems its difficult and unfathomable subject through a consistent and well-rendered sense of humor, which gives this obviously fanciful work an imprimatur of smiling philosophy. (quoted in Hammond, *L'age d'or* [BFI Film Classics] 131)

9. To supplement Naremore here, the name for such a linguistic singularity is a hapax legomenon—a word that occurs *only once* in a work, body of works, or, in the most extreme case, the entire written record of a language. The significance of the existence of such a scene is that it makes the grotesque both general (aesthetically) *and* singular (as a word) in Kubrick. Opposites thus coincide in both the concept of the grotesque (terrifying and funny) and in the grotesque's form of appearance (aesthetically general and linguistically singular) in Kubrick's films.

10. Erika's life shares parallels with the life of the author of the novel on which the film is based. Like Erika, the author, Elfriede Jelinek, had a domineering mother, a musical upbringing, and today is haunted by debilitating neuroses.

11. The Andantino is famously and incessantly used in Robert Bresson's *Au Hasard Balthazar* (1966), as Haneke is surely aware.

12. Like the Andante con Moto from the Trio in E flat, the Andantino shows trace influences of Beethoven, who also included operatic imitations in his late piano sonatas, as in his previously mentioned Sonata in A flat major, Opus 110.

Works Cited

Adler, Renata. "Movie Review: *Weekend*." *The New York Times*, 28 Sept. 1968.
Adorno, Theodor. "Music in the Background." 1934. *Essays on Music*, edited by Richard Leppert, translated by Susan Gillespie, Minnesota UP, 2003.
———. *The Philosophy of New Music*. 1949. Translated and edited by Robert Hullot-Kentor, Minnesota UP, 2006.
———. *Alban Berg: Master of the Smallest Link*. 1968. Translated by Julianne Brand and Christopher Hailey, Cambridge UP, 1994.
———. *Mahler: A Musical Physiognomy*. 1963. Translated by Edmund Jephcott. Chicago UP, 1996.
Adorno, Theodor, and Hanns Eisler. *Composing for the Films*. 1947. Althone, 1994.
Ames, Eric. "Herzog, Landscape, and Documentary." *Cinema Journal*, vol. 48, no. 2, 2009.
Baldwin, James. "Sonny's Blues." *The Jazz Fiction Anthology*, edited by Sascha Feinstein and David Rife, Indiana UP, 2009.
Barlow, Priscilla. "Surreal Symphonies: *L'Age d'or* and the Discreet Charms of Classical Music." *Soundtrack Available: Essays of Film and Popular Music*, Duke UP, 2001.
Barthes, Roland. "The Grain of the Voice." *Responsibility of Forms: Critical Essays on Music, Art, and Representation*, translated by Richard Howard, UC Press, 1991.
Baudelaire, Charles. "The Painter of Modern Life." *The Painter of Modern Life and Other Essay*, translated by Jonathan Mayne, Phaidon Press, 1995.
———. "Richard Wagner and Tannhäuser in Paris." *Baudelaire as a Literary Critic: Selected Essays*, translated by Lois Boe Hyslop and Francis Hyslop, Pennsylvania State UP, 1964.
Baum, Dan. "The Price of Valor." *The New Yorker*, 12 July 2004.
Bazin, André. "The Myth of Total Cinema." 1967. *What Is Cinema?*, translated by Hugh Gray, vol. I, UC Press, 2005.
Beckett, Samuel. "Worstward Ho." *Nohow On: Three Novels*, Grove Press, 1996.
Benjamin, Walter. "Theses on the Philosophy of History." 1968. *Illuminations*, translated by Harry Zohn, Schocken, 1997.

———. *The Origin of German Tragic Drama*. 1928. Translated by John Osborne, Verso, 1999.

———. *The Arcades Project*. Translated by Howard Eiland and Kevin McLaughlin, edited by Rolf Tiedemann, Harvard UP, 1999.

Benjamin, Walter, and Theodor Adorno. *The Complete Correspondence: 1928–1940*. Translated by Nicholas Walker, edited by Henri Lonitz, Harvard UP, 2001.

Biancorosso, Giorgio. *Situated Listening: The Sound of Absorption in Classical Cinema*, Oxford UP, 2016.

Biskind, Peter. *Easy Riders, Raging Bulls: How the Sex-Drug-And-Rock 'N' Roll Generation Saved Hollywood*. Simon and Schuster, 1998.

———. *Gods and Monsters*. Nation Books, 2004.

Bloch, Marc. "The Advent and Triumph of the Watermill." *Land and Work in Mediaeval Europe*, UC Press, 1967.

Bordwell, David, and Noel Carrol, editors. *Post-Theory: Reconstructing Film Studies*, Wisconsin UP, 1996.

Brody, Richard. *Everything Is Cinema: The Working Life of Jean-Luc Godard*. Metropolitan, 2008.

———. "An Exile in Paradise." *The New Yorker*, 20 Nov. 2000.

———. "Taking a Breather from 'Breathless.'" *The New Yorker*, 9 Dec. 2010.

Brown, Royal. *Overtones and Undertones: Reading Film Music*. UC Press, 1994.

Büchner, Georg. *Danton's Death. Complete Plays, Lenz and Other Writings*. Translated by John Reddick, Penguin, 1993.

Bujić, Bojan. "The Impact of Wagner." *Music in European Thought: 1851–1912*, Cambridge UP, 1988.

Buñuel, Luis. *My Last Sigh*. Translated by Abigail Israel, U of Minnesota P, 2003.

———. "*Land without Bread*." *An Unspeakable Betrayal: Selected Writings of Luis Buñuel*, translated by Garret White, UC Press, 1995.

———. "On *Viridiana*." *The World of Luis Buñuel*, edited by Joan Mellen, Oxford UP, 1978.

Buruma, Ian. "There's No Place like Heimet." *The New York Review of Books*, 20 Dec. 1990.

Cabral, Amilcar. "The Weapon of Theory." *Marxists Internet Archive*, 31 May 2017.

Cavell, Stanley. *The World Viewed: Reflections on the Ontology of Film*. Rev. ed., Harvard UP, 1979.

Citron, Marcia. *Opera on Screen*. Yale UP, 2000.

———. *When Opera Meets Film*. Cambridge UP, 2010.

Cooke, Deryck. *I Saw the World End*. Cambridge UP, 1979.

Cooke, Mervyn. *A History of Film Music*. Cambridge UP, 2008.

Donnelly, Kevin, editor. *Film Music: Critical Approaches*. Bloomsbury, 2001.

Duncan, Dean. *Charms That Soothe: Classical Music and the Narrative Film*. Fordham UP, 2003.

Durgnat, Raymond. *Luis Buñuel*. UC Press, 1977.

Eggen, Dan, and R. Jeffrey Smith. "FBI Agents Allege Abuse at Guantanamo Bay." *The Washington Post*, 21 Dec. 2004.

Eldredge, Niles, and Stephen Jay Gould. "Punctuated Equilibria: An Alternative to Phyletic Gradualism." *Models in Paleobiology*, edited by T. J. M. Schopf, Freeman Cooper, 1972.

Eliot, George. *Middlemarch*. 1872. Wordsworth Editions, 2000.

"Erland van Lidth." *Wikipedia*, 20 Apr. 2011.

Estève, Michel. "The Exterminating Angel: No Exit from the Human Condition." *The World of Luis Buñuel*, edited by Joan Mellen, Oxford UP, 1978.

Flinn, Caryl. *The New German Cinema: Music, History, and the Matter of Style*. UC Press, 2004.

Freedman, Carl. "Polemical Afterword: Some Brief Reflections on Arnold Schwarzenegger and on Science Fiction in Contemporary American Culture." *PMLA*, vol. 119, no. 3, 2004.

Freud, Sigmund. "The Interpretation of Dreams." 1900. *The Basic Writings of Sigmund Freud*, translated by A. A. Brill, Modern Library, 1995.

———. "The Unconscious." 1915. *The Freud Reader*, edited by Peter Gay, translated by James Strachey, Norton, 1995.

———. "Negation." 1917. *The Freud Reader*, edited by Peter Gay, translated by James Strachey, Norton, 1995.

———. "The Uncanny." 1918. *Writings on Art and Literature*, edited by Neil Hertz, translated by James Strachey, Stanford UP, 1997.

Frisch, Walter. *Brahms: The Four Symphonies*. Schirmer, 1996.

Fuentes, Carlos. "The Discreet Charm of Luis Buñuel." *The World of Luis Buñuel*, edited by Joan Mellen, Oxford UP, 1978.

Fuentes, Victor. "The Constant of Exile in Buñuel." *Luis Buñuel: New Readings*, edited by Peter Williams and Isabel Santaolalla, BFI, 2004.

Gengaro, Christine Lee. *Listening to Stanley Kubrick: The Music in His Films*. Scarecrow Press, 2013.

Geck, Martin. *Richard Wagner: A Life in Music*. Translated by Stewart Spencer, Chicago UP, 2013.

Gibbs, Christopher. *The Life of Schubert*. Cambridge UP, 2000.

Gilman, Sander, and Jeongwon Joe, eds. *Wagner and Cinema*. Indiana UP, 2010.

Goehr, Lydia. *The Quest for Voice: Music, Politics, and the Limits of Philosophy*. UC Press, 1998.

Goldmark, Daniel, Lawrence Kramer, and Richard Leppert, editors. *Beyond the Soundtrack: Representing Music in Cinema*. UC Press, 2007.

Gorbman, Claudia. *Unheard Melodies: Narrative Film Music*. Indiana UP, 1987.

———. "Ears Wide Open: Kubrick's Music." *Changing Tunes: The Use of Pre-Existing Music in Films*, edited by Phil Powrie and Robyn Stilwell, Ashgate, 2006.

———. "Auteur Music." *Beyond the Soundtrack: Representing Music in Cinema*, edited by Daniel Goldmark, Lawrence Kramer, and Richard Leppert, UC Press, 2007.

Gould, Stephen Jay. 1979. "The Nonscience of Human Nature." *Ever Since Darwin: Reflections on Natural History*, Norton, 2007.

———. "Return of the Hopeful Monster." *The Panda's Thumb: More Reflections on Natural History*, Norton, 1982.
———. *Time's Cycle, Time's Arrow: Myth and Metaphor in the Discovery of Geological Time*. Harvard UP, 1987.
———. "Nurturing Nature." *An Urchin in a Storm: Essays about Books and Ideas*, Norton, 1987.
———. *Wonderful Life: The Burgess Shale and the Nature of History*. Norton, 1990.
———. *The Mismeasure of Man*. 1981, rev. and expanded ed., Norton, 1996.
Grover-Friedlander, Michal. *Vocal Apparitions: The Attraction of Cinema to Opera*. Princeton UP, 2005.
Gubern, Roman, and Paul Hammond. *Luis Buñuel: The Red Years: 1929–1939*. Wisconsin UP, 2009.
Gunning, Tom. "The Cinema of Attraction: Early Film, Its Spectator and the Avant-Garde." *Early Cinema: Space-Frame-Narrative*, edited by Thomas Elsaesser and Adam Barker, BFI, 1990.
———. "Early American Film." *American Cinema and Hollywood: Critical Approaches*, edited by John Hill and Pamela Church Gibson, Oxford UP, 2000.
Guzzetti, Alfred. *Two or Three Things I Know about Her: Analysis of a Film by Godard*. Harvard UP, 1981.
Hammond, Paul. *L'age d'or* (BFI Film Classics). BFI, 1997.
Henderson, Brian. "Toward a Non-Bourgeois Camera Style." 1974. *Film Theory and Criticism*, edited by Leo Braudy and Marshall Cohen, 6th ed., Oxford UP, 2004.
Herr, Michael. *Kubrick*. Grove Press, 2000.
Herzog, Werner. "Minnesota Declaration." *Werner Herzog Film*, 27 Apr. 2011.
Hillman, Roger. *Unsettling Scores: German Film, Music, and Ideology*. Indiana UP, 2004.
———. "Wagner as Leitmotif: The New German Cinema and Beyond." *Wagner and Cinema*, edited by Sander Gilman and Jeongwon Joe, Bloomington: Indiana UP, 2010.
Hirschman, Charles, Samuel Preston, and Vu Manh Loi. "Vietnamese Casualties During the American War: A New Estimate." *Population and Development Review*, vol. 21, no. 4, Dec. 1995, pp. 783–812.
Jameson, Fredric. *Marxism and Form*. Princeton UP, 1971.
———. "Modernism and Imperialism." *Colonialism, Nationalism, and Literature*, Minnesota UP, 1990.
———. *Postmodernism; Or, The Cultural Logic of Late Capitalism*. Duke UP, 1991.
———. *A Singular Modernity: Essay on the Ontology of the Present*. Verso, 2002.
Joe, Jeongwon. *Opera as Soundtrack*. Ashgate, 2013.
Kael, Pauline. "Trash, Art, and the Movies." *The Making of 2001: A Space Odyssey*, edited by Stephanie Schwam, Modern Library, 2000.
Kagan, Norman. *The Cinema of Stanley Kubrick*. 1989. 3rd ed., Continuum, 2000.
Kant, Immanuel. *Critique of Pure Reason*. 1781, translated by Werner Pluhar, unified ed., Hackett, 1996.
Kerman, Joseph. *The Beethoven Quartets*. 1966. Norton, 1979.
———. *Opera as Drama*. 1955. UC Press, 2005.

King, Martin Luther. "Beyond Vietnam." *Martin Luther King Online*, 18 Apr. 2011.
Koss, Juliet. *Modernism after Wagner*. Minnesota UP, 2010.
Kramer, Lawrence. *Classical Music and Postmodern Knowledge*. UC Press, 1995.
———. *After the Lovedeath: Sexual Violence and the Making of Culture*. UC Press, 1997.
———. *Opera and Modern Culture: Wagner and Strauss*. UC Press, 2004.
Lane, Anthony. "Happy Haneke." *The New Yorker*, 5 Oct. 2009.
Lennig, Arthur. "Myth and Fact: The Reception of 'The Birth of a Nation.'" *Film History*, vol. 16, no. 2, 2004.
Locke, Arthur Ware, and Hoffmann E. T. A. "Beethoven's Instrumental Music: Translated from E. T. A. Hoffmann's 'Kreisleriana' with an Introductory Note." *The Musical Quarterly*, vol. 3, no. 1, 1917, pp. 123–33.
Ma, Jean. "Discordant Desires, Violent Refrains: La Pianiste (The Piano Teacher)." *A Companion to Michael Haneke*, edited by Roy Grundman, Blackwell, 2010.
MacCabe, Colin. *Godard: A Portrait of the Artist at Seventy*. FSG, 2003.
———. "Godard at Cannes, Part Two." *The Criterion Collection*, 12 July 2014.
MacMillan, Margaret. *Dangerous Games: The Uses and Abuses of History*. Modern Library, 2008.
Mallarmé, Stéphane. "Homage to Richard Wagner." *Selected Poetry and Prose*, edited by Mary Ann Caws, translated by Hubert Creekmore, New Directions, 1982.
———. "Richard Wagner, Reverie of a French Poet." *Music in European Thought: 1851–1912*, edited by Bojan Bujić, Cambridge UP, 1988.
Marks, Martin Miller. *Music and the Silent Film: Contexts and Case Studies, 1895–1924*. Oxford UP, 1997.
Masschelein, Annalein. *The Unconcept: The Freudian Uncanny in Late-Twentieth-Century Theory*. SUNY Press, 2011.
McGowan, Todd. *The Real Gaze: Film Theory After Lacan*. SUNY Press, 2007.
McQuiston, Kate. *We'll Meet Again: Music Design in the Films of Stanley Kubrick*. Oxford UP, 2013.
Mendelson, Jordana. *Documenting Spain: Artists, Exhibition Culture, and the Modern Nation 1929–1937*. Pennsylvania State UP, 2005.
Michelson, Annette. "Bodies in Space: Film as 'Carnal Knowledge.'" 1969. *The Making of 2001: A Space Odyssey*, edited by Stephanie Schwam, Modern Library, 2000.
Michaels, Lloyd. *Terrence Malick*. Illinois UP, 2009.
Morgan, Daniel. *Late Godard and the Possibilities of Cinema*. UC Press, 2013.
Naremore, James. *On Kubrick*. BFI, 2007.
Nietzsche, Friedrich. *The Case of Wagner*. Translated by Walter Kaufmann, Vintage, 1967.
Neumeyer, David, editor. *The Oxford Handbook of Film Music Studies*. Oxford UP, 2014.
———. *Meaning and Interpretation of Music in Cinema*. Indiana UP, 2015.
Oudart, Jean-Pierre. "Cinema and Suture." *The Symptom: The Online Journal of Lacan.com*, vol. 8, 2007.
Palmer, Christopher. *The Composer in Hollywood*. Marion Boyars, 2000.

Patterson, David. "Music, Structure and Metaphor in Stanley Kubrick's *2001: A Space Odyssey*.'" *American Music*, vol. 22, no. 3, 2004.
Powrie, Phil, and Robynn Stilwell, editors. *Changing Tunes: The Use of Pre-existing Music in Film*. Ashgate, 2006.
Rosar, William. "Film Music—What's in a Name?" *The Journal of Film Music*, vol. 1, no. 1, 2002.
Rosen, Charles. *Sonata Forms*. Norton, 1988.
———. *The Frontiers of Meaning*. Hill and Wang, 1994.
———. *The Romantic Generation*. Harvard UP, 1995.
———. "The Ruins of Walter Benjamin." *Romantic Poets, Critics, and Other Madmen*. Harvard UP, 1998.
———. "The Aesthetics of Stage Fright." *Critical Entertainments: Music Old and New*. Harvard UP, 2000.
———. "Brahms the Subversive." *Critical Entertainments: Music Old and New*. Harvard UP, 2000.
———. "Brahms: Classicism and the Inspiration of Awkwardness." *Critical Entertainments: Music Old and New*. Harvard UP, 2000.
———. "Should We Adore Adorno?" *The New York Review of Books*, 24 Oct. 2002.
———. "From the Troubadours to Frank Sinatra, Part I." *The New York Review of Books*, 23 Feb. 2006.
———. *Music and Sentiment*. Yale UP, 2010.
———. "Mallarmé and the Transfiguration of Poetry." *Freedom and the Arts: Essays on Music and Literature*. Harvard UP, 2012.
Ross, Alex. "Mahlermania." *The New Yorker*, 4 Sept. 1995.
———. "Young Adorno." *Transition*, no. 69, 1996, pp. 160–77.
———. *The Rest Is Noise: Listening to the Twentieth Century*. FSG, 2007.
———. *Listen to This*. FSG, 2010.
———. "Secret Passage; Decoding Ten Bars in Wagner's 'Ring.'" *The New Yorker*, 25 Apr. 2011.
———. "The Music of The Tree of Life." *Alex Ross: The Rest Is Noise*, 29 May 2011.
———. "Encrypted: Translators Confront the Supreme Enigma of Stéphane Mallarmé's Poetry." *The New Yorker*, 11 Apr. 2016.
———. "Wagner Weekend: A Bleak "Tristan and Isolde" at the Met, and a Playful "Das Rheingold" at the Lyric Opera of Chicago." *The New Yorker*, 17 Oct. 2016.
Rourke, Sean. "Ligeti's Early Years in the West." *The Musical Times*, vol. 130, no. 1759, Sept. 1989.
Russell, Catherine. "Surrealist Ethnography: *Las Hurdes* and the Documentary Unconscious." *F Is for Phony: Fake Documentary And Truth's Undoing*, edited by Alexandra Juhasz and Jesse Lerner, Minnesota UP, 2006.
Sanglid, Torben. "Buñuel's Liebestod—Wagner's Tristan in Luis Buñuel's Early Films: *Un chien andalou* and *L'age d'or*." *The Journal of Music and Meaning*, vol. 13, 2014/2015.

Sarris, Andrew. "Notes on the Auteur Theory in 1962." 1974. *Film Theory and Criticism*, edited by Leo Braudy and Marshall Cohen, 6th ed., Oxford UP, 2004.

———. "The Devil and the Nun—Viridiana." *Movie: A Journal of Film Criticism*, vol. 4, 2013.

Scemana, Céline. "La partition des Histoire(s) du cinema de Jean-Luc Godard." *Centre de Recherche sur l'Image*, 14 Apr. 2016.

Schoenberg, Arnold. *Theory of Harmony*. 1922. Translated by Roy Carter, UC Press, 1978.

———. "New Music, Outmoded Music, Style and Idea." 1946. *Style and Idea: Selected Writings of Arnold Schoenberg*, edited by Leonard Stein, translated by Leo Black, UC Press, 1975.

Schubert, Franz. 1827/1828. "Die Winterreise." *Complete Song Cycles*, edited by Eusebius Mandyczewski, Dover, 1970.

"Sesame Street Breaks Iraqi POWs." *BBC*, 20 May 2003.

Shaw, G. Bernard. "The Perfect Wagnerite." 1898. *Major Critical Essays*. Penguin, 1986.

Sheer, Miriam. "The Godard/Beethoven Connection: On the Use of Beethoven's Quartets in Godard's Films." *The Journal of Musicology*, vol. 18, no. 1, Winter 2001.

Shin, Paul. "'Valkyries's Swoop in Iraq: Opera Blares, G.I.s Hit Guerillas." *New York Daily News*, 23 June 2003.

Smith, Matthew Wilson. "American Valkyries: Richard Wagner, D.W. Griffith, and the Birth of Classical Cinema." *Modernism/modernity*, vol. 15, no. 2, 2008.

Solomon, Maynard. *Beethoven*. 1977. Schirmer, 2001.

Sontag, Susan. "Eye of the Storm." *The New York Review of Books*, 21 Feb. 1980.

Steinitz, Richard. *György Ligeti: Music of the Imagination*. Northeastern UP, 2003.

Stevens, Wallace. "The Noble Rider and the Sound of Words." *The Necessary Angel: Essays on Reality and the Imagination*. Vintage, 1965.

Talens, Jenaro. *The Branded Eye: Buñuel's Un chien andalou*. Translated by Giulia Colaizzi, U of Minnesota P, 1993.

Taruskin, Richard. *The Oxford History of Western Music*. Vol. 2, 4 June 2013.

Torbett, Rachel June. "The Quick and the Flat: Walter Benjamin, Werner Herzog." *Essays on Boredom and Modernity*, edited by Barbara Dalle Pezze and Carlo Salzani, Rodopi, 2009.

Tovey, Donald Francis. "Seventh Symphony in A Major, Op. 92." 1935. *Essays in Musical Analysis. Volume I: Symphonies*, Oxford University Press, 1972.

Tunbridge, Laura. "Schumann as Manfred." *The Musical Quarterly*, vol. 87, no. 3, 2004.

Von Trier, Lars, and Thomas Vinterberg. "Vow of Chastity." *A Tribute to the Official Dogme95*, 13 Mar. 1995.

Wagner, Richard. *Judaism in Music and Other Essays*. Translated by William Ashton Ellis, U of Nebraska P, 1995.

Warren, Charles. "The Unknown Piano Teacher." *A Companion to Michael Haneke*, edited by Roy Grundman, Blackwell, 2010.

Weiner, Marc A. "Hollywood's German Fantasy: Ridley Scott's *Gladiator*." *Wagner and Cinema*, edited by Sander Gilman and Jeongwon Joe, Indiana UP, 2010.

Wierzbicki, James, Nathan Platte, and Colin Roust, editors. *The Routledge Film Music Sourcebook*. Routledge, 2012.

Wilde, Oscar. "The Soul of Man Under Socialism." *Marxists Internet Archive*, 24 Mar. 2013.

Williams, Linda. *Figures of Desire: A Theory and Analysis of Surrealist Film*. UC Press, 1992.

Wittgenstein, Ludwig. *Culture and Value*, edited by G. H. von Wright and Heikki Nyman, translated by Peter Winch, U of Chicago P, 1980.

———. *Philosophical Investigations*, 1953. Edited and translated by G. E. M. Anscombe, Blackwell, 2001.

Wood, Michael. "Bangs and Whimpers." *The New York Review of Books*, 11 Oct. 1979.

———. "Viridiana: The Human Comedy." *The Criterion Collection*, 22 May 2006.

Wood, Robin. "'Do I Disgust You?' Or, tirez pas sur *La Pianiste*." *CineAction*, Spring 2002.

Zinman, Gregory. "Lumia." *The New Yorker*, 27 June 2011.

Žižek, Slavoj. *Enjoy Your Symptom: Jacques Lacan in Hollywood and Out*. Routledge, 1992.

———. "'In His Bold Gaze My Ruin Is Writ Large.'" 1992. *Everything You Always Wanted to Know About Lacan (But Were Afraid to Ask Hitchcock)*, edited by Slavoj Žižek, Verso, 2002.

———. *The Plague of Fantasies*. Verso, 1997.

———. *The Fright of Real Tears: Krzysztof Kieślowski Between Theory and Post-Theory*. BFI, 2001.

———. "'Ode to Joy,' Followed by Chaos and Despair." *The New York Times*, 24 Dec. 2007.

———. Preface. *The Case of Wagner*, by Theodor Adorno, Verso, 2005.

———. "Why Is Wagner Worth Saving?" *Journal of Philosophy and Scripture*, vol. 2, no. 1, 2004.

Index

Note: Italicized page numbers indicate illustrations.

Adler, Renata, 110
Adorno, Theodor, 97, 126–28, 132, 134, 140; Benjamin and, 144; Mahler and, 152–53; neoliberalism and, 151; *Philosophy of New Music*, 11–12
allegory, 96, 99, 132
Altman, Robert: *Shortcuts*, 124
Ashby, Hal: *Coming Home*, 2
Augustine of Hippo, 144
auteurism, 5, 14–15; Buñuel and, 53; Coppola on, 148; Godard and, 104

Bach, Johann Sebastian, 14, 122, 136
Badiou, Alain, 18
Bakunin, Mikhail, 25
Baldwin, James, 141–42
Barenboim, Daniel, 29–30
Barthes, Roland, 10, 67–68, 71, 76
Bartók, Béla, 12
Baruma, Ian, 5
Baudelaire, Charles, 8
Bazin, André, 9
Beethoven, Ludwig von, 30, 43, 48, 156n12; Godard and, 97–105, 147; late style of, 84, 91, 95, 98, 102, 119–20, 143
Beethoven, Ludwig von, works of: *Fidelio*, 98, 102–3; Grosse Fugue, 84, 99; Opus 59, 95, 101; Opus 110, 102; Opus 131, 99, 101; Opus 132, 103–4; Opus 135, 95, 96, 99–101; Sonata Pathétique, 117; Symphony No. 3 ("Eroica"), 78; Symphony No. 7, 118–19, 143; Symphony No. 9, 72, 102
Benjamin, Walter, 6, 8–9, 11–12, 98–99, 153; Adorno and, 144; on allegory, 96, 99, 132; on cultural memory, 2; on genre, 124; Wittgenstein and, 144, 145
Berg, Alban, 122, 140, 151
Berlioz, Hector, 153
Bertolucci, Bernardo, 108
Bizet, Georges, 101
Brahms, Johannes, 37; Symphony No. 4, 47–51, 145–46, 150
Brecht, Bertolt, 33–35, 97
Breil, Joseph Carl, 22
Bresson, Robert, 156n11
Breton, André, 8
Büchner, Georg, 151
Buñuel, Luis, 7–10, 37–63, 141–42, 154; auteurism of, 53; Brecht and, 34–35; Handel and, 37, 51–54, 143; Liszt and, 40, 49, 145; Mallarmé and, 62–63; Sartre and, 55–56; Wagner and, 6, 34–35, 37–63, 145

Buñuel, Luis, works of: *L'âge d'or*, 35, 42–47, *45*, 145; *El Bruto*, 50–51; *Un chien andalou*, 35, 38–42, 59, 74, 74–75, 145; *Discrete Charm of the Bourgeoisie*, 42, 58, 62; *Exterminating Angel*, 42, 53–57, *55*, 60; *Las Hurdes*, 47–51, *51*, 145–46; *Milky Way*, 47, 62; *My Last Sigh*, 6; *Nazarín*, 46; *Phantom of Liberty*, *57*, 57–63; *Simon of the Desert*, 53; *That Obscure Object of Desire*, 6, 42, 58–61; *Viridiana*, 51–54, 60; *Wuthering Heights*, 42, 61–62

Cabral, Amílcar, 56
Carmen Jones, 103
Carrière, Jean-Claude, 62
Cavell, Stanley, 112–13, 117
Cézanne, Paul, 77
cinema of critique, 122–26
"cinema of narrative integration" (Gunning), 22–23
Clarke, Arthur C., 67
Cocks, Geoffrey, 92
Cohn-Bendit, Daniel, 111–12
Conrad, Joseph, 2
consumerism, 96, 98, 147
Cooke, Deryck, 19
Cooke, Mervyn, 20
Coppola, Francis Ford, 19; *Apocalypse Now*, 1–3, 15–16, 19–26, *20*, 145; on auteurs, 148; on battle scenes, 24; on filmmakers, 15–16

Darío, Rubén, 7
Darwin, Charles, 4, 43
Deutsch, Karl, 155n6
Dogma 95 movement, 125
Dohnányi, Christoph von, 18
Domingo, Plácido, 29
Doors, The (music group), 21
Dreyer, Carl Theodor, 108
Durgnat, Raymond, 34–35

"ecstatic truth" (Herzog), 26
Eliot, George, 122

Faltermeyer, Harold, 32
film music studies, 4–6
film within the film, 71–73, 106
Franco, Francisco, 7, 47, 51
Freud, Sigmund, 71, 73, 86, 139, 143
Frost, Robert, 135
Fuentes, Carlos, 7

Gesamtkunstwerk (total work of art), 34, 101
Godard, Jean-Luc, 7, 10, 95–120; *Breathless*, 97, 111–13; *Detective*, 97; *Every Man for Himself*, 97; *Film Socialisme*, 117; *First Name: Carmen*, 96, 97, *100*, 100–105; *For Ever Mozart*, 97, 110–12; *Goodbye to Language*, 117–19, *119*, 147; *Histoire(s) du cinéma*, 117–18; *Keep Your Right Up!*, 97; *King Lear*, 99–100, 116; *Love: Departure and Return of the Prodigal Children*, 106–9; *A Married Woman*, 95, 98; *The New World*, 98, 99; *One Plus One*, 97; *Passion*, 97; *Tout va bien*, 109; *Two or Three Things I Know about Her*, 95–96, 98, 117, 147; *Weekend*, 97, 105, 110, 113–17, *114*
Goehr, Lydia, 18
Goethe, Johann Wolfgang, 132–33
Goldschmidt, Richard, 110
Gorbman, Claudia, 88
Gould, Stephen Jay, 54, 66
Griffith, D. W.: *Birth of a Nation*, 1, 20, 22
Guadeloupe, 27
Gunning, Tom, 22–23, 39
Guzzetti, Alfred, 117

Haggis, Paul: *Crash*, 124
Handel, George Frideric, 37, 51–54, 143
Haneke, Michael, 7, 121–42; *Amour*, 124, 140–42, 147–48; *Benny's Video*, 123, 125; *Caché*, 124, 125; *Code Unknown*, 124, 125, 142; *Funny Games*, 122, 125, 142; *The*

Piano Teacher, 10–11, 14, 121–41, 127–30, *138,* 147–48; *The Seventh Continent,* 123, 125; *71 Fragments of a Chronicle of Chance,* 123–24; *Time of the Wolf,* 124; *The White Ribbon,* 124
Hanslick, Eduard, 133–34
Hasford, Gustav, 71
Haydn, Joseph, 48
Herr, Michael, 85
Herzog, Werner, 5, 19, 26–30, 145; *Fitzcarraldo,* 26; *Lessons of Darkness,* 27–29; *Lo and Behold,* 145; *La Soufière,* 27; *Transformation of the World into Music,* 5, 26, 29–30
Hindemith, Paul, 12
Hitchcock, Alfred: *Psycho,* 74–75, *75*; *The Wrong Man,* 6
Hoffmann, E. T. A., 87

immersion, phenomenology of, 74–75
Iraq Wars, 21–22, 27–29

Jameson, Fredric, 7, 96
Jelinek, Elfriede, 156n10
Job, Book of, 150
Joyce, James, 7

Kael, Pauline, 68
Kafka, Franz, 3
Kaiser, Joachim, 2
Kant, Immanuel, 123, 125, 142
Kerman, Joseph, 102
Kierkegaard, Søren, 144
Kieślowski, Krzysztof, 11, 149, 151
King, Stephen, 31
Kubrick, Stanley, 7, 10, 65–92, 143; documentaries about, 92–94
Kubrick, Stanley, works of: *Barry Lyndon,* 66, 78–83, *84,* 129, 133; *Clockwork Orange,* 66, 71–76, *72,* 78; *Eyes Wide Shut,* 13, 66, 78, 84–92, *87, 91,* 146; *Full Metal Jacket,* 66, 69–71, *70,* 78; *The Killing,* 85; *Paths of Glory,* 70–71; *The Shining,* 78, 86, 92; *2001: A Space Odyssey,* 13, 66–68, 76–78, *77,* 85–86, 146–47

Lacan, Jacques, 88
Legendre, Maurice, 47
leitmotifs, 22–23; in Godard, 96, 98–101; in Kubrick, 13, 66; in Wagner, 33, 40, 42, 97
Lenin, Vladimir, 112–13
Ligeti, György, 13, 66, 76, 78, 84–91, 143; *Musica Ricercata,* 13, 84, 86–88; Steinitz on, 146
Liszt, Franz, 30, 40, 49, 145

MacCabe, Colin, 117–18
Mahler, Gustav: Symphony No. 1, 11, 149, 151–53
Malick, Terrence, 149; *Tree of Life,* 11, 148–53
Mallarmé, Stéphane, 33–34, 62–63, 118
Marshall, S. L. A., 70
McGowan, Todd, 68–69, 146
McQuiston, Kate, 88
Mendelssohn, Felix, 43
"meta-commentary," 69
Michelson, Annette, 76
Milius, John, 1–3, 19–22
Morgan, Daniel, 111
Mozart, Wolfgang Amadeus, 43, 110–16; Clarinet Concerto, 112; *Marriage of Figaro,* 98; Requiem, 112
Müller, Wilhelm, 121, 123
Murnau, F. W., 108, 110

Naremore, James, 69, 86
neoliberalism, 38, 151
New German Cinema, 4, 7
New Wave, 14
Nietzsche, Friedrich, 66, 67

Oedipal complex, 44
Ophüls, Max, 84

Paradisi, Domenico, 54–56

Persian Gulf Wars, 21–22, 27–29
Plato, 72
Preisner, Zbigniew: *Requiem for a Friend*, 11, 149–51
Preminger, Otto, 103

Rachmaninov, Sergey, 12
realism: psychological, 14; surrealism and, 10
Red Dawn (film), 21
Romanticism, 87, 118, 123; modernism and, 148; Schubert and, 131–34; surrealism and, 10, 37–63
Ronson, Jon: *Stanley Kubrick's Boxes*, 93–94
Room 237, 92–94
Rosen, Charles, 4, 48–49, 65; on Adorno, 12; on hermeneutics, 18; on musical systems, 104–5; on Romanticism, 148, 149; on Schubert, 132, 133; on scientific inventions, 13; on Wagner, 18, 19
Ross, Alex, 17–19, 33, 40, 145, 150
Rouche, Jean, 108
Running Man (film), 19, 30–33
Ruskin, John, 69

Sade, marquis de, 43–47
Sarris, Andrew, 52
Sartre, Jean-Paul, 55–56
Schnitzler, Arthur, 87
Schoenberg, Arnold, 3–4, 6, 96, 115; Adorno on, 12; on Brahms, 48
Schubert, Franz, 43, 78–83, 147; Adorno on, 132; Impromptu No. 1, 140, 141, 147–48; Impromptu No. 3, 141; Piano Trio No. 2 in E flat, 14, 78–83, 128, 134, 156n12; Sonata in A major, 126–27, 136; *Winterreise*, 10–11, 121, 127, 133–40
Schumann, Robert, 48, 126, 140
Schwarzenegger, Arnold, 19, 30–33
Shaw, George Bernard, 19, 25–26

Sheer, Miriam, 98
Sibelius, Jean, 12
Smith, Matthew Wilson, 20
Spanish Civil War, 50
Stanley Kubrick's Boxes, 92–93
Stevens, Wallace, 42
Strauss, Johann, 76–77
Strauss, Richard, 67; *Also Sprach Zarathustra*, 66, 76
Stravinsky, Igor: Adorno on, 12
surrealism, 141; Romantic, 10, 37–63; Sade and, 47
Swanson, Gloria, 16
Syberberg, Hans-Jürgen, 5; *Our Hitler*, 5–6
symbolism, 99

Tlatelolco massacre (1968), 57
Toscanini, Arturo, 30
Total Recall, 30
Truffaut, François: *400 Blows*, 14–15

van Lidth, Erland, 32, 32–33
Vinterberg, Thomas, 125
von Trier, Lars, 125; *Melancholia*, 6

Wagner, Richard, 7, 17–35, 131; anti-Semitism and, 25, 30; Brahms and, 146; Brecht and, 33–35; Buñuel and, 6, 34–35, 37–63; Coppola and, 1–3, 15–26, 33; *Gesamtkunstwerk* of, 34, 101; Herzog and, 5, 26–30, 33; leitmotifs of, 33, 40, 42, 97; Mallarmé on, 33–34; patron of, 25; Rosen on, 18, 19; Ross on, 17–19, 145; Syberberg and, 5–6
Wagner, Richard, works of: *Götterdämmerung*, 25–27; *Lohengrin*, 29; *Parsifal*, 2, 56; *Das Rheingold*, 28, 145, 151–52; "Ride of the Valkyries," 1–3, 20–24, 32; *Der Ring des Nibelungen*, 9, 17–19, 23–35, 43, 145; *Tristan und Isolde*, 6, 10, 35, 37–40, 42–46, 145; *Die Walküre*, 17–18, 24, 37, 59–60, 145
Wagner, Wolfgang, 29

Weidner, Jay, 92
Wilde, Oscar, 52, 76
Wilder, Billy: *Sunset Blvd.*, 16
Wittgenstein, Ludwig, 144, 145
Wood, Michael, 20

Wood, Robin, 121, 125–27

Žižek, Slavoj, 18, 39, 56; on fantasy, 87–88, 146; on Hitchcock, 6; on "Ode to Joy," 73

THE SUNY SERIES
HORIZONS OF CINEMA
MURRAY POMERANCE | EDITOR

Also in the series

William Rothman, editor, *Cavell on Film*

J. David Slocum, editor, *Rebel Without a Cause*

Joe McElhaney, *The Death of Classical Cinema*

Kirsten Moana Thompson, *Apocalyptic Dread*

Frances Gateward, editor, *Seoul Searching*

Michael Atkinson, editor, *Exile Cinema*

Paul S. Moore, *Now Playing*

Robin L. Murray and Joseph K. Heumann, *Ecology and Popular Film*

William Rothman, editor, *Three Documentary Filmmakers*

Sean Griffin, editor, *Hetero*

Jean-Michel Frodon, editor, *Cinema and the Shoah*

Carolyn Jess-Cooke and Constantine Verevis, editors, *Second Takes*

Matthew Solomon, editor, *Fantastic Voyages of the Cinematic Imagination*

R. Barton Palmer and David Boyd, editors, *Hitchcock at the Source*

William Rothman, *Hitchcock: The Murderous Gaze, Second Edition*

Joanna Hearne, *Native Recognition*

Marc Raymond, *Hollywood's New Yorker*

Steven Rybin and Will Scheibel, editors, *Lonely Places, Dangerous Ground*

Claire Perkins and Constantine Verevis, editors, *B Is for Bad Cinema*

Dominic Lennard, *Bad Seeds and Holy Terrors*

Rosie Thomas, *Bombay before Bollywood*

Scott M. MacDonald, *Binghamton Babylon*

Sudhir Mahadevan, *A Very Old Machine*

David Greven, *Ghost Faces*

James S. Williams, *Encounters with Godard*

William H. Epstein and R. Barton Palmer, editors, *Invented Lives, Imagined Communities*

Lee Carruthers, *Doing Time*

Rebecca Meyers, William Rothman, and Charles Warren, editors, *Looking with Robert Gardner*

Belinda Smaill, *Regarding Life*

Douglas McFarland and Wesley King, editors, *John Huston as Adaptor*
R. Barton Palmer, Homer B. Pettey, and Steven M. Sanders, editors, *Hitchcock's Moral Gaze*
Nenad Jovanovic, *Brechtian Cinemas*
Will Scheibel, *American Stranger*
Amy Rust, *Passionate Detachments*
Steven Rybin, *Gestures of Love*
Seth Friedman, *Are You Watching Closely?*
Roger Rawlings, *Ripping England!*
Michael DeAngelis, *Rx Hollywood*
Ricardo E. Zulueta, *Queer Art Camp Superstar*
John Caruana and Mark Cauchi, editors, *Immanent Frames*
Nathan Holmes, *Welcome to Fear City*
Homer B. Pettey and R. Barton Palmer, editors, *Rule, Britannia!*
Milo Sweedler, *Rumble and Crash*
Ken Windrum, *From El Dorado to Lost Horizons*

www.ingramcontent.com/pod-product-compliance
Lightning Source LLC
Chambersburg PA
CBHW030827230426
43667CB00008B/1415